The Wheel

of

Life

The Wheel of Life

A Life of Safaris and Romance

by
Bunny Allen

Illustrations
by
Harry Claassens

SAFARI PRESS INC.

Allen, Bunny

Second edition

Safari Press Inc.

2002, Long Beach, California

ISBN 1-57157-308-9

Library of Congress Catalog Card Number: 2001089634

10 9 8 7 6 5 4 3 2 1

Printed in USA

Readers wishing to receive the Safari Press catalog, featuring many fine books on big-game hunting, wingshooting, and sporting firearms, should write to Safari Press Inc., P.O. Box 3095, Long Beach, CA 90803, USA. Tel: (714) 894-9080 or visit our Web site at www.safaripress.com.

To Jeri, David, Anton, and Lavinia

Table of Contents

Foreword

I first met Bunny Allen in the summer of 1964. From that first moment on the asphalt of the old Nairobi Airport, a friendship developed that will furnish enchanting memories throughout the remainder of my life. And there are thousands of others like myself whose lives Bunny's person and personality have everlastingly touched.

During the summer of 1964, Bunny introduced me and my son, John, and my lifelong friend and hunting companion, Dr. L. S. "Buddy" Thomson Jr. and his son, Sandy, to the enchantment of Africa and to the excitement of big-game hunting and the pleasures of the safari. That was not a new role for Bunny, but one he has filled with charm and vigor countless times. Bunny's global reputation as one of the outstanding ladies' men of all time—and his casual and romantic appearance and style of social engagement—provides a charming veneer for a man totally dedicated to serving his clients fully, completely, and professionally.

After that first safari, my relationship with Bunny grew richer over the course of the numerous safaris that followed. Bunny has given clients like me and my friends excitement, adventure, and new perspectives on the world and the various societies that inhabit it. At the same time he has become a close, loyal, and dependable friend.

Bunny Allen is unique. His life has been filled not only by thrilling encounters with Africa's majestic wildlife, but also with exciting adventurers, professional hunters, royalty, movie actresses, Hollywood moguls, and celebrities from throughout the world. To review his life in book form, told by Bunny himself, is itself an adventure.

Ben H. Carpenter
Dallas, Texas
January 1999

Chapter 1

Arrival in Kenya

I t was a pleasant sensation. A gentle rocking up and down, together with a slow and swaying to and fro. I was in dreamland, and it was delightful. It was dark, but the sky was alight with stars. A shooting star went on its way, and, maybe, I had a dreamy wish. How could I tell? I was in dreamland, where nothing is distinct—in fact, where everything is splendidly vague. Nothing from the field of dreams should ever cause worry or harassment. The dreamer should be peacefully prepared only for the beauties of the coming day.

The horizon to one side was bathed in a silver glow, while the other side showed just the smallest touch of warmth. The stars twinkled once more, and then everything was dark. Time stopped; nothing registered. I had moved from sweet dreamland to plain sleep. Time passed, but how much? Then the rocking, swaying began again. But it was more urgent this time, a true shaking, and a voice calling, "Bunny, Bunny." I opened my eyes; golden hair fell over me. "We are here," she said. "Beautiful Kenya, come and see."

I got to my feet, wrapping my sleeping apparel more securely around me, and followed the golden girl, whom I will call She, to the rail of good ship *Ussukuma*. And there it was, beautiful Africa at last: the Kenya coastline, green and golden and wonderful, bathed in the light of the glorious rising sun. I was completely silenced by the beauty of the scene. It was a tremendous contrast to the miles of sand down the coast to Egypt, Suez, the Sudan, and Somalia. As She had said, "Africa does not start until you arrive at the coast of Kenya." I held her hand and thanked her for waking me to see this fabulous sight. She put her fingers to her lips and indicated over her shoulder the still-slumbering forms behind us. The previous night, we had had a farewell dance on board, and then our party of six or seven had decided to sleep on deck, as several of us had been doing since Suez. It was much more pleasant sleeping out in the air than in the close quarters below. She and I stood by the rail and devoured the beautiful shoreline for several minutes in absolute silence. Then She relented and called to the others to join us. Like me, all of them were seeing this coast for the first time. She, however, was an "old hand." This was her sixth or seventh trip to Kenya, where her parents had a coffee farm at Kiambu.

By now, more and more people were arriving along the rail. I caught a glimpse of Philip Percival, one of the real old-time white hunters. I'd had the luck to be introduced to him only a few days out from Southampton. A charming man, he became a very sound friend in the years to come. Then there were Sir John Ramsden and his family. Sir John was a very well-to-do farmer in the Naivasha area. Mervyn Soames was another passenger. He gave me my first job in Kenya, and his brother Jack was more or less responsible for my becoming a professional hunter.

The ship's company was in a happy, buoyant mood, all ready for our arrival in Mombasa that morning. The trip had been an enjoyable one. Three and a half weeks previously, friends and relations had seen me off at Southampton, and on my arrival in Nairobi in two days' time I would join my brother Ba. While en route I had made some good friends, but the trip didn't really start for me until we reached Genoa. There She came aboard, having come overland from England. She proved a marvelous companion from the very first moment. She was lighthearted yet serious, and full of knowledge about Kenya and its people. This I feasted on, and She proved a willing provider. She told me many amusing and interesting tales of the first settlers in Kenya, stories that had been passed on to her by her parents.

Some of them were fabulous tales, both fact and fiction, of the white hunters of Kenya. Almost all of the first clutch of these gentlemen were, in fact, settlers. She had met a great many of these fine men, many of whom had visited her home. She had also met them at Muthaiga Country Club, where the whole of Kenya gathered to see in the new year—or at least it sounded like that to me. She made me feel that I had made the right decision in deciding to come to Kenya.

It had not been an easy decision to make. Back home in England, I had become very attached to a rather beautiful Irish girl. We had planned to marry sometime in the future, but I was only twenty-one then and knew, in my own mind, that I was not ready to be anchored. Also, I had made some splendid friends among the Thames Valley Gypsies, who had instilled in me a great love of the outdoors. They also encouraged me to hunt and shoot and trap—everything from a rabbit to a deer. My grandfather, on my mother's side, owned some fine farmland adjacent to the Great Forest of Windsor. It was a great opportunity for a little hunting, not to mention a little poaching.

But those early days are another story. Suffice it to say that my love for the great outdoors had grown to such an extent that when the first opportunity occurred for me to make a move from cramped England to wider horizons, I seized it. My two elder brothers were both in Kenya, and they wrote advising me to join them. With very little delay I packed my bag and bade my farewells to my mother—my father had left us for a better world a few months before—and to my Gypsy friends. I was sad to leave behind my splendid lurcher dog, Bill, who was a fine sporting companion. And so I made the break, and here I was about to enter into a brand-new life in a very new country. With something under £100 in my pocket, I was stepping into the unknown, and I was thrilled.

As we passed along the coastline of Kenya, still very green with the odd patch of pale golden sand, She, said: "Ah, we must be just off Lamu Island. You must go there, Bunny, a most lovely, different place." Then: "Here we are opposite the Tana River Estuary. Do you see the red water? That's Mount Kenya losing all its wonderful soil from the heavy rains." Then we passed Malindi and Kilifi. Finally, She pulled me aside from the others to say: "I wanted to tell you about Takaungu— we are opposite it now; I can tell from those huge baobab trees. Here is where Denys Finch Hatton and Karen Blixen come, whenever they can, for a quiet time." Finch Hatton was already established in my mind as a great hero. He was one of the first great white hunters. Karen Blixen was the author of *Out of Africa*, which she wrote under the pseudonym Isak Dinesen. Their love affair was a rather beautiful fairy story. She knew them both fairly well. I was to get to know them, and the more I knew them, the better I loved them.

Late in the afternoon of 28 December 1927, I landed at Kilindini Harbor, on the island of Mombasa. The adventure was on. I was happy, and I was in good company.

Well before dark, the Nairobi Express steamed out of Mombasa station, to the accompaniment of cheers, whistles of all sorts (including that of the express), catcalls, and good-byes in a multitude of dialects. Before leaving Mombasa, I had taken leave of my shipboard friends, who either remained there or went to other destinations at other times and by other means. At this time there was no workable road between the coast and Nairobi. The first automobile had actually made the journey in 1927, but in many places no road existed; the pioneer driver and his mate had carved out their own route.

The train journey was to take about eighteen hours, stopping on the way at various dark bungalows for the passengers to alight and partake of meals and refreshments. It was my good fortune that She was still with me to point out things of interest en route. Halfway up the hill out of Mombasa, the train did a loop on itself in order to beat the steep gradient.

"Look," She said, pointing out the window. I looked, and there we were, passing over a bridge that crossed the line where we had been five minutes earlier! I asked her, as I laughed, "Have you got any more tricks like this?"

"Plenty. In this gorgeous country there is a trick every minute." That girl was a card. No! She was a whole deck of cards! Just before darkness finally descended on us, She suddenly pointed through the window. Then I saw my first African elephant, a handsome old bull with its trunk up in the air, sniffing and snorting, as though in competition with our locomotive. Other gray shapes were melting into the bush. At the crack of dawn, She came to join me again, explaining, "As it gets light, we will see plenty of game in this rather more open country. I didn't want you to miss them." I thanked her and said, "What am I going to do without you? Will I see you again?" She switched on a country girl smile and replied, "*Labda.*" That was the first Kiswahili word I learned, without knowing the meaning of it, for She would not elaborate. But She knew her Kenya.

As we went up onto the higher, more open country, we saw great masses of game: impala, Grant and Thomson gazelle, zebra, thousands of wildebeest, and hundreds of eland. It was exciting. I was thrilled. I was in Africa. I was really here amid it all.

About midday, our train chugged into Nairobi station. The platform was alive with—nay, a seething mass of—people of all colors—white, black, and coffee. After a while I spotted Ba. We registered with a wave. As my luggage was coming out, I noticed that She had located her parents. They were a handsome, distinguished-looking pair. She came running over to me. "Good-bye, Bunny, and enjoy lovely Kenya." She allowed me to give her a very brief kiss. Then away She went. I did not see her again until twenty years had passed. But that is another story.

Well, here I was. She had gone, but brother Ba had come to take over. He told me of the adventures he had had with lion a few days previously. The Gypsy blood immediately started working within me. I wanted to get out on a hunt.

"Don't worry," said Ba. "Buster has laid on a hunt for you this coming weekend." Buster Cook was a school friend of ours who had come out to Kenya with Ba the previous year.

Chapter 2

My First Safari

Buster arrived right on time. His car was a box-body of mixed parentage but looked very smart and well cared for. Buster, I should explain, was a "well-clued-up" mechanic: Everything he had was well cared for and had the extreme merit of functioning. The difference between Buster's motorcars and the Allens' was that Buster *knew* his car would go, while the Allens *hoped* theirs would.

Buster and I drove to the campsite, which was on the upper reaches of the Tana River about forty miles east of Mount Kenya, that beautiful, beautiful mountain. There we met John Adams, a friend of Buster's. The hunt was in fact for him. The camp was simple but adequate. The site was delightful, situated between two rivers just before they met and tumbled into the Tana. Our camp beds were out in the open under the stars. In fact, the only cover in the camp was a tarpaulin, strung between two trees over the stores. I suppose we hoped it wouldn't rain. After an excellent supper, cooked over the wooden embers by a most splendid chap called Njerogi, we retired to bed. I, for one, was quite worn out, more from excitement and anticipation than anything else.

John was looking for a very good rhino, and Buster was keen on a buffalo hunt. He had said: "Bunny, they are tremendous animals. The old hunters say that buffalo will very often hunt you!" What a fine story to go to bed on. Maybe for that reason I did not sleep well. All night I dreamt either of a buffalo over my shoulder or a snorting, charging rhino.

The next morning, we set out from the camp in Indian file. A tall African was in the lead, followed by Buster, John, another African, and then poor me, bringing up the rear. I was feeling lonely and a little nervous. As we progressed, I kept glancing over my shoulder to see if I had been joined by anything. We were walking in the half-light, when every dark shade is a thing of terror. Furthermore, I did not have a gun in my hand—our armaments did not stretch back that far.

A little later, the lead African, Kikunyu, came up to me, detached a fine-looking knobkerrie from his belt, and, with a huge grin that went from ear to ear, handed it to me. I grinned back, gave him a pat on the shoulder, and on we went. He was armed with a most splendid spear and wore only a blanket over one

8

shoulder, held around his waist by a belt. He was extremely impressive to look upon. I felt happier now. I was armed, and I had made a new friend.

We continued on our way for a mile or more, with, from time to time, the noise of something or other scurrying away into the bush. However, all these noises were of small animals, maybe of only one animal. Then, when we were somewhat farther from the river, the bush thinned considerably, and at once we started to see animals. First a fine-looking waterbuck. He was standing on a small hillock, with the light of the coming sun throwing him up in relief. He looked very proud, and stayed put until we passed from his sight behind a clump of bush.

From early youth, I had read and studied as many books on Africa and its game as I could lay my hands on; therefore, I was familiar with the appearance of a lot of the animals. Among others, I had read Karamojo Bell, and that grand, bearded giant of a fellow and unforgettable "jungle man," Pretorius. Now it was happening. Wonderful.

Suddenly we stopped. Then I heard some subdued crashing in the bush, followed by the weirdest noise. It was a combination of a bellow, a squeal, a whistle, and a snort— all four of them, and more. Indescribable. However, within a few moments the matter was resolved. After a loud, watery whistle without any music in it, a great crashing brought a rhino out of the bush. It headed straight for us. We all took to our heels, but that was not necessary; the old rhino stopped in its tracks, turned like a polo pony, and trotted back into the bush. As it went, we could see it had a miserable pair of horns that were clearly not up to John Adams's standard.

We rounded a bend in the bush, and, as we took a turn back toward the river, there was suddenly a barking snort and a crashing of vegetation. A huge buffalo came straight at us. Buster upped his .318 and fired. At the same moment, the great Kikunyu made an amazing leap to the right and threw his spear, with great power, into the flank of the buffalo, which sank to the ground. I forgot to use my *rungu,* and John didn't have time to do anything. The buffalo made a brave effort to get up and attack again while Buster gave it the quietus. I thought the hunt was over, but not a bit of it.

As we were all beaming at one another and Kikunyu, having retrieved his spear, was straightening it, we heard a further loud crash and snort. A second buff came out from the exact same spot. This time, John got into the firing line, and his shot went on its way just before the one by Buster, who hadn't reloaded immediately after his last shot. I threw my *rungu,* but I have to admit it was a clear miss. The buffalo veered off into the nearest bush just as Kikunyu finished adjusting his spear. He took off after it like greased lightning and disappeared in the bush. Then we heard noises of battle from within. We followed as quickly as we could, but by the time we had caught up, the fight was over. Kikunyu had given a final thrust into the heart of the dying animal.

We then looked at the heads of the two buffalo, and even I could tell that as trophies they were not much. They were all body, but I was amazed at their size. After the second African had tied a piece of cloth to a stick, to flutter in the breeze over the buffalo carcass in the open, we set off for camp. There was always the chance that the elusive trophy rhino might appear, so we kept quiet as we made our way to camp. Nothing happened, and after one hour's walking we were back, as hungry as the proverbial hunters.

At camp we kept to the rules that come into play after a hunt: We held a postmortem. Buster and John were puzzled as to why the rhino, having winded us, had not carried on his charge. Furthermore, why had the buffalo broken their usual rule and charged upwind? And not only one buff, but two.

"It's very odd," said Buster.

John nodded, as Buster went on: "I noticed that the first buff appeared to be knocked about a bit, but I had only a brief look because of the start of the second episode. After that I was too shaken to think or to look further."

John nodded again, while I was just a keen listener. John suggested: "Why don't you ask Kikunyu what he thinks of it?"

They called Kikunyu, and a short discussion took place among the three of them. I could only guess at what they were saying; however, I heard one word repeated several times. It was my *She* word, *labda*. Finally, Kikunyu returned to the kitchen to cook his tripe.

Buster enlightened me concerning Kikunyu's opinion. First, the rhino had not carried through its charge because it had other, more interesting, ways of passing the time—namely, Mrs. Rhino. Second, both buffalo were badly knocked about and had without doubt been fighting. Perhaps their fight had been caused by a flirtatious cow. In years to come I was to remember this, my first lesson on the buffalo. Many times some buff would charge me, but always there was a good reason: The animal was sick, or sorry, or angry—maybe because it had been turned down by some fair, or unfair, lady.

It all sounded like a reasonable enough explanation for what the others called odd behavior. As the breakfast table broke up, I asked about my mystery word.

"One moment, Buster, what does *labda* mean, in plain English?"

"Oh, just 'perhaps' or 'maybe.' Why?"

"Nothing much. I've just decided that I must learn Kiswahili as quickly as possible."

Then and there I decided to buy a little notebook and learn a number of new words every day. I kept to that resolve, and in a very few weeks I had a fair working knowledge of the language. As it happened, very soon the splendid Kikunyu became my first mentor.

With the hunt over, it was now time to travel to where I'd be staying in Kenya. The idea was to drop me at Sagana, about thirty-five miles from the camp, where I would catch the train to Naro Moru, which at that time was the railhead. There my eldest brother, Denys, would meet me, and we would drive to his house. That was going to be my first base in Kenya. Having duly thanked Buster and John for a most interesting—nay, thrilling, time—I sat upon my baggage to await the train while they departed. Both of them had to return to work on the morrow: John to Maragua and Buster to Makuyu. They were both on sisal estates.

As I sat on my tin box, an old native woman came by selling bananas. I thought I'd have a few, so I gave her a shilling. She then proceeded to count out one hundred bananas! I gasped in astonishment, selected five of the bananas, and then indicated to her that she could take the rest. She scooped them up into her basket and went off, muttering something about the mad English. At last my train arrived, and many natives came out of it. Some of them probably bought the other bananas, as well as various other foods from stalls alongside the tracks. Then the train hooted three times and set about the long climb to Naro Moru. Halfway between Sagana and Nyeri, Mount Kenya came out in its full glory. The sight was truly magnificent.

I arrived at my destination, and my good brother Denys was there to meet me in the pouring rain. I noticed that he had chains on the car and four natives accompanying him.

We wasted not a moment, and in no time we were squashing through the mud toward his house, which I gathered was ten miles away. Several times along the alleged highway the four men and I had to get out and push the car up inclines and out of ditches. However, we made pretty good time until we turned off the muddy highway onto the farm track. Then it was sheer black cotton soil. We sank in, pushed a bit, made a few yards, and sank in again. The poor old car snorted, sneezed, steamed, and finally gave up. The radiator was throwing off so much steam that I expected at any moment to hear a whistle. Denys got out of the car, saying, "Well, that's about it. We have to walk now; it's only about a mile and a half." Thankfully it had stopped raining. We trudged home through the mud.

At the house, Denys got up from his chair, looked at his watch, and strode quickly out of the room. He was back in a minute, carrying a bottle of champagne and two glasses. "Let's drink in the New Year," he said, with a broad smile on his face. The old year had finished its span, and with all the excitement of my new life I had quite forgotten this festive occasion. The two of us made merry as best we could. At any rate, we had the right lubricant, thanks to the forethought of brother.

The next morning a young African led me along the muddy track of the previous night. At the car I found a team of fourteen oxen, their driver (who was carrying a long whip), and a small child who apparently led the oxen. In no time they had attached the rear oxen to the car by a chain, and my guide intimated that I should get behind the steering wheel. After a couple of cracks of the whip, away we went. At first the oxen really had to put their backs into it, and there were many cracks of the driver's whip in the air above them. Also, the driver called the oxen by name to encourage them.

Once the car was out of the ditch, it went along fairly well, and within twenty minutes we were back at the house. I took the opportunity to have a good look around. The house was an all-timber building set up on wooden piles about three feet above the ground. The walls were off-cuts from large cedar logs, the floor was of wood, and the roof was made of wooden shingles. It was a roomy house with three bedrooms, and there was a separate guest house adjacent. It looked out upon a very green meadow with a nice trout stream on the far side. Beyond it and reaching up into the heavens was Mount Kenya. I knew already that I was going to be very happy in this magnificent country. I also knew that I had two great needs. One was a horse and the other a dog, and it took no great time to satisfy these needs.

The farm belonged to Jack Soames, an Etonian and the brother of Mervyn Soames, who had been on the boat. Denys pointed out that, without a doubt, they were both now at Muthaiga Country Club for the New Year's celebrations. After a few days they would go to Jack's house, which was on the other side of the farm on another river.

When Jack Soames arrived on the farm with his brother Mervyn, he very soon came to see Denys and to meet me. I immediately liked him immensely, and I could tell that this feeling was mutual. I was very encouraged by one of his first remarks: "Mervyn told me about you. I must get him to buy a farm, and then we can put you in to run it." I murmured something in reply, which implied that I thought that would be wonderful; I was so bowled over by the very idea of it that I was not capable of coherent thought. However, whatever I said must have passed muster. Jack patted me on the back, and he said, "We'll see."

Jack was a very good-looking man and a great charmer. He was over six feet tall but had a slight stoop. I later learned that he had been gassed in the Great War, and for that reason he was not always feeling entirely well. However, this did not appear to interfere with the life he led. He was a great "party man"; in fact, he was usually the life and soul of any party he attended. Naturally, with his life and his associates, he drank quite a bit. Before he left, he pulled me aside and said: "Look, let me give you a tip. Learn the language as quickly as possible. I've got some ideas, but you must speak Swahili."

The next time I saw him—two weeks later, on his return from buying some dairy cows near Machakos—I proudly informed him that my knowledge of Kiswahili was already growing. I had a vocabulary of two hundred words. Then he enlightened me: Raymond Hook was getting a safari together for a visiting British M.P., Freddie Guest, and his daughter, Diana. Jack could arrange for me to help on this trip. God, I was excited. What a chance! And so quickly!

In the meantime, Jack had not been idle regarding scouting for a suitable farm for Mervyn to buy. He arrived just after breakfast one morning, with brother Mervyn. "Come on, Bunny," he said. "We are off to see Mervyn's farm." One hour later, having forded two rivers, each with good stony bottoms, we drove to a deserted farmhouse. It was derelict, having been empty for about six years. The long and the short of it all was that they offered me the job of farm manager at the salary of £15 per month. It was very little in exchange for doing very little. I was to continue to live with Denys and from time to time ride over to supervise the cleaning up of the place. In fact, we did not intend to start any work there until March, the beginning of the next rains. In the meantime, I would go to meet Raymond Hook and prepare for the safari project.

A few days later, I rode over to see Raymond—and what a character he proved to be. A shaggy, bearded giant: raw-boned and rough-shod at first appearance, but on further acquaintance a very gentle man. Shortly after lunch, Raymond started to brief me on the coming Guest-and-daughter safari. They wanted to do about ten days up and around Mount Kenya, onto the moorlands, and onto Meru on the northern end. All this would be by horseback and pack animals. Raymond said, in his very precise way: "Now this is where you come into it. I want you to go ahead of the customers and set up camp." I started to ask how I would know how to do that, but he held up his hand and said, "Oh, yes, yes, that is all taken care of. Kikunyu will show you where to camp. Oh, yes, he knows." How wonderful! Kikunyu was coming with us.

Having gotten all the information about the safari, I started to prepare myself for the ride back home. As I went to fetch my horse, little pups bounded up to me, and one almost jumped into my hands. I petted him, patted him, and generally made much of him. Raymond noticed, remarking: "Would you like him?" I nodded my head keenly. "Right, he's yours."

I named the pup Poppleton, the combined names of two professors Raymond had been talking with that morning. It was only about eight miles across country, and although carrying the pup made my progress somewhat slower than usual, I arrived home to the awaiting Denys just before dark. He was eager to hear my news and was delighted with it.

I continued my swotting up on Kiswahili and soon found that I was able to carry on an adequate conversation with the house servants and farm labor. Whenever I came on a new word, down it went in the book. By the end of the month, Jack told me that the Guest safari was going to start on 7 February. That meant I would go off on the fourth with Kikunyu and the camp company. He also told me that Raymond was presenting me with a horse, as payment for the work I was to do. So my first two needs were satisfied. I had a dog and a horse. What now? I had four days to obtain a gun! Once again my Gypsy luck was with me, and the very next day the local forest officer came riding by and had lunch with us. In the course of conversation, he let us know that he was just going away on long leave to England: "Do you know of anyone who would like to buy my 10x75mm Mauser rifle?" Denys, in answer, just pointed to me. So as easily as that I came into possession of my first rifle for the price of £25, which included fifty rounds of ammunition.

That night, the most amazing noises aroused me from my sleep. I knew it was a lion, but I could not believe that its voice could be so loud. The roar went on and on. An old lion was claiming the land for its own. First the question: "Whose land is this?" and then the grunting reply: "It's mine, it's mine, it's mine." The animal was roaring up the river valley, and its voice reverberated in a rocky gorge. It was a magnificent performance. Some of the lion roars I've heard since then have been more exciting, more sudden, more frightening. This roar was not in the least frightening. I was lying securely in bed, and I certainly had no thought of being snatched out of it, like the poor man in *The Man-Eaters of Tsavo*. Yet it was my first real lion roar in the wild, and one I would remember.

I awoke the next morning; the great day and hour had come. The Guests arrived in camp escorted by Jack Lucy, an assistant of Raymond's. They all seemed pleasant enough after what had, quite obviously, been a good luncheon party. Freddy Guest, by all accounts, liked his gin, and on this occasion, by the look of his nose, he'd been drinking the pink variety. His daughter Diana was a good-looking girl, though not pretty. She was handsome, a bit horsey, quite tall, and had a good leg for slacks. I took to

Jack Lucy at once. He was as cheerful as they come, and I realized that with him around I was certainly going to enjoy my first professional safari. Make no mistake, that's what it was. This was something that I had dreamt about.

The original plan had changed somewhat. Jack Soames and Raymond Hook would still join us several days later at the Mukogodo camp. On the following two days Jack Lucy took the Guests by horse up the forest track to the moors. Meanwhile, I went with Kikunyu to inspect various glades in the forest to see if there was any sign of bongo. We didn't find any.

I got along very well with Freddy and Diana. They both had a keen sense of humor, and she had a most delightful chortle. He had a dry, ginny cackle. They certainly didn't seem keen to shoot anything from the mountain camps, but it sounded as if it would be different in the lower country. Freddy remarked, "I'd dearly love to get a greater kudu." And she quietly said, "That rather goes for me, too."

Jack, between puffs on his pipe, replied: "We'll do our best for you. They are elusive, but they are there."

I nodded knowingly at the red fire and then quickly hoped I hadn't been noticed.

After the Guests had bid us good night and headed for bed, Jack remarked, "Well done, Bunny. I noticed your nod of agreement. She did, too. She now knows she's got a definite ally in helping her get a greater kudu." It was a fine pat on the back. No bed in the whole world could have been as comfortable as mine that night.

I found the ride across the moors interesting but uneventful. Every now and then beautiful Mount Kenya showed in all its glory; then the next moment it became shrouded in cloud. Slightly nearer was the rocky, craggy, and awe-inspiring Sendeyo.

Even though it was still fifteen miles away, it appeared to be right on top of us.

After midday, we descended the moors and crossed two wide and deep river valleys to get to our campsite. We did not waste much time in getting something to eat and in getting into our blankets that night. However, we did not manage to get much sleep. Inadvertently, we had set up camp among a herd of cow elephants. They had been drinking at the river when we arrived, and so they had left us undisturbed. But shortly after we were all tucked in bed, the yelling and bawling started. From my reading, I knew exactly what it was. Nevertheless, that splendid Kikunyu came to my heather bed. "*Mama na watoto,*" (Mothers and their children) he whispered. I nodded, as he went off to give some instructions.

Small fires soon sprang up all around camp to ward off the elephants. These small fires became bigger fires, and they burned all night. Throughout the darkness there were elephant noises, chiefly the trumpeting of angry cows. There were also high-pitched shrieks of pain as calves were delivered, and a thump of trunks on calves' rumps for stepping out of line. From time to time, one or two cows would make a false charge toward our camp, and now and then we could see their shapes in the firelight. Once I saw fearsome eyes reflecting back at me. Or was that nervous imagination? I was frightened. It is always frightening to be among a herd of cow elephants, and here we were in their maternity ward!

It was nice to see dawn approach, and luck was on our side. The females and children moved off, and we had our tea and settled down for a belated night. After a few hours' respite, we started setting up the camp.

When Jack Lucy and the Guests arrived around noon the following day, they told us that, on coming round a bend in the forest track, they had bumped right into our maternity ward. Two irate cows immediately charged the car. Jack quickly reversed back around the corner, blowing the horn continuously, while in the back the Africans beat on the sides of the car and shouted their loudest. The two cows came rushing onward but luckily veered off down an elephant track to the right. Jack then fired off a couple of shots into the air, causing the herd to disperse, trumpeting and screaming. It was nerve-racking for everyone concerned, to say the least. But about six pink gins later, Freddy and Diana were beginning to feel normal again, and Jack was still laughing.

Very early the next morning, a grinning Kikunyu with a cup of steaming tea in his hand awakened me. He was shaking his head as he said, *"Ndovu hii, mbaya kabisa,"* and telling me exactly how bad the elephants were. After a good breakfast, Jack and I set off on our recce. Kikunyu and two other trackers accompanied us.

Within three-quarters of an hour, we were up with the herd. Jack had explained to me that he did not intend to get entangled with them. He just wanted to find out exactly where they were so that he could determine if we could use the desired trail. We could hear them feeding. The wind was right as we made our way toward the trail, which Kikunyu informed us was close by. At that moment the wind changed, and before we knew it two youngish cows charged us out of a patch of bamboo twenty-five yards away. Quick as a flash Jack had his rifle to his shoulder and two shots rang out almost as one. Then, at the top of his voice, he shouted for us to run. We ran, and by sheer luck, or fine judgment, Kikunyu had us on the trail, down which we could make a quicker retreat. After running about a hundred yards and around two corners, we pulled up. We were not being followed, although we could hear the herd churning around.

As we walked quickly away, Jack explained to me what he had done to halt the elephant charge: He had put a shot close over the head of each cow. "It very often works," he casually remarked. I must say that I was glad it had worked this time.

As we walked back to camp, Jack discussed this "abominable herd of women," as he called them. "They have been around for years. They are always on this corner of the mountain, sometimes east and sometimes west, but within thirty miles of Meru, you can be certain of that." He paused, put a hand to one ear, shook his head, and continued his monologue: "This is the first time I've mixed with them, and I won't do it again." I was to remember that, and I never once "mixed with them" myself.

Thirty years later, my two sons, doing elephant-control work for the game department in this area, had a real battle royal with this same herd. They had to shoot eight elephant before they were able to extricate themselves. The elephant had been raiding the maize fields of the forest squatters on the edge of the plantations night after night. My sons went out to drive them from the area. The elephant positively pinned them down in one small clearing in the forest, repeatedly charging them, sometimes one at a time, usually two at a time, and once three together. After eight were on the ground, almost touching one another, there was a slight lull in the attack, and my sons were able to leg it to safety. They returned the next day and found that the herd had moved off. They collected the ivory and informed the game department that they were not keen to attempt to control uncontrollable elephants again.

On the following day of the Guest safari, we decided to hunt for greater kudu. The customers went off by car, and Kikunyu and I moved the camp out of the Mount Kenya forest, away from the rain clouds and into the sunshine. Owing to the excellent time we made on the downhill journey, Kikunyu and I found that we had a spare day before Jack Soames and company arrived. We decided to have a mounted look at the area by the Uaso Nyiro River, with the intention of bringing back some camp meat. There I saw fresh animal tracks. I could tell they were neither eland nor waterbuck, but they were sizable. Could they be greater kudu?

Kikunyu returned, looked at the spoor in the sand, grinned in his most pleased manner, and commented: *"Tandala tu."* (Only a kudu) He pointed downhill and made indications with his fingers so that I could easily follow the two greater kudu tracks, which led downstream. We followed the tracks through a riverbed and onto the dry, rock-strewn surface.

We tethered our mounts and climbed up about a hundred feet on some rocks, and I started to search with my binoculars. Kikunyu was just using his keen eyes. After a while, during which time I had seen nothing but bushes, trees, and rocks, Kikunyu lightly touched my arm and pointed down the valley. I switched my aim with the glasses, and I saw a greater kudu bull in all its glory come from beneath the shadow into the sunlight. A moment later a second bull came into full view. We really were in greater kudu country. At this moment, I had some retrospective thoughts on the advice my Gypsy hunting mentor, one Piramus Berners, had given me some years before. Piramus had said, "Watch for movement," and it was precisely movement that had shown the hideout of the animals. The glints were nothing other than the reflection of the sun on a horn. I would have liked a closer view of the animals, but on Kikunyu's sound advice I fought off this desire and we rode back to camp.

The next day Jack Soames and Raymond arrived, and so did the rest of the safari party. We broke the glad news of the kudu to them. Everyone was delighted, and they all drank several pink gins. Jack Soames and Raymond had arrived in two hunting cars this time. The second one, belonging to Jack Soames, carried almost entirely liquor and other such refreshments. It looked as if we were in for a party! But none of us knew how great the party was going to be.

Jack Soames was overflowing with joy and enthusiasm. "Well done, Bunny," he said. In actual fact, I hadn't done anything. We had just been lucky. I smiled back at Jack, crossed my fingers, and said, "I hope the luck holds." Raymond gave me a shaggy smile, from which I gathered he was pleased with me. Having had a cup of tea, he and one of his men rode off toward the bushland and broken-up forest to see how his honey barrels were doing. We did not see him again until well after dark, when he returned with a goodly supply of wild honey. He really was a nature man.

In the meantime, we had a very good and jolly luncheon in camp, with good food and good wine. During the meal, there was a certain confusion caused by the two Jacks at the table. Somebody or other would say "Jack" and two voices would answer. The bright and quick-witted Diana said, "We can't have two Jacks. One of you will have to be John." She tossed an imaginary coin in the air, caught it, looked at it, and, pointing to Jack Lucy, said: "You are John." And that little matter was resolved.

Over the campfire, we laid the plans for the coming day. John and I were going to take the Guests after what they all called "Bunny's kudu." Jack and Raymond were going by car to another area below a little escarpment to search for greater kudu. They would be another string to our bow.

After an early breakfast, we mounted our steeds, mules, and zebroids and started off for the Uaso Nyiro River. After much glassing we spotted some kudu. I suggested to Diana that she should rest against the rock for a while, but she would have none of it. She whispered nicely and closely into my ear, "No, I want to watch how Pa gets on." So we watched them until they were out of sight in the runnel. After that we caught a vague glimpse of them from time to time as they made their approach by walking up the sand riverbed. The two kudu had by then wandered slowly around a small thicket of thornbush and were out of sight to us. I waited two or three minutes, hoping I would see our quarry again, but they did not reappear. Therefore, acting on John's instructions, I signed to Diana that we were off, gave her gun to the extremely youthful tracker, who looked keen to take it, and away we went. My heart was pounding, my legs felt slightly weak, and my mouth became a little dry. This was my first solo hunt in Africa. This was history.

We made for a hill, and, as we got to some big boulders at its foot, a shot rang out. We halted at once. I then heard the crunch of rocks as they went flying under the feet of a running animal. It came into sight around 120 yards from us. The first shot was quickly followed by a second. Now two kudu were angling in front of us. I said quickly: "Take the first one." She took it immediately, and the kudu was down and out. The second bull was over the crest in a few moments. Diana had made a fine shot into the thick of the neck. We congratulated her, and she was obviously very happy with her trophy. Then I noticed a second wound in the kudu. Freddy had hit him with his shot! It was a little too far back, probably just touching the lung. The kudu might have gone a long way had Diana not made her excellent shot. Just then John and Freddy came over the rise, huffing and puffing. On seeing the kudu, Freddy threw his hands in the air and cried out, "We got it, we got it." At which Diana rushed up, put her arms around him, and said, "Yes, Pa, we got it." She emphasized the "we" as she smiled over his shoulder at me.

Back at camp, we discovered that Jack and Raymond had not yet returned. John asked me to take his car as near as possible to the kudu so that we could collect the head, skin, and meat. One of the trackers came along as my helper, and we talked as I drove.

"*Jina lako nini?*" (What's your name?) I asked.

"*Tabei Arap Tilmet,*" he replied, with a broad smile.

So at least I knew his name. *But what a long name,* I thought. Then, by question and answer, I gathered that Tabei was his own name, Arap meant "son of," and Tilmet was his father's name. He also enlightened me about Kikunyu. Kikunyu was a nickname, meaning "caterpillar," given him by the Wakikuyu. His real name was Memasabom Arap Meteget. They were both of the Kipsigi tribe, coming from West Kenya. By the time I had gotten all this information, we were within a stone's throw of Kikunyu and his skinning party. They had to manhandle everything across one small, deep, and sandy *lugga.* In half an hour we were back in camp.

They had started celebrating with pink gin, Jack and Raymond had just returned, and everyone was happy. However, Raymond was not drinking gin. He never touched alcohol. Instead, one of his Ndorobo friends had brought him some ready-mixed blood and milk. I joined the pink-gin group for a matter of two drinks; then I heard a loud *pop* and saw champagne glasses, and champagne became the drink of the moment. *Much better than gin,* I thought. I was never fond of gin, and after that party I gave it up entirely.

Soon after, the excitement and exhaustion of the day started to tell. John and Freddy slipped off to bed. The rest of us continued to enjoy the fire for a while, until Diana got up, kissed Jack good night, kissed me good night, and thanked me for giving her such a wonderful hunt. I said, "But it was not me at all. . . ."

"Nonsense," she said, "you did splendidly."

She turned to Raymond to say good night, gave him a peck beside his goatee, and walked off across the firelight to her tent. The fire silhouetted her legs very prettily through her thin night apparel. She waved to us as she misted into the darkness. Raymond turned his head back to the fire and said, "That girl has a good pair of legs."

As he bade Jack and me good night, he went on to suggest that I join him on his activities the next day. He was going to catch Grevy zebra by horseback. It sounded good to me, so I quickly nodded in agreement. We then talked quietly to the accompaniment of the gentle noises from the dying campfire: There were *cracks* and *hisses* and *spits*, *woofs* and *oofs* and *spoofs*. Jack finally got up, put his hand on my shoulder, and said, "Bunny, you did very well today. You pleased Diana very much indeed." He hesitated, then continued. "The important thing on a safari is to keep the girls happy. If the girls are happy, you have a happy safari." How true that was. In the years to come, I have often remembered Jack's words, as well as how adept he was at keeping the girls happy. They all loved him.

How different was the next day! It was brimming with excitement but quite, quite different. Raymond and I rode away from camp after a good breakfast—and how wise it was, to have it, for we did not eat again for the rest of the day. Raymond's only remark about food was, "Oh yes, we don't bother very much about that, you know." And we certainly didn't. But it was a wonderful day. I was on my brand-new filly; I called her Nell, after my mother. Raymond was mounted on his stallion, Bronze, and the horse was exactly that color. In fact, with Raymond in his old slouch hat, the pair looked exactly like a bronze statue depicting the Boer War.

After riding down a steep but short escarpment, we found ourselves in open, sandy bush country. Within two hours, we arrived at Raymond's Grevy-catching camp. We were very soon in the hunt. There were four of us: Raymond; his man in charge, Sigira; a Kikuyu named Ndirango; and me. We soon sighted the right size Grevy, separated it somewhat from the herd, and gave chase. I noticed that either Sigira or Ndirango always kept to the flank where the herd had been to prevent our quarry from breaking back. After riding three to four hundred yards, Raymond was up alongside the Grevy. He had his rawhide noose looped around a light stick. He pushed out the noose till it went over the Grevy's head and then slipped it down the neck. Raymond pulled the rawhide tight and cried out for help. I learned that the important thing was to get to the Grevy quickly to secure it; then it would be remarkably easy to quiet it down. Within ten minutes, two of Raymond's men were leading the Grevy back to camp between their horses.

As we went, I commented on Raymond's stick with the rawhide noose and the fact that I didn't have one. "Oh yes, you need a stick," he said. "You had better get one, and perhaps we can have another little tilt as we return." I collected the right sort of stick. Raymond passed it as good and, within five minutes, it was tally once more. This time only Raymond and I gave chase; the other two carried on with the catch to camp. I selected what I thought was the right size Grevy, which Raymond confirmed by shouting, "Yes!" All went according to plan, but just as I was about to slip the noose on the animal it jinked round a thornbush. My mount jinked also, but I didn't. I parted company with my splendid mount and landed smack in the middle of the thorns.

A few minutes later, a laughing Raymond led my horse back to me. "Yes, yes, you know. This sort of thing is always happening. Just as well to get some of the falls behind you." "Behind" was about right; mine was full of thorns. The ride back to our main camp was a little painful. All together, twenty-three thorns came out of my back and side.

We found the camp and the Guests in splendid form. Jack had taken them out on a bird shoot with great success. We now had a larder full of guinea fowl, spur fowl, and some sand grouse; and in a patch of long, green grass, Jack had combed out a few quail. We were going to live like so many kings—and one princess. And Princess Diana deigned to take the last two thorns out of me. To spare my blushes, these two were in the back of my shoulder, making twenty-five in all.

H CLAASSENS.

Chapter 3

Learning to Be a Professional Hunter

fter Jack Soames and the guests had gone back to England, I thought it a good idea to move over to Mervyn Soames's farm and really do a bit of managing. Also, I wanted to spend some time with my fine dog, Poppleton, and enjoy Nell, my filly. The rains were due to start, so it was a good time to get going. Mervyn had all sorts of wild ideas about growing sisal there. I planted a few hundred suckers. I believe the sisal is still there, looking as ragged as when I first planted it.

It was a lovely wild farm. Five thousand acres of rolling plains country, pretty bush, two permanent rivers, and one river that was only part-time. The whole area was covered with a great game population. At times lion, rhino, buffalo, and leopard, as well as *kongoni*, eland, and oryx, could be seen on the plains. It was another Serengeti, a Serengeti without wildebeest. At first living on the farm was a bit lonely, but overall I enjoyed it immensely.

During this time, several people came to hunt within the confines of the farm. One girl I recall very well. Her name was Billie Limpey, and she was from Southern California. She was short and blonde, used a strong perfume, and was not unkind to look upon. As I recall, she hunted a buffalo, on which I helped her, and several of the lesser game in the able company of either Kikunyu or Tabei. And then there was one famous hunt when she went entirely on her own.

One morning, just after breakfast, she slipped out unbeknownst to anyone. About noon that day she returned. "D'you know what?" she asked in her high-pitched Southern-Californian voice. "I've gotten me a dandy impala." I was so relieved to see her back in one whole piece that I ran up to put my arms round her and kiss her, but at the last moment I was repelled by her perfume. I just took her by both hands, saying, "Well done, Billie, well done." It then occurred to me that the vultures had probably eaten the carcass by now. Also, all the bush for several miles around looked exactly alike. I asked her if she could find her kill.

"Of course, sure," she said. "D'you think I am stupid?"

As we approached the bush, I saw a white flutter in the breeze. Clever girl; she had hung a little white handkerchief on a thorn tree. Now what? Another hundred yards away, more flutter. This time a piece of toilet paper. Fifty yards more, another piece. On it went, flutter after flutter. Finally we arrived at the dead impala to find on it—as a bird-scare and, maybe, to claim ownership— Billie's little pink panties. She saw me viewing them and ran up to me, saying: "You see, I ran out of handkerchiefs."

As a result of Billie's safari, my bank balance doubled, and I was able to invest in my first safari car. It was a box-body Rugby Durant. It had wooden spokes on the wheels, which creaked and groaned, and a radiator that whistled, snorted, and steamed. In time I found a remedy for all these ailments. The car gave me comic pleasure, helped me with some of my safari work, and cost the princely sum of £50.

I still continued to use horses and mules for weekend hunts up Mount Kenya. These were chiefly on my own account, to get experience. From time to time, though, I took a customer along in the Rugby. I was also on the lookout for a suitable trophy rhino for John Adams. I wanted to do something to repay him for my fine first hunt at Embu. I was to let him know if I saw something good. He would then come up posthaste.

One day, Kikunyu, Tabei, and I—not forgetting Poppleton—came on John Adams's rhino. As soon as possible I sent a telegram to John, telling him that his animal was "all tied up." Within three days, he replied that he would come on Saturday for a long weekend.

We began the hunt by following rhino tracks up into the forest. The rhino were feeding a bit as they went, but they never stopped. It was hard going, and I could see that John, who was not particularly sturdy, was beginning to wilt. Then, in the glade amidst the bamboo, were two rhino. One was definitely John's; the other was not so big but obviously had the same genes. We made ready for battle.

We moved closer and from time to time could see the shape of the two rhino through the lacy bamboo. Then, all of a sudden, as if alarmed, they threw their heads in the air, showing the tips of their horns above the short bamboo. One rhino appeared to have a considerably longer horn than the other. Very rightly, John selected that one, and with a finely judged shot he hit it fair and square in the neck. Down it went for the count. But imagine our horror when the second rhino came snorting out. This one was undoubtedly John's. A huge horn reached up to heaven. It looked to be about fifty inches as the animal crossed our path at a range of thirty yards.

But John had expended his license, and his rhino was behind the bamboo. We went to look at it, and when compared with that of the monster, its horn did look quite small. I tried to cheer him up. "John, my God, that was a good shot. Smack in the middle of the neck, and through that bush." He was in no mood for it. He answered, "I wish I had missed."

Kikunyu and Tabei, who had quickly rejoined us, improved the situation by measuring the horn by spans, and it wasn't at all bad: about thirty inches. "That's about three times as good as anything you could get in Embu, from all accounts," I said. He actually combed a smile out of his dour face and nodded. In days thereafter, that rhino head became his pride and joy. It was his showpiece amongst all his trophies. And the big one was left to sire others.

✕ ✕ ✕ ✕ ✕

All the time I was on the farm, I was getting hunting experience. Often on the weekends, I would go with my little safari party to the far ends of the farm, pitch camp, and study the game. The two permanent rivers, Uaso Nyiro, from the Aberdare Range, and the Naro Moru, from Mount Kenya, met on the farm, in very thick bush amidst big forest trees, cedar and Podocarpus. There were always buffalo here and very often rhino and hippo, together with a variety of lesser game. On the opposite side of the river was a vast acreage, an absolute wild corner, belonging to Lord Delamere. Lion in great numbers were on the Delamere acres, and very often they visited me for a cow feast. Almost always we tracked them down and did battle with them at the river junction. Elephants trekked across the farm, from Mount Kenya to the Aberdares, once a year. Leopard continually killed our calves, and we hunted them chiefly up and down the Naro Moru River. After our weekends in our camp we would load everything back onto the pack animals and head for home. At other times we would go to Mount Kenya, with the same methods of transport, although I added the safari car when I had to get back to the farm more quickly.

One way or another, the next two or three years passed quickly and pleasantly. Some episodes, of course, were not so pleasant. A case in point was the shooting of the unlucky Bill Ryan on a rhino hunt. Mind you, it's a great wonder to me that there aren't more accidents on hunts, especially when there are too many people on the scene. At this particular time we had four guns. That was probably two too many. We were on the lower slopes of Mount Kenya trying to chase off an insistent rhino. The wretched old rhino insisted on chasing Jack Soames's cattle off a salt lick that really belonged to any who cared to use it. The rhino apparently had other ideas. As we approached the salt lick, with not a cow in sight, the rhino winded us and came on like an express train. This was almost completely open country with no bushes to dive into, and we were a large target of seven, with the three trackers. Four rifles fired, almost as one. Down went the rhino—and Bill. One of the shots had gone through his right arm, and the shock put him flat for a moment or two. However, he was up in a trice and put a finisher in the great beast. Poor Bill. He was in great pain, but full of guts. He blamed no one. It might have been any one of us, but he did not make accusations. Needless to say, we got him off to Nairobi, into hospital, as quickly as possible. The roads were very bad in those days, and the journey took many hours. It must have been absolute hell for him. He took a long time to recover, and when he did he had only about 50 percent use of his right arm. It was yet another lesson learned: not to have too many guns.

✗ ✗ ✗ ✗ ✗

Jack Soames had often said that he must take me down to Nairobi to meet the chief game warden, Archie Ritchie. As we drove there in his Chevrolet hunting car, Jack discussed my safari future: "Very shortly, Lady Alice Scott is coming out.

She wants you to take her onto Cole's Plains to catch game. You remember, in the same style as you caught the Grevy with Raymond?" Of course I remembered, and several times after my thorn-catching experience I had taken myself out on my lovely Nell and had, more or less, perfected the art of game-catching by horseback.

So that was splendid news. But there was more. Jack told me of the Rawson family, friends of his from England. They consisted of Captain Rawson R.N., his wife, and two daughters. They wanted to hunt in the Mount Kenya forest for rhino and buffalo. As we trundled through to Fort Hall, I said to Jack: "Thank you for all this. You are a wonderful friend to me." In response, he turned on his most lovely smile, and said: "And I'll lend you one of my Rigby .470s." I really was in heaven. The gun I had dreamed about, and soon I was going to use it.

We had a night at Muthaiga Club, where we had drinks with Denys Finch Hatton and Karen Blixen. She was a most gentle, delicate girl, and I just could not imagine her running a coffee farm, or living by herself anywhere. She had a strange beauty. I had heard that Karen was not an easy person to get to know, and I think that was very much the case. Yet, there were two Karens. One was when she was in a party of several people; then she was extremely guarded in all she said and did. The other was when she was more or less on her own, with perhaps a close friend and, of course, with Denys. In fact, when you saw Karen and Denys in a group of people you never for a moment would think that they were having a love affair. But when on their own, or with a person they liked and trusted, everything was different. They were very much in love.

The following morning, after breakfast, Jack drove me down to the center of Nairobi, asking me to meet him at the game department at 11:30. At the appointed hour I followed Jack up the steps to meet the great Archie Ritchie. He was great in every meaning of the word.

A big, fine-looking man with a great mop of silky white hair and a silky white mustache, he was sitting behind an enormous desk that was in apple-pie order. He got up to meet us, and I was surprised at the length and breadth of the man. His voice was deep and melodious: "Jack has let me know something about you, and from him, it is a recommendation that I take notice of." He indicated two huge leather chairs for us and continued: "Apart from your taking out some of Jack's friends and contacts, I'll be able to use you at times on control work." I thanked him, and I was thrilled at the prospect.

As we sat in the leather chairs, Archie opened a handy cupboard at his desk, produced a bottle of gin and a bottle of Angostura bitters, and proceeded to mix three pink gins. It was like being in a very private little club. As we sat and drank, Jack told Archie his future plans for me as regards Lady Alice Scott and Captain Rawson R.N., and more "coming up in the lift." After the third pink gin, Jack decided it was time to go. For myself, I was always ready to give the drinks the go.

✕ ✕ ✕ ✕ ✕

Lady Alice arrived soon after for her game-catching safari, and what Jack had told me about her was dead right: She was a very fine horsewoman. In fact, for the first part of the chase I found myself watching her. She was well up on the chase all the time, and within a short space we had two zebra safe and sound. The game-catching team consisted of Lady Alice, myself, Kikunyu, Tabei, and four other mounted helpers. While Jack was seeing to it that the two zebra got up to my farmhouse, we spotted a small herd of eland. We had decided to look them over to see if there was one of catchable size when a half-grown impala came over an adjacent rise, hotly pursued by two cheetah. Alice's eyes lit up beautifully. I knew she wanted to have a go. We went, followed immediately by Kikunyu and Tabei.

35

The Wheel of Life

The two cheetah were after the impala, four humans were after the cheetah, and I noticed over my shoulder that Jack was bumping along in the rear with his car. First the cheetah ran down the impala, and then we ran down the cheetah. For a few seconds none of us knew what to do next. Then Kikunyu and Tabei arrived, and they knew exactly what to do. They were off their horses like greased lightning. Kikunyu rushed up to the nearest cheetah, threatening it with his whip, and it immediately cowed down. Kikunyu clamped a sack down hard on its head, and all struggle ceased. The inevitable piece of rawhide appeared. They tied its four feet together, and when Jack's car arrived, into another sack it went.

The next day, the whole party joined by Raymond and his men went out again to the cheetah country. We parked the truck under a convenient shady thorn tree whilst the rest of the party rode out looking for cheetah. After a short while, one of Raymond's men pointed to a little cone-shaped hill a mile away. Above it circled telltale vultures. It could be a lion kill; we hoped it was a cheetah kill. It was.

There were five cheetahs enjoying their kill, a youngish zebra.

Then I saw a most spectacular performance from Raymond and his men—a splendid team operation by a group who definitely knew their job. As we approached the cheetah, Raymond's men split up into two parties. One moved slightly left and one, with Raymond, slightly right. As the cheetah showed signs of disquiet, but before they actually started to move, Raymond gave the order: "Charge," followed immediately by "*Kimbia tu.*" Without ado the two parties galloped for their respective sides of the cheetah, which at this stage broke, three to the left and two to the right. Naturally I followed Raymond. I had to see that great man in action, in a sport that he himself had surely created. I noticed that our "Alice in Wonderland" was with me.

The two cheetah running from Raymond's group got a flying start and continued to outspeed the horses for about three hundred yards. Raymond and one of his men, I think Ndirango, came up level with the biggest of the animals. As the tired cheetah shot out under Raymond's horse, Raymond appeared to fly out from the saddle and landed smack atop the cheetah. Now Raymond was no mean weight. He was 210 pounds of solid meat and bone, and I suppose at this stage he was at his strongest. I noticed that he had a large piece of blanket, or some such, wrapped round his arm. This he stuffed right into the cheetah's mouth, by which time Ndirango had arrived to help and I had arrived to gape. In three trices the large animal was bundled up in a sack and tied up with rawhide. In a moment Raymond was on his horse again and after his second cheetah.

From a slight distance I observed Raymond emulate the flying trapeze artist three times more. The man seemed immune to hurt. The final cheetah was really an anticlimax. It was a deadbeat that took refuge in a pig hole, and we pulled it out by its tail. So there it was. In about forty-five minutes, Raymond and his merry men had caught five cheetah.

Jack Soames got himself back from England just in time for the Royal Naval safari—as we decided to call it—with Captain Rawson and his family. I put up a very nice camp on the lower slopes of Mount Kenya in a lovely glade surrounded by cedar trees. We had the most beautiful views all over the lower plains country.

"The Old Captain would like to get a rhino," Jack told me. "Also a buffalo. Apart from that it's just what shows up and what we advise. Maybe, just two or three other trophies." They were a very sweet, very attached family. The elder girl was Evelyn, the younger Elizabeth. "She, the mother," Jack informed me, "likes to be called Mrs. Rawson. We call him Captain till he asks you to call him Bill." Jack was amazingly good at these sorts of points, and I learned, in the fullness of time, that these diplomatic details did really count for a lot. Without them one could manage all right, but with them one would safari along with a sail full of wind. In this particular case Jack's advice to me was 100 percent sound. Furthermore, after setting out the first morning to hunt a buffalo with "Captain," I came back a few hours later with "Bill."

Within half a mile of camp, we came upon a small herd of cows and calves with two big bulls walking along behind. I decided to try a Gypsy trick, which I whispered in the ear of Kikunyu. He quickly nodded his head, tested the wind, and went off stealthily to the right. I got the captain into position by the side of a stout cedar tree. I was right beside him. Without spoken word I had made it clear that he was to be in readiness to shoot the second bull, if I approved of it and gave the sign. Sure enough, after Kikunyu had proceeded round the glade sufficiently, the buffalo got the wind of him, threw up their heads, and milled around a bit. With good luck, the second bull showed itself at this instant as it came up onto a higher piece of ground. I evaluated it at once as a good head and gave the captain the sign to shoot. He certainly hit it well and solidly, but like a flash the buff turned and was away at top speed. As it was about to disappear over the rise, I swung a shot at its rump; the shot sounded like a hit, but in a moment the animal was out of sight. I turned to the captain, saying: "You hit it a good, solid shot." He replied: "I took its heart. I hope it was good."

We hurried after the buff. Right beyond where the big bull had gone out of sight we found its tracks and, within a few yards, flecks of frothy blood and one spot where the beast had obviously nearly come down. Then it had turned off into a small patch of bush. We all stopped, and I sent Tabei around to the other side of the bush to see if the bull had gone straight through. It hadn't.

The captain insisted on going into the bush with me. We went in very slowly and cautiously. Then we heard the snorting, grunting, and bellowing that only a charging buffalo can produce, and it came at us. Our royal naval captain was as steady as the Rock of Gibraltar. The captain shot the gallant bull straight and true, smack between the eyes, and it came to rest six feet from us. And it was a beautiful trophy: at least a 48-inch span and a wonderfully deep boss.

The next morning we got on a terribly good motor track in the forest and went along it for a few miles, watching out for rhino tracks. But we saw a rhino before we found any tracks. I say we saw a rhino; in fact, we saw only the rear end of the animal disappearing into the forest. Just as we studied the tracks, the oddest series of noises came from within the forest. We pushed our way in while the odd screaming and grunting-cum-snorting noises continued. I felt that the rhino, both of them, would be more interested in sex than in us. Fortunately, that proved absolutely right. We were rewarded with a very pretty sight. There was old papa rhino serving mama rhino. Young master rhino suddenly became aware of us and came trotting up to have a closer look. Thankfully, he thought Ma and Pa were putting up a better performance than we, so he went back to cheer them on and take notes. I was relieved when Bill said no to the bull, which had a good pair of horns. Bill was suitably rewarded. The next day he got a very good rhino—a bachelor.

Shortly after the Royal Naval safari, Jack arrived on my doorstep early one morning. He was clearly very upset: "Those bloody elephants," he said, "are uprooting all the lucerne I've planted. They are making a hell of a mess. There must be a hundred of them. I want you to come over, spend a night or two, read Bell's book on elephants, see where to shoot 'em, and drive them off." I got over to Jack's in double-quick time and immediately started studying the heart shot on an elephant from Karamojo's book and half a dozen others. The mistake I made was to study only the heart shot. That is, I thought I would go and stalk an elephant, get it into a position I liked, and shoot it in the heart. And do you know, it didn't happen like that at all.

Instead of my stalking the elephant, the elephant stalked me. Instead of my getting a nice side view of an elephant, with the heart shot standing out a mile, a very fast-walking elephant came round a corner in the trees, looking down at me with its enormous head. I did not have time to think what to do; I just had to do. I flung Jack's poetic Rigby .470 to my shoulder as the elephant raised its trunk in the air. Thankfully, the great animal went straight down. I had shot at the only target I could see, and that was the middle of that huge head. I thought I had brained him, but of course I had done no such thing. The great animal was up on its feet in almost no time. I shot again, at the only target available, the head. Down it went. At that stage there was a tremendous crashing of bushes, and I turned off to where Kikunyu was pointing. Great gray shapes ran through the nearby trees and bushes. Fortunately, they were not on our line.

With a great feeling of relief I was able once more to turn my attention to the downed bull. But it was not so down. This time I stepped to one side to shoot through the bushes at where I judged the heart to be, and I finally found it. This hunt was a great lesson to me. I had not done my homework sufficiently; I had not studied all the shots, from all the angles. I was planning to shoot for the heart, but I had to try for the brain. It was just our good fortune that I was near enough to the brain to down the animal. These mistakes I never made again. But I went on learning. Does one ever know it all? The answer is: Never! Never! Never!

That period of elephant trouble went on and on. The Mount Kenya forest suddenly seemed to burst its seams with the huge animals. They overflowed continuously onto the adjoining farms, especially onto Jack Soames's farm. There was a large salient of forest that extended into the farm, and that made it easy for the raiding elephant. They did not have to travel back into the forest reserve; they just hid up in the salient and raided the crops at night. At least once a week I would answer Jack's call for help: "Come and shoot an elephant." This I continued to do, but with a difference. I now carried my own beautiful Rigby .470, one I had acquired from one of my near neighbors, Segar Bastard, who had a wife and a beautiful young daughter named Joy. Kikunyu carried Jack's .470. We were well equipped.

However, we would kill an elephant, and the next day they'd be back again. Then, really quite by chance, we lit on the answer. We had just downed one jumbo, and I had not even had time to reload the one expended barrel when two more elephants came tearing down our path. I shouted to Kikunyu to take the left one: *"Piga ili ya Kushoto."* So, in a moment or two more, we had three elephants on the ground within a radius of fifteen feet. That did the trick. During the night the whole herd moved back into the mountain, and they did not trouble us for a full month. It was of no avail to shoot one elephant. Shoot two or three and away they went. That was the pattern for the future, and it always worked.

At the next New Year's celebrations at Muthaiga, Jack invited me to come along and join his party. I had a wonderful time, as everyone else did. At the party, Denys Finch Hatton came up to me without any preliminary warning and said: "Jack has been telling me of your safaris for his friends. Now, I'm wondering if you can help me out. I am in a somewhat tricky situation." He went on to explain. Apparently he had been contacted by a friend in Canada to take out three French Canadians from Montreal. It was all laid on and the deposit for the safari paid. Then, as a bolt from the clear blue sky, two of the men suddenly refused to take out the third man with them. Denys was in a complete quandary as to what to do. This was before the days of the "random harvest" of professional hunters.

Denys looked at me, and I looked at Jack. He nodded to me and then answered for me: "You can take it from me, Denys, Bunny will certainly do the job for you. And I'll give him every assistance." So that was that.

Puffing Billy, my safari car, chugged into Nairobi with hardly a creak. I walked onto the platform at Nairobi station and awaited the train from Mombasa. In it came with all the usual noises to accompany its arrival. They were in fact identical to those that had heralded my arrival several years before. On that occasion I searched for a face I knew; now I was searching for a face I did not know. Yet I picked him out immediately. There he was, leaning out of the window, as plain as if advertised.

Starting at the top, he had an enormous double terai hat, obviously bought a few days previously at Simon Artz in Port Said. Covering his tiny, dark, almost black eyes were the thickest glasses imaginable. His face was as white as a slightly dirty sheet. Round his neck he had a red bandanna handkerchief, tucked into a long-sleeved safari coat of heavy material. I guessed he also had a red-lined spine pad. He did. He looked at me. He blinked. Then he opened his very small mouth: "Bunny Allen?"

"Yes," I replied, "welcome to Kenya." He then smiled very nicely, and I could see a warmth in the man. He climbed down through the carriage door with the help of the various handles and one luggage porter. It was then I saw the size of him. He must have been only five feet tall—including his Simon Artz hat! As he stepped onto the platform, the hat fell over his eyes, where it came to rest on his glasses. He pushed it back into position, and it was then I noticed his large, protruding ears.

Next morning we set off for camp after buying the drinks that Macabbie—that was his French-Scottish name—asked for and a few fresh provisions. My customer proved to be a really nice little man. He wanted to enjoy himself, but most of all he wanted to beat his two former friends. "It is like this, Bunny. I must beat them. If I get one or two good animals, I know I will."

Owing to Macabbie's minute build, I decided that we would hunt from horseback—that is, keep on horses until such time as we had located the animal that we wished to hunt. Otherwise the poor chap was going to get completely lost in the high grass and the bushes and quickly become exhausted.

Next morning, shortly after dawn, we were riding over the plains between the Thika and Rupengazi Rivers. We spied a rhino fast asleep under a tree. At a distance of ten yards I intimated that it was time to shoot. He knelt down, but, of course, the grass was too long for so short a man. Then, as he stood with the rifle positively trembling at his shoulder, the enormous hat tumbled over his eyes. The rhino quit its snoring, probably missing its lodgers, the tick birds, and got quickly to its feet. It looked somewhat belligerently at us, the trespassers into its domain, and then came on like an express train. As I shouted, "Shoot," I fired, and the shock of my bullet made Mac pull off his rifle. By a sweet piece of good fortune, Mac's bullet connected to the rhino's chest, and the animal was down and out.

The next day the good fortune continued. After riding for an hour, Tabei spotted some buffalo tracks. We dismounted, and there, for all to see, were the buff signs, wet, polished, and steaming hot. In next to no time we located the animals in a clump of bush, and before I could think of the next move, one old bull poked out its nose. I certainly expected it to act on usual form and run away. But, not a bit of it—it came right on out at us from about fifty yards. "Shoot, shoot," implored a somewhat frightened Macabbie, as his hat fell over his eyes. It was second nature for me, by now, to have my hand ready to adjust it. That done, I said: "Right, you shoot too. Ready—now." The two guns went off together, and the buffalo crunched to the ground fifteen yards away.

Before Mac could do a jump of delight there came a surprise. A second bull buff came roaring out of the same bush, again straight at us. This was just too much for Mac. He dropped his gun and took to his heels. I brained the charging bull, and very conveniently it dropped in splendid photographic position right alongside the first.

Not long after, a game scout arrived by bicycle with news of troublesome lions. The note he handed me read: "I am sending a game scout down first thing in the morning on his bicycle. He can guide you to the lions. Good hunting. Tom."

After discussing the prospects with the game scout while Mac took forty winks, I decided to go out in the evening, put a bait up if necessary, and see what the chances really were. It sounded a good possibility. After a cup of "English four o'clock tea," we went out to look into the lion story. Kikunyu was optimistic.

"There are many lions about, bwana. There is one big one. I have seen his footmark; I have heard his grunt. He is big."

Upon our arrival close to the spot where the lions had been seen, some local river fishermen told us that the animals had moved on. Nobody had any real clue which way they had gone, and the matted grass cover made it quite impossible to spoor them up. We put up a zebra after a long drag, and on the way back to camp Mac made a very neat shot on a reedbuck. There was no doubt that the man could shoot straight enough if he didn't get excited.

First thing in the morning we crept up on the bait but found, to our disappointment, that it had not been touched. Some fishermen said the lions had been about all night. Their roars had kept them all on tenterhooks and some up trees. I was wondering what should be our next move when the bicycle arrived once again. The face of the fine game scout was wreathed in smiles. "We have it, sir. It is in a large patch of makindu near the river, one mile up."

We decided to use beaters, and they arrived shortly thereafter with an assortment of drums, tins, and other cacophonous materials. We soon heard them working their way through the palms; they were coming closer, and doing a splendid job. Kikunyu had them well under control. A lioness broke cover and came ambling along, close to us. "Shoot, shoot," came the plaintive cry from Mac. "It's a lioness. Wait," I breathed. Then in rapid succession came three more lionesses and two half-grown cubs. This time an absolute begging came from the client: "Shoot, shoot, please shoot." This pantomime went on three more times, on each occasion with the same beseeching cry from big-hatted Mac: "Shoot, shoot, *pleeese* shoot." At last it happened. Out came the grandfather of all lions. It came trotting along, giving a wonderful shot. Now, it was my turn. I did the imploring this time: "Mac, shoot, shoot, please shoot." Nothing happened. The lion came on and was level with us. I slowly lifted Mac's big hat and said: "Ready—now—shoot!" It worked like a dream. As I shot harmlessly into the air, Mac shot straight and true. It was a dead lion. I walked up and bent over it, remarking: "Well done, a fine shot."

It was truly a magnificent lion, one of those very rare peroxide-blonde jobs. Mac walked up and glowed as he examined it. Then he looked puzzled as he quizzed me: "I missed it with my shot. There is only one shot there." He pointed to the lion's shoulder.

"No, Mac, that's your shot. I missed it." Knowing Mac would just not believe this, I continued: "I wanted you to shoot your lion, completely on your own, as I knew you could. I shot in the air just to get you started."

Mac shook me by the hand, and in nodding his head in agreement, over went the hat once again. For the last time I set it back into place, fair and square on the two large ears. All he wanted to do was beat his "friends." That he did, hands down, as I subsequently learned from Denys Finch Hatton. His rivals got, between them, one miserable lion, two poor buffalo, and sundry plains game, none of which amounted to anything.

Chapter 4

Two Wonderful Characters

I break off now to tell of a rather lovely experience with two very lovely people. Through the machinations of my brother, I had been invited down to Mombasa to box against the British Navy. Jack Soames passed this news onto Denys Finch Hatton, who in turn invited me to his place at Takaungu. Immediately I thought back to my arrival at Mombasa in company of that nice girl She, and how She had told me of Takaungu and Denys and Karen. Thus I was thrilled at the invitation. Now I would be able to get firsthand information on what everyone considered to be a beautiful fairy story. Mind you, I did not know that Karen would be there, but I certainly imagined she would be. She was. And what a difference from the Karen Blixen one met at Muthaiga Club, at a polo tournament, at a race meeting, or anywhere with a lot of people about. Under those conditions she was so reserved as to be almost cold. You could almost feel the icy blast of a Scandinavian snowstorm—not the wonderful glow of her heart. Denys reacted in complete sympathy to her feelings.

Until Takaungu, I had not seen their warm, loving side. It was a complete revelation. There, they lived for one another. As soon as I arrived, they accepted me as a good friend and an ally. They behaved exactly as if I were not there, and that was a rare compliment! Whenever he left her he kissed her. When he returned he kissed her. She did exactly the same. They would go for long walks on the beach, holding hands the while. They would pick up a shell, putting their heads together as they examined it. Constantly he would read to her as she sat at his feet. Usually it would be poetry, but always something of value.

As I saw it, their love was only just coming to fruition. The sadness is that it ended so abruptly. Theirs might have been one of the world's most beautiful love stories. They were two wonderful characters. All they needed was time, and time for them ran out. Within two weeks of my few days with them at Takaungu, Denys Finch Hatton was dead. That splendid man, that fine example of an English gentleman, climbed into his little aircraft for what proved to be his last safari. He crashed near Voi.

Many, of all races, mourned him. Karen kept her broken heart wonderfully under control as she saw to his burial in the Ngong Hills. She then sold out, packed up, and returned to Denmark, to live with her own precious feelings and write her beautiful books. *Out of Africa* tells her love story very sweetly. It is a love of Africa and a love of Denys.

I had arranged for a safari with Baron Bror Blixen, Karen's former husband. Time was in a rush, and before I knew where I was, the safari, which I had arranged at the last New Year's celebration and which entailed my guiding a German, was close at hand. The German client, Walter Wolter, had written me a long letter, telling in detail what he wanted to hunt. He finished up: "I am a big man. I need a big bed. I need a big bath. I look forward to meeting you. Walter Wolter." Later, a cable arrived: "Am getting married. Now need double bunk, double tub."

The great day arrived. Walter and his new wife, Orlanda, got off the boat train at Nairobi station. He certainly was a monster of flesh. She was a tiny slip of a thing. And gorgeous!

Two days later we took off for Tanganyika following the load-carrying truck, which was awaiting us at Arusha. We then proceeded to the camp, which was delightfully situated right on the Great Rift Wall, under monster shade trees and among cascading rivulets. There were tsetse flies here and there, but not in the great numbers we were going to encounter at Bror Blixen's place some days later. The first morning's hunt was a great success. We went out primarily to sight in their rifles and pick up some camp meat. They did all that and on the way home collected a rhino.

One day, as we made our way through some thick cover below the wall, a venerable old hippo came bundling out of the bush. Walter had an odd sort of rifle-cum-shotgun, called a drilling. It was an over-and-under job with a single-barrel 9mm up above and 12-bore barrels below. On seeing the hippo, Walter fairly frothed at the mouth with excitement. The poor old hippo was only about thirty yards away and a very easy target for the 9mm. Instead of which his bullet expended itself in midair. Walter immediately let drive with one of his under-barrels, a 12-bore lethal ball, with quite surprising results. It hit the hippo now, rapidly running, square in the neck. Down it went as if poleaxed, to the excited cry of Orlanda: "*Bene, molto bene.*" (Good, very good.) But in actual fact, all was not very well. The poor old hippo had only been shocked to the ground. It was up immediately and off like a Derby winner. I took careful aim with my .470. One through the neck did the trick. A few minutes later, while I took a picture of this huge man beside his hippo, I had to have a quiet titter behind the camera. It was positively hard to tell which was the hippo. Two days later the remains of the hippo brought further excitement, and a little danger.

The Wheel of Life

Lions had come to the kill. At first light we moved off from camp and made our way through the forest. On approaching the hippo, we were aware of lions, sure enough: a lion's grunt and a growl as two of them argued over a choice piece of meat. At this moment a monkey, in a tall, wild fig tree overhead, dropped its "morning card" smack on Walter's shoulder. A large, beaming smile expanded over his enormous face: "Ah, sheet luck, goot luck." And that was what it proved to be. He didn't deserve it—but he had "goot" luck.

We crept round another couple of clusters of bush, where I signed for a halt while I peeped through. Two rather young lions were there. However, I was aware of other lions away to both left and right. Just as I was having a further look, he squeezed the trigger. The bullet passed an inch or two over my head and into the sky, and the blast sent me headlong into the bush. I was merely shocked and up in a moment to see a very fine sight. The two young lions had scampered at the noise. In their place, with its front feet resting on a small anthill, was as fine a king of beasts as anyone could desire. There he sat, monarch of all he surveyed. I indicated round the bush: "Take him," I whispered. He did. It was a beautiful trophy.

We hunted for a few more days from our pretty, foresty, water-cascaded camp while my customers collected the plains game they wanted. Then I received a letter from Bror Blixen. He very briefly wrote: "Come to my place, Bunny. We are having a game drive out of the tsetse bush. The clients will like it." The great Blix had ordered, and so we obeyed. We loaded up Puffing Billy with a minimum of baggage, guns, and ammunition, and off we drove the eighty-odd miles to Blix's house near Babati. I took just Kikunyu and Tabei for staff. The rest stayed in the camp, to pack up and await further instructions.

Late in the evening we made our arrival at the Blixen farmhouse. There was Bror Blixen with his expansive smile to meet us: "Ah, I am so glad you 'ave come. Now we can spread the guns right across." In the morning I was to see what this meant. He then took us to meet his partner, Raf Cooper, a very nice man, former R.A.F., and his initials were R.A.F.! He kept his own little plane at the airstrip near Babati. He had a very delightful American wife, who at once made us feel at home. The house was in a marvelous position, looking down a spider web of valleys, which in turn all led down to the Great Rift. We stood on the verandah of the house as the last rays of the sinking sun made the colors and shadows within the valleys more fantastic than ever. Blix looked intently in one direction, then reached for his binoculars. "Yes, there they are, have a look, Bunny—roan—on the left-hand rock hill." Walter had a look, too, and immediately drooled at the mouth.

The object of the shoot was to try to drive the game out of the area. That, together with clearing particularly shady bushes, which the flies used as a breeding ground, would eliminate the tsetse. They could then farm it. "At the moment," remarked Raf, "we can't go near it with our stock. If we do, they are as good as dead. We can't even graze the top of the valleys." His wife also bemoaned the fact that she could not go there to pick the wild orchids that grew there in abundance. "The damned tsetses bite me to bits."

Blix went on with the story: "D'you see, this is the position. Down there," a large thumb went over his shoulder, "we have the best grass on the place. Before we can use it we must get rid of the goddamn tsetse flies. And then they tell us that in order to get rid of the tsetse we must get rid of the game. If we get rid of the game, we get rid of my living. It is—it is—what you call it? Ah, yes, it is a vicious circle." He laughed somewhat bitterly, then added: "Funny, isn't it?" I could tell he was genuinely upset.

"So that, Bunny, is what we are after tomorrow. We are doing what we have been doing for two years now, killing the game, so that we kill the tsetses. So that our cattle may live. How it will all work out, I do not know." He lifted his hands in the air. Raf added: "It's the department's policy. We are trying it. Tomorrow you will. You will see buffalo in the thousands."

In the morning, after an early breakfast, the members of the shooting party made their way down to their positions. Three more guns off neighboring farms joined us. Raf, in the meantime, had gone off to the airstrip to ready his plane. Blix put the guns in position where the largest draws came together from the main valley far below. Kikunyu and Tabei joined the beaters, who must have numbered at least fifty.

Almost immediately a dozen buffalo were out in the open, and their numbers were increasing every moment. Suddenly there was a bang of a gun over to the left, followed quickly by two more shots. Then a call from Blix: "Here comes a big bull. Tell Walter to take 'im. He's a trophy."

I signed to Walter, who, I noticed, was shaking like a jelly. He fired; the buffalo turned for the bush. I shouted: "Give him another." I then fired as Walter fixed his second. The bull continued into the bush. In the meantime, that splendid Orlanda picked a nice bull and brought him down there and then.

When the shooting stopped, the count of buffalo was nine bulls and one old, very large cow that someone had shot in error. Blix came up to me, saying: "What about that wounded one that cut back into the bush?"

"Yes, I'll go for him now. He's pretty well hit."

"I'll come with you," answered Blix. As soon as we were well and truly in the thick bush the buffalo came on. Blix brained him before I could fire, and remarked: "Ya, he was hit goot, but a buffalo is never dead until he is . . ." and the baron pointed to the one at his feet.

After a couple more days' hunting, Walter collected a good trophy eland. Then Walter talked our hosts and our hostess into letting him try for a roan. Our hostess was absolutely against it, but the two hosts were not so adamant. Walter inveigled the necessary permission, but he made an absolute nonsense of his shooting, with the result that a wounded roan got away. With

Walter, we followed the roan for an hour. He was then totally exhausted, so I sent him back to the house with Kikunyu. I continued on for a further two hours with Tabei, without a sign or sound of the wounded animal. The blood spoor gave up entirely, and I gave up, too.

I got back to the house to find the sparks fairly flying. Our pretty hostess was really laying on the treatment to Walter for leaving a wounded animal in the bush, and when I arrived to announce that I also had failed, she turned her venom onto me. "You call yourself a white hunter, and you leave a lovely animal wounded in the bush?" Quite obviously she had been having a healthy prelunch session of gin, which made matters worse. Neither her husband nor Blix rallied to my support, and I really didn't know what to say. As it happened, she was very ready to carry on, both with her volley of words and her gin. She accepted another glass from Blix and went on: "Well, I can tell you that I am disgusted with you and your clients. The sooner you leave, the happier I will be."

Within an hour we were on our way. And that was the last time I saw Blix. Actually, in his own domain he was a more likable man and, I could tell, a great organizer. He ran the little shoot for the buffalo most efficiently. From his talk, it was obvious that he knew the safari business from A to Z. However, I will still say that he was at times rude in his manner and inclined to ride roughshod over others. I do not know when exactly he left Kenya, but my fancy is that he was back in Sweden in time to make ball bearings for the Germans. He was not a man who ever missed a chance, whether it be for a grand trophy, the hand of a lovely lady, or the collection of golden shekels.

Walter, Orlanda, and I camped one night beside the track on the way to Singida and then settled in close to the Itigi thicket for an elephant hunt. From a hilltop we spotted some bull elephants in perfectly horrible thorn scrub. Two great heads poked out of the thick trees, for a moment, before melting back in. We went after them. Suddenly, I saw a rather larger tree trunk than I had been seeing, just a few yards ahead. I had wonderingly started to glance up when the tree came for us. One of the bulls had "waited."

I threw my .470 up and just fired into the gray. The shot stopped and turned the great beast. I gave a shout over my shoulder: "Come on, Walter," followed by a quick look behind. Walter was not there. Not wanting to lose the wounded animal, I gave chase, signing Tabei to fetch Walter. I very soon saw the gray mass again and let it have another shot. The bush was so thick that I had no idea where I was firing. Nor did I have time to think, except, Where in the hell is that fool Walter?

In a few moments Walter arrived, puffing, blowing, and fuming: "Vy did you shoot, Bunny, vy did you shoot?" I was not absolutely certain, but I rather thought that the heel of Orlanda's little foot came down rather smartly on Walter's instep just then. Anyway, he said no more, and I indicated that the elephant had waited.

Walter was not exactly talkative on the march back to the camp, and, on arriving there, he went straight to his tent. Orlanda appeared for lunch, but he did not. She implied, with a few words and much sign language, that he wanted a little food and drink in his tent. The same thing happened at night. During the afternoon I was from time to time aware of a wordy argument going on in their tent. Once or twice it sounded like real strife. The next morning Walter let me know that he wished to get back to Nairobi at once. The safari was over. He paid in full.

✗ ✗ ✗ ✗ ✗

On my return to the farm I found that there were things to be caught up with, and therefore I decided to stay around for a while.

I kept to short safaris, one or two for Jack Soames's friends, and spent quite a bit of time on the farm. My sweet Nell, apart from breeding, gave me a few chukkas of polo, friendly country stuff, but nonetheless enjoyable. Life was becoming fun—but it was not only dogs and horses. Suddenly a girl came into the scene. At one of the local race meetings at Nanyuki, I saw, or thought I saw, Ethne, my beautiful Irish girl. She was away some distance and looking wonderful.

I was puzzled and bemused. I knew it could not be she, but it was the image of her. She was with three men, and I was to learn she always was with men. One of them was Jack Soames, who told me: "Oh, that girl! Yes, she is a beauty. Sylvia, the Afghan princess." I thought, What a splendid description. And what a most beautiful Afghan princess.

The next day she was there again. I talked with her a little and found her rich yet resonant and beautiful voice like the rest of her. In a word, I became one of her many admirers. Her two constant companions both wanted to marry her, and she was equally fond of both of them. She finally tossed a coin for her decision! Be that as it may, she married and lived happily for a while. However, what was important, she stayed with us so that I could go on admiring her beauty and her splendid character.

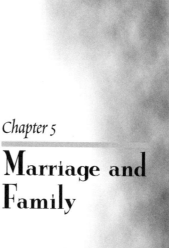

Chapter 5

Marriage and Family

y next safari of note came as a result of my knowing Denys Finch Hatton. A doctor, Kurt von Wedel of Oklahoma City, got in touch with me. He had been planning, in the first instance, to go out with Denys. Then came Denys's untimely end. The doctor had also been in touch with Macabbie of Montreal. He wrote: "Mr. Macabbie highly recommends you. I shall be coming with a friend, Mr. Robert Johnson, and his son, Gantry. We would like to hunt for a month or six weeks." It sounded a nice enough possibility. I would have to get everything in apple-pie order.

What about my poor car, Puffing Billy? I decided that I certainly couldn't afford a new one, but I could afford to give old Puffer a good face-lift. With a new radiator, some new wheels, and new tubes and tires, together with a thorough overhaul, the old car came out ready to take on anything. It even had a horn that worked. Everything was raring to go, and in the bad weather ahead good old Puffing Billy pulled several cars out of the Tanganyika mud and always got us through.

The hunt started off in great style and went from strength to strength. The very first morning out Gantry got an elephant with eighty-pound tusks under the Rift Wall, where normally fifty-pounders were just about the best. Then one night as we sat around the campfire, chatting, I told them of the tremendous buffalo drive on Blix's place. They were really interested.

"But would Blix give us permission?" asked the doctor.

"Blix has long since gone," I said. "My guess is that the country there has all gone back to the buffalo and tsetse flies."

We went, and the doctor took a buffalo with a spread of only 42 inches. But the boss was 14 inches across, and that was what made it so impressive. The following morning we took a walk into a piece of open meadow, where Kurt took an elephant.

There was no doubt that there were more buffalo and more tsetse now than before. The past shooting hadn't helped in the least: The buffalo and the tsetse flies had won hands down.

The next morning, we left camp well before the crack of dawn and went north, parallel to the wall. After we had traveled about ten miles, Tabei tapped me on the back and signed for me to stop the car. Kikunyu apparently had heard a lion roar. We heard the roar at once, immediately ahead of us, but still way off.

We got Kurt out of the car and ready for battle. Then the four of us—Kurt, Kikunyu, Tabei, and I—advanced toward the lion roar. An anthill moved, and I knew it was a lion. At any moment, I expected the lion to poke its nose up—they always did. Up indeed came the great head from behind the anthill, with a fair slice of shoulder showing. "Now," I whispered, as I guided Kurt past me to level his .300. He fired, and the lion, with a tremendous growl, bounded off. I took any shot I could. I hit it several times as it made distance, but it didn't stop. The lion ultimately disappeared into a clump of thick grass and bushes.

In a few more moments I could hear labored breathing. We sat and crouched there; finally, it was the lion who could stand it no longer. It poked its nose through the grass to see what was going on. It saw us perched on and around an anthill and immediately came out. It came fast, and when the combined shooting from Kurt and me brought it to earth it was only nine feet from us. A cheer went up from the remainder of the party, who had moved up behind us and were about six hundred yards away. With binoculars, they could see exactly what was happening. Puffing Billy came chugging up and brought them along to join in the postmortem. "What a beautiful lion," Bob said. Later he asked: "What now, do we head for home?" I pointed to the wall and swept my arm toward camp: "I thought we'd go down past the swamp and back along the other track."

"Oh, that's fine," quickly came from Gantry. "Always follow up good luck." I almost sang as I climbed into Puffer.

From the top of the hill above the swamp we looked through our glasses. There were the usual hundreds of zebra and wildebeest going to and from water, nothing more. We were just about to make a move when Tabei suddenly raised his hand: "*Ngoja,* bwana, wait—I see something." I handed him my binoculars and he looked again. His face lit to a great smile.

Within twenty minutes we were close to a lion, which had moved up on a wildebeest; it was standing quite frozen, apparently looking straight at the lion, transfixed by fear and fascination. Meanwhile the lion was moving up on it, slowly but surely. Gantry got ready to take the lion and I prepared to back him up if necessary.

Suddenly the lion increased speed and went straight for the wildebeest, which still did not move. Gantry's shot was a beauty, clean through the heart, and the lion dropped twenty yards from its intended prey. The wildebeest then emitted a loud snort and took off at a great rate. It looked as if it were not going to stop this side of the border!

"Good shot," I enthused. "That was really a smasher."

"Wal, wal," said Bob. "Two lions in the bag and not yet 9:30 in the morning. I'll say you've done swell work, Bunny."

However, there was more to come. A further mile or so along the wall we collected a rhino for Bob, without any bother or strife. Then, just for good measure, a pride of six lions presented itself on the edge of some thick grassland. I looked the lions over with the glasses, and there was certainly one worth having.

We got into a good position for a shot, then had to wait for the selected lion to move off from among the rest. The moment came. Bob fired, and a lion rushed for the tall grass. I gave it one just before it disappeared, and the remainder of the pride followed it into thick grass.

"God, did I miss it?" asked Bob.

"No, you got it all right. It's in there." I indicated the tall grass.

"And so are the other five," he replied somewhat ruefully, with his tongue in his cheek.

"Actually, Bob, my chief worry is that I don't want to shoot another by mistake. We'll have to be very careful."

"You mean, you'll have to be very careful." This was said with great emphasis. "I'm off back to the car to look after my one and only son."

"Good, that's exactly where I'd like you. God, Bob, how I wish all customers were as easy as you."

The car arrived nearby and Bob got in at once, saying, "I'm a darn poor hero, but a fair good father," as he passed his arm around Gantry with affection.

After a few minutes I gave up the search as hopeless. Someone was going to get hurt, and the wrong lion might well be shot. I was not going to risk it. I called up old Puffer and climbed onto the roof with Kikunyu: "Bob, I'm going to follow your good example. After all, discretion is the better part of valor."

We advanced very slowly in low gear and stopped every few feet to have a good look from the roof. We had progressed about twenty yards in this manner when suddenly Kikunyu touched my arm and pointed ahead. "It is there, down dead."

And, sure enough, there it was. All's well that ends well. We loaded in the lion, by which time the splendid Puffer was carrying a lot of excess weight.

The next morning before breakfast Kurt ferreted me out on my own. I was at my tent, shaving, before going on a "late start" photographic morning. "Bunny," he said, "I noticed that your safari car is getting rather old. It was fairly groaning and creaking its way back home yesterday."

"Yes, it was. Mind you, it had quite a payload on it. Poor old Puffing Billy will have to be retired soon."

"Well," he announced, "I thought of bringing you a new car when I come next year. How will that be?"

"That'll be fine. That's a kind offer. We can take it off the safari cost."

"Well, we can see about that. I thought I'd send an International chassis and you can get the body built in Nairobi."

"Fine idea."

So that was settled. I was delighted and relieved; the good and wonderful Puffing Billy really had only just made it with the great load of the previous day. It was not going to last much longer. It was already a museum piece.

On the final day's hunting we had a thrill, with very nearly a spill. We had gone on a long walk up into the Rift Wall itself, to photograph hippo in a very beautiful lake. Suddenly, from nowhere at all, there were several whistling snorts as three rhinos charged from just to the left of the gunbearers. Kikunyu and Tabei threw themselves into the bushes, off the track. My dear .470 was up to the shoulder in near record speed and two bullets put two rhinos down, shoulder to shoulder. Young Gantry acted with great speed and judgment, and his .375 caught the third fair and square and turned it about, back into the forest.

Yelling "Come on, Gantry," I took off after the rhino and found it a few yards away: "Finish it off, in the neck." This Gantry did, and I complimented him: "You did damn fine." I shook him by the hand, and he looked pleased. On that exciting note the safari ended, and the next day we chugged and puffed our way back to Nairobi. There had been a lot of rain, and the journey took us two and half days.

X X X X X

About this time, and right out of the blue, I got myself married. Nothing was further from mind, when I suddenly saw this beautiful girl. She arrived in Nairobi in a little two-seater moth airplane. The pilot was doing a publicity trip for a big Jo'burg firm, and, being an opportunist, he thought that having a lovely girl alongside him would be good for business as well as good company. Well, the upshot of it all was that as soon as I saw her, I wanted to meet her. She had the most beautiful eyes in the world. She danced divinely, and, meeting another opportunist, she was talked into doing exhibition ballroom dancing in the newly opened Torr's Hotel. That's where I met her, and I was "done for" immediately.

She was a really sweet girl, and far too good for me. However, I talked her into marrying me, and we had several good years. Jack Soames approved of her and was always very thoughtful about her. I also rather think that he imagined she would steady me down— keep me at home a bit more, make me less nomadic. Yet, in actual fact, the effect was the exact opposite. I began to wander off more than ever. And with the advent of more and more safaris, the wandering became sort of "built in." So, despite the fact that my wife, Babs, was a loving companion, produced three wonderful children for me, and made the best rich fruitcake in the world, I left her. The final break came when the 1939–45 War took me into its arms. I never recovered from those "arms" and did not go back to Babs. I feel that she was far better off without me. I was not good to or for her. She was a splendid, lovely girl and a wonderful mother to my three children, David, Anton, and Lavinia.

✕ ✕ ✕ ✕ ✕

After a few months of short, near-to-the-farm safaris, I then had to prepare for the return of Dr. Kurt von Wedel and his friend, Ben Susan. By a stroke of luck I found that Buster Cook was due some leave, and he agreed to come along on the safari as the second hunter. It was good to see Kurt again, and his companion, Ben Susan, seemed a very nice man. The International chassis had not yet arrived, but it was expected at the coast any day. I suggested to Buster that he could take the customers up to the northern frontier for a few days' bird shooting, while I slipped down to Mombasa by train to collect the International. This I did, enjoying the train trip as always.

Then the fun started. I saw the chassis off the boat, tied a soapbox on behind the steering wheel, filled up with gasoline, and headed through the dust to Nairobi. The road was a road in name only. Even at this stage it was still very much up and down, round about, and dust six inches deep in places. Thankfully, there was very little traffic. During the whole journey, which took me three days, I saw only three other vehicles until I got to within twenty miles of Nairobi. Without a windshield, the drive was no joy. I was immensely relieved when I was able to hand the International over to the body builders.

In the meantime, Buster had looked after the customers well; the bird shooting had been good, and local scouts and trackers were laid on for the latter part of the safari. Nevertheless, I found Kurt a little fractious because I had been away so long from the safari. He was also upset because the International was not ready. In a word, he was being childish. I realized I would have to handle him with great care on this safari. He had aged quite a bit since his first safari and now was fragile. Finally we got off to Tanzania on the first leg of the safari proper.

Right away we had good hunting, good luck, and, at long last, smiles from Kurt. From our camp near Lake Manyara we had a most interesting lion experience. Ben had shot a zebra and, after skinning it, Buster left the carcass under a thick thornbush, hoping a lion would come along. We came back later to discover that a lion had already been there—and it was a most tidy lion! It had consumed a sufficiency of nice, juicy zebra meat, and it intended to come back. Furthermore, it did not intend the vultures to descend on its private larder. The wise old king of beasts had dragged the carcass back into the deep shade of the thorn tree, and it completely covered the spilt-out cut-track with loose sand. It had made as neat a job as any trained domestic cat could have done. I had neither seen nor heard of the like before, and, in fact, I never have again. Buster took Ben back to sit on the bait late that evening, but the lion did not show up. Later that night we heard Ben's lion grunting away near the swamp. "Let's hope it's moving over to the bait," commented Buster. It was. Very early next morning, as the sparrow was feeling its first wind, Buster and Ben crept into the blind. There in front of them was the "tidy" lion, licking its chops and cleaning its paws. A little way behind were five or six hyena, waiting for the remainder.

As Kurt and I left camp, we heard Ben's shot. We stopped to listen—no more shots. I said, "That sounds pretty good. I could say Ben's collected the lion."

"I certainly hope so," said Kurt.

We then took a walk up some sandy flats between folds of the valley. "Looks a good place for birds," remarked Kurt. We carried our shotguns, and the gunbearers had the rifles. Sure enough, there were birds aplenty. A couple of volleys of lefts and rights accounted for three francolin—but that was not all! Oh, dear no, that certainly was not all. A large lion bounded out of the grass. In a trice Tabei gave Kurt his .300, and when the lion stopped, at about 120 yards, Kurt hit it. It crashed off. I took it as it went but did not bring it down either. I fired the second barrel, reloaded, and fired two more. One of these was a clean miss. It sang its way into the grass on the opposite side of the sand flat. However, the lion had three shots in him. As we stomped after the wounded lion, which had gone into a small clump of wait-a-bit thorn scrub, I said somewhat ruefully: "Kurt, we seem destined to have trouble with our lions."

"We do," he said, as he polished his glasses. We made a slow and careful approach until we were about fifty yards from where we knew the lion to be. Then out it came. "Take it," I said, and Kurt made no mistake.

"Well, I'll be doggoned," remarked Kurt as we examined the lion. "Well, if he ain't a dandy."

All ended well that day. As we had surmised, Ben had gotten his lion, all right. Everyone was happy and ready for the move on to the next camp, under Fiume Mountain.

There we camped only a mile or so from a village of the Wafiume people, a good-looking tribe indeed, more like Egyptians than Africans. I surmised that they were probably of Nilotic origins. The national sport of the women seemed to be the development of perfect breasts, a richly endowed portion of their anatomy. Very finely made women they were. Each day around lunchtime they would come along and perform their ablutions at the spring just above the camp. Then came the breast massage and manipulation.

"Quite a show," Ben remarked one day. "Are they trying to upset me?" He had a nice sense of humor. For future safaris in this area, when I noticed the clients training their binoculars on these girls, I knew it was time to move camp.

The first day's hunting from Fiume brought us a herd of female kudu, then a lone bull buffalo, and finally a really breathtaking roan: It was a fine, big bull. "Come along; he's a beauty," I encouraged Ben. I was keen to have a walk through this interesting country. It was no place for a car, being full of large rocks, tree stumps, and washed-out gullies. We followed the roan for about half a mile, and when it showed itself on a slight ridge, Ben made a good shot to collect a fine trophy.

Back at camp that evening, I followed Kurt over to his tent. There he was, sitting on his bed, clasping and unclasping his hands, with his eyes full of tears. A fully grown, elderly man, mad with jealousy, because his friend had shot a trophy he had not yet gotten! It was incredible, but it was true. I hit him rather hard on the back, pretending not to see his tears.

"Well, Kurt, we'll go out this evening and get a roan for you."

"Oh, Bunny, d'you really think so?" He perked up at once.

"I should say it's a certainty. Roan are two penny round here."

Luck was with me that day. Kurt got a roan, and all was peace within the camp.

Chapter 6
A Royal Safari

The war years put an end to my hunting for a time, but at last I found myself with an honorable discharge from the Kenya Regiment of His Majesty's Forces with the rank of captain. After the turmoil of war, I was for home and hunting. I must say that I did not foresee that hunting would not get going immediately. Owing to the world's being in such chaos at the end of the war, that, however, was the situation.

Jack Soames, once again, encouraged me in every way: "Don't you worry, it will come along fine. May take a little time, possibly a year." In the meantime he wanted me to build a house on his farm for myself. In fact, he presented me with fifty acres, saying: "There you are, build when you like. It will be nice to keep you about." His wife, Gloria, whom he had married during the war years, was also a great ally of mine. She said: "You help to keep Jack years younger. He's very fond of you." She was a very sweet, charming woman. Some years before the war I had taken her on a safari.

So I had to raise some money to build a house down on the river, near where I had had so much fun hunting before the war.

The hunting was, in fact, still good there, and I was to have some fine hunts out of this bush in the next years. Jack was very generous: Apart from giving me the land, he also gave me a substantial cash payment to help with building the house. He added: "You'll need more. Ivory has a good price. Why don't you go out and bag a few elephant while you're waiting for the white hunting trade?" That was brilliant thinking. As luck would have it, I bumped into Buster Cook, just back from his war service. "What about an elephant hunt?" I asked. "Grand," he replied, and what was more, he had a friend named Hugh who wanted to come too. With three to share the expenses we figured to be able to do much better financially. Ivory was selling better day by day.

Within a week we were all packed up and off we set, but with no luck after five days, we held a conference. Said Buster: "Look here, chaps, I bumped into Pat Ayre in Garbatula today, when I went in for gasoline. He said we ought to try the Lorian Swamp." We all agreed there and then, and next morning we were on the move at first light.

By evening we pulled into the edge of the great Lorian Swamp, where we encountered immediate good fortune. Three fine big bull elephants were besporting themselves in the water, right in front of our eyes. Rifles were unbundled in nothing flat, and three buoyed-up hunters ankled into the swamp. The elephants were only a hundred yards away, behind some tall papyrus. We were soon up to our waists in water and making quite a noise thrashing through. However, that did not matter, for the elephants themselves were very busy. Buster sidled over to me and whispered: "They look like seventy- or eighty-pounders." Hugh and I were to shoot and Buster to stand in reserve, in case of trouble.

There was no trouble. The jumbo went neatly into the water. Then from far and wide we saw elephants, in and out of the swamp. In the failing evening light they went in all directions. There was only one odd thing: All the elephants were a great distance away. The only ones close at hand were the dead one and the two that had packed their bags and were heading for the next port! The rest were far away across the swamp.

Later in the evening, around the campfire, I heard the gunbearers discussing the matter. It was a happy camp. We had an elephant at last. I edged up to listen.

"*Sijui*," said Tabei, "*walikuwa ndofu, kweli?*" He was saying: "I don't know, were they really elephant?" Then spoke Kiptaiga, Buster's man, telling of a type of elephant mirage that could sometimes occur. I rejoined Buster and Hugh, feeling a bit bewildered. I was still more bewildered the next day, when I made, I think, the biggest hunting mistake in my life.

We went along the edge of the great swamp, and, after going a couple of miles, sure enough, there were elephants. I put up my glasses. "Oh, golly, yes. I see a beauty." Hugh agreed: "Yes, I see him. He looks good." We went closer, and I was still certain. Beautiful, glistening, thick, and very white ivory. Without ado, down it went. It was an enormous cow, but the beautiful white ivory was only thirty pounds a side! I have never lived down that mistake. To this day I cannot account for it.

The gunbearers and the rest of our staff declared it to have been the mirage they had been discussing the previous night: black magic on white tusks. I seized on this excuse also; I had to do something. Buster nearly packed up and went home. He was really down at the mouth. "After all," he complained, "we are out on safari to make money. You two must remember that, whether we get elephants or not, our overheads are mounting all the time." Hugh butted in to help matters: "I know, Buster, we'll cut down on beer to help with the overhead."

It was agreed: less beer, more walking, and great big tusks must come in. However, nothing more came out of the Lorian.

We saw only cow herds with bulls carrying about sixty pounds a side, maximum. "Not good enough," declared Buster, and for a while I was happy to let him make the mistakes.

A few days later we moved to the Tana River, setting up a pretty camp in the riverine forest. For a couple of days we did a lot of walking through the dense bush without seeing anything worthwhile. As the three of us sat in camp on that second evening, morale was not very high. We were each imbibing from our one-bottle ration of beer. Both Hugh and I polished off our bottles pretty smartly. It was thirsty work going through that bush. Buster was sipping his beer slowly as he read a book. He still had a large half-bottle left. Hugh and I exchanged glances; then Hugh bravely said: "Bunny, like to split another bottle with me?"

I was about to agree but was cut short by Buster, who, without a word, thumped down his half-bottle between us. He did not even lift his eyes from the book. Hugh and I exchanged smiles before I slowly remarked, "What's the matter, Buster, frightened of the overhead?" That thawed the ice that had descended on the camp. We all three had a big laugh together, and each had another bottle of beer. Our luck changed. The next day we collected a nice big elephant.

Report of it had come in from across the river. After a hunter's breakfast sufficient to keep us going all day, we crossed the river in a dugout canoe. We then walked a couple of miles in and out of dense bush. Elephant signs were everywhere. It was very dry away from the river, and, consequently, they had to come to the water. Our guide eventually stopped and made a birdlike whistle. This he repeated several times until eventually he got the bird to call back. A few minutes later another local guide appeared out of the bush. His face wore a large grin, and he pointed back from whence he had come to signify that the jumbo was there. His face lost its grin, however, when he muttered: "*Lakini mzito sana.*"

Hugh knew very little Kiswahili, so I enlightened him: "He says the old elephant is in hellish thick bush."

We then went quietly forward for about four hundred yards. The guide stopped and pointed. With a strong imagination I was able to see a small piece of gray in amidst the green of the foliage. There was no movement. It was impossible to speak, even to whisper, so I indicated to Buster that I was going up closer to have a "look-see." Buster and Hugh were to keep their eyes skinned in case the elephant showed. As a final reminder from the ever careful Buster, I observed a sweeping movement by one arm and then the holding up of two fingers. This message read: "Make certain it's got two tusks."

It was vilely thick bush to creep through, but at last Tabei and I got to within a few feet of the bull. Luckily its continuous stomach rumbles covered the slight noise of our approach. The wind was steadily perfect, and the grand old man was far away in dreamland. I could now see one tusk, a truly huge one, resting in the fork of a tree, easing its weight somewhat. But there was no sign of the second tusk as yet. The enormous backside was toward us, with the loose skin hanging down, looking to all intents and purposes like a pair of extremely baggy trousers.

If there was another tusk, it was keeping it well tucked away! However, we could not get around to the other side. The trees and bushes were all meshed together. By this time we were so close that the swishing of the tail hairs touched Tabei on one occasion. My mind thought back to exploits of the old-time ivory hunters, when it was said that they used to stick postage stamps on elephants' bottoms for a playful bet. I had no postage stamp, but in mild desperation I reached up and smartly smacked the gray bottom, and then we retreated as best we could a few yards. The elephant's reaction was quite astonishing, and lucky.

It crashed round in the bush, fully exposing two tremendous tusks. Buster roared: "Stand clear, Bunny," and with that two shots went off almost as one. Down went the elephant and completely out. It certainly had a splendid pair of tusks. They were going to go well over a hundred pounds apiece all right.

Now the hunt was on in earnest. The next day we got another one. Buster was as happy as a pig in mud. "That's at least four hundred pounds of ivory in a couple of days," he beamed. In actual fact, it turned out to be 475 pounds. For three days after the sleeping beauty we saw plenty of elephant but did not take any. They were all around the 70- and 80-pounds-a-side mark. The 100-pounders had made us a bit choosy! However, on the fourth day we had to shoot a bull, irrespective of ivory weight. It came at us, in a small clearing, from about forty yards, ears well out, trunk right up, and tail "on high." It meant business, all right. We dropped it twenty yards from us. When we extracted the tusks we found the reason for the animal's ill temper. At the root of one tusk was a large, festering abscess. We were lucky. The tusks went 85 and 81 pounds.

We concluded a most successful ivory hunt two days later when we bagged a really beautiful pair of tusks, weighing 150 and 142 pounds. That made the total weight of ivory shot on the safari 1,138 pounds.

✕ ✕ ✕ ✕ ✕

After the ravages of meat hunters during the war years, the plains game in the Nanyuki district had to a large extent disappeared. The shooting of the game had apparently been a necessity. Prisoners of war, several hundred thousand of them, had had to be fed, but at the same time it was a great sadness. These beautiful plains used to look so magnificent with the thousands of head of game on them. It was a sight to feast the eyes on.

The animals in the forest, on the other hand, had not taken so colossal a hammering. The prisoners themselves had taken a few:

They had dug pits to snare buffalo and such, but they took few indeed. The number of buffalo had increased at an enormous rate during the war years, and there had been a severe outbreak of rinderpest. On top of that very little control work had taken place. The forest was positively stiff with buffalo, and they were overflowing onto the farms below to raid the crops.

During this period, while I was building my house, I was continually on buffalo-control work. By good fortune, my eldest son, David, who had joined the game department, was sent up as game warden in the Nanyuki area. We had a few good buffalo-control hunts together, but it was hard going. At times we would hunt with dogs, and on one of those forays I managed to take an unexpected ride on an unwilling buffalo.

I had just downed two buff and had an empty double .470 in my hands when another buffalo came at me out of the bush. It lowered its head, hit me on the shins, and then lifted me up through its horns onto its neck—this all at top speed, with dogs yapping at its heels. As it galloped along, I gradually slid farther up its neck. By good fortune the path the buffalo took went right past David, in the next little forest clearing. He took a quick shot through the lower neck of the buff—and down we went. By sheer luck no hard horny part of the buff fell on me. I finished up under its soft belly, with a useless double still in my hands.

We went on with the hunt for a couple more buffalo. Then we called it a day. Apart from a somewhat bloody pair of shins, I had sustained no real damage. However, I took a week off as black and blue bruises came and went all over my body.

At other times we set upon the buffalo at night, with the help of a good flashlight. However, it was the same old story. We would knock down a few buff and a night or so later they would be back in the crops in the hundreds. Jack Soames's wheat, right next to my house, was disappearing. Finally David said to me: "Look here, let's give those buff a real pounding tonight."

That night we got into David's hunting car, in which Tabei was already waiting, and drove out to the wheat fields. Hundreds of large green eyes greeted us, and David drove at breakneck speed right at them. The herd divided as I collected a right and a left, almost off the end of my barrels. Tabei took the empty rifle from me to reload and handed me David's rifle. The battle went on with a left here, a right there, and quite often a double.

At dawn we drove out to the scene of the battle. We found fourteen dead buffalo and the spoor of a wounded one going off into the bush. We followed and killed it within a hundred yards, a fine, big bull with a spread of 50 inches. So the count was fifteen buffalo in ten minutes. Only three were cows. David and I grinned rather weakly at each other. We were a little disgusted. However, no meat went to waste. Africans from far and wide came to collect it.

✗ ✗ ✗ ✗ ✗

Signs soon started to show that there might be a safari revival. Jack Soames drove up to see me one evening, and his eyes sparkled with excitement. "Bunny, I've got a short safari for you. A young Brazilian I met at the club. He must have an elephant." Naturally I was very interested. "But it has to start tomorrow. He positively has to be back in São Paulo in ten days' time, with a pair of tusks under his arms!"

It was too good a chance to turn down. I told Jack I'd set up camp near Isiolo the next day. The little Brazil nut could fly up to the airstrip at the DC's *boma* in the evening. Jack had told me that Juan Tarodos was a man of under five feet, but he had the heart of a lion. As Jack went off, he said: "I reckon if you do Juan well, he'll bring you some good business." And he was right. As a result of that one-week safari, all of which took place within seventy miles of my house, three large safaris came to me over the next two years. When Juan Tarodos climbed aboard the aircraft at Nairobi airport, he had, as accompanying baggage, one goodly pair of elephant tusks, a handsome buffalo head, and a very homely pair of rhino horns. The rest of the trophies followed by freight express.

Juan, who was twenty-two, had rather stolen this safari out of his father's business time. He had been on a selling trip to South Africa. He stepped into Kenya for an illicit hunt on his way home. He needed the trophies, especially the ivory, as an alibi. Apparently it worked. Within six months, Juan was back. What is more, he had with him his father, two uncles, and two cousins. Before the year was out he was back again on his honeymoon safari, and seven months after that he was back with a party of nine.

About this stage in the safari business, the four-wheel-drive vehicle made its appearance. First, one or two former American army Jeeps came along, and that certainly did revolutionize hunting, up to a point. One could get more easily to inaccessible places, and you did not have to walk so far. It took a little of the romance out of a hunt, however. Instead of hiking to a special spot, spending a slightly uncomfortable night—mind you, there could be compensations—and then hiking back, you could do it all with four-wheel-drive, getting there and back in a day. For me, the chief advantage of four-wheel-drive was that I spent far fewer nights stuck in the mud, in the *bundu* (bush), fifty miles from camp.

My first experience with a Land Rover was when Kris Aschan and I took out Prince Aly Khan and his entourage. Kris had a Land Rover, about the first in the country. We chose the Narok area, as we judged that to be the best place for getting a good buffalo, which was Prince Aly's first wish. The prince also wanted his followers to have a good view of the buffalo hunt in order to film it, if possible. The party wanted to fly in with the prince's own plane. It would have to do two trips.

We set up a very fine camp in a beautiful spot, one certainly fit for Rita Hayworth, if she chose to come. It was a distinct possibility, since she was Aly Khan's wife at the time. We also cut out an airstrip within half a mile of camp. Two days before the party was due to arrive the heavens opened up and the rain did not stop. The whole place became a quagmire, and the airstrip absolutely useless. After a great struggle, Kris, with his brand-new Land Rover, got through to Narok and from there was able to phone Nairobi to put off the departure of the safari party.

For his gallant trouble, on the way back he spent the night out in a swollen riverbed—very tired, very wet, very cold, and very hungry. However, he was delighted with the performance of the Land Rover, which suffered no harm from the experience. I must say I decided to get a Land Rover at the first opportunity.

The following day the rain let up, and at night a radio message came through to say that the Aly safari would come along to Narok the next day, weather permitting. Weather permitted, and in they came. Furthermore, I suggested that the pilot might consider it quite safe to land on our strip. They landed safely and soundly, and the pilot immediately took off again for Nairobi to bring in the balance of the party. From there on we had better weather: rain, but not heavy.

The following morning I went out early to look for buffalo. I left a couple of scouts in the bush to watch and listen for any movement of the buffalo while I went back to report to Aly in camp. I suggested a buffalo drive, which the rest of the camp party could watch from their cars at the top of the slope.

"Nothing could be better," enthused Aly, "and Jackson can take movies from the car hatch." Jackson was a friend of Rita Hayworth's from Hollywood. He was an excellent professional photographer, and had "the lot" in equipment.

I judged that I wanted to get Aly into position, his followers up on the slope, and the beaters to work by 3:30 P.M. We left camp in three cars, drove quietly, and arrived at the appropriate spot to let off the beaters. Kikunyu was in charge of them. He carried a big gun, just in case.

As luck would have it, the situation was ideal if the buffalo broke cover anywhere near the spot where I expected them. After only a few minutes, Tabei's large eyes opened even larger as he pointed one finger toward the clump. "I hear the beats," he breathed. I heard them, and then Aly heard them, and his eyes smiled in sweet anticipation. At that moment the worst possible thing happened. A buffalo broke cover way down, a good three hundred yards off, and came lumbering along pretty fast. I said vigorously: "Damn and blast," and thought that the hunt was lost.

Then out burst two wonderful "face-saving" buffalo. They came angling along so as to pass about twenty-five yards from Aly, but going fast. They were striding neck and neck, with the slightly bigger head somewhat behind. "Take the back one," I advised. The "back one" must have heard me, for it shot forward until it was completely hidden by the other.

I promptly seized Aly's elbow and worked him over a few yards, but the "golden moment" had passed. The shot that Aly now took was a difficult one. Nevertheless, it connected all right. It went in with a dull *guddumf*.

"Well done, you got him," I said as I closely watched the buffalo disappear into a small riverbed. We continued to watch and with relief noted that only one bull came out on the far side. The wounded one had stayed in there. I turned and said to Aly: "I want you to stay here while I go along to finish it off."

"Hell I will," firmly replied the prince. "I'll come along too. I put him in there, wounded, and I'll see the thing through."

I told Tabei to signal Kikunyu to tell the others to bring the cars down closer, in order for Jackson to get pictures of the end of the hunt. "Get them into position so they can get some good closeups," I said.

In a moment or so Prince Aly, Kikunyu, who had joined us, and I followed the spoor of the bull, which turned off in a circling movement to the left. Suspiciously, Kikunyu's head swept round the circle, and I immediately knew what was in his mind. I alerted Aly to the left just as the bull crashed out at us from twenty feet away. Aly made no mistake with his shot: It went smack through the lowered boss into the brain. Down the buffalo tumbled, to Ismaili cheers from the cars up the slope, a mere thirty yards away.

"Thank you, Bunny, thank you. That was a damn fine hunt."

"I hope Jackson got good pictures," I replied.

As it turned out, he did get good pictures, and the professional in him knew he had got good ones that very same day.

"Bunny," Jackson told me, "that was wonderful. I can't wait to tell Rita. How I wish she had been along. She would have loved it."

Then he looked a bit pensive. He tilted his hands one way, then the other. "You know, the situation between Rita and Aly is a bit dicey. Maybe it's best she didn't come along this time."

I had to wait several years before I met Rita Hayworth. When I was over in Hollywood helping to publicize a film on which I had been working, she came to see me. She was a charming girl. We laughed a bit together about the hunt she had missed, and she told me how good the buffalo pictures were.

"Jackson was right, I would have loved to have been there. But, you know?" Her large expressive eyes said quite a lot, but I was left to wonder what exactly happened between this beautiful, fascinating woman and her charming prince.

Chapter 7

A Bitter Rivalry

My next safari was one of the trickiest I have ever undertaken, and if it had not been for a very unexpected happening it would have been perfect hell. As it was, the pearly gates to Heaven actually showed themselves.

Before the safari set off from Nairobi, everything sounded all right. There they were, two old friends from the States who had hunted together several times over there. They looked rather alike and even their names were similar. One was Smith, the other Smit.

As we drove off to Tanganyika, Smith, who had been out on a previous hunt in Africa, spoke kindly and encouragingly to Smit: "See here, Rudolf, I've been out before so that you can take everything first. Then when we get down to the sable country, I can have a go."

It sounded so easy, but it wasn't. For the first week the safari went with great accord. Then suddenly it happened. Rudolf Smit one day got himself a magnificent greater kudu on the edge of the Masai steppe. That really upset the applecart.

Alfred Smith, on his former safari, had apparently gotten only a rather poor kudu. For two solid days he would not speak to his hunting companion. On the third day matters improved somewhat because Alfred shot a very fine buffalo. His willingness to wait to get into sable country before shooting had gone quickly by the board. Even so, their conversations did not get beyond the monosyllabic. However, up to this point they still were willing to share the same tent.

The safari moved more and more south, into the sable antelope country. Here they each quickly got a good trophy, and so the peace was maintained. But this was just a little quiet before the storm. One early morning, as we were out looking for Alfred's second sable, Kikunyu spotted a good-looking lion. He suddenly exclaimed: "*Simba*, bwana, a very big one, over there." He pointed to a large, tree-covered anthill. Without ado I spun a coin and asked Alfred to call: "Heads," he said quietly. It was tails. It was Rudolf's shot.

We crept up on the anthill, and as we got close I moved Rudolf into a good position to take a shot as soon as the lion showed itself. I noticed that Alfred was lurking close up in the background. Suddenly the lion showed its head and shoulders and Rudolf got ready to fire. But at that moment a second and far better lion walked out onto the scene.

Alfred saw it and immediately flung his rifle to his shoulder, but Rudolf was right in the line of fire. Just as Alfred pulled the trigger, my hand came across and hit the gun into the air. The bullet whistled an inch or two over Rudolf's head. It was as close as that! Rudolf, it must be said, recovered quickly, and before his companion could reload he had put a good shot into the better lion. However, he did not kill it, and it rushed off into the undergrowth. Strange to say, the other lion did not go away quickly and was just meandering across the open country, about twenty-five yards away. Alfred shot at and hit that one before I could stop him. There were now two wounded lions to deal with. I must say that neither of the men was a coward. They both went after the wounded lion—the better one—immediately. Here, however, I called a halt.

"Stop, you two, and listen to me. You've got to go carefully or someone is going to get hurt."

They both saw reason. "You're the doctor," said Rudolf, while Alfred added: "Just tell me what to do and I'll do it."

After that, the finish of the hunt was not so bad. We killed both lions without any undue bother. Then both clients claimed the better lion. I knew that it was Rudolf who had first shot at and hit the better trophy. It was, therefore, his. Besides which, Alfred had very nearly "drilled" his friend Rudolf. The way they had behaved, neither of them deserved a trophy at all, but in fact they had each gotten a very good lion, by any standards.

Back in camp, each of them came up, in turn, with the same request.

"Look here, Bunny, you must give me a separate tent. I can come in with you. I can't spend another night with that goddamned Dutchman," said Alfred Smith.

"Say, Bunny, put me in with you. I can't stay on with that son of a bitch of a Mormon," said Rudolf Smit.

While I fully realized that I must separate them, I did not intend to share a tent with either the one or the other. Both snored terribly. I'd heard them in action, and, furthermore, I made a point of sharing my tent only with very, very special customers. Therefore, making the excuse that I needed a tent of my own as an office to deal with the constant stream of business concerning the safari staff, I produced a spare tent and moved Rudolf into it.

From that point on, the two customers did not exchange one solitary word for the rest of the safari, a matter of forty-five days. Each one was most pleasant to me; in fact, each one of them sort of wooed me. It was a terribly wearing safari, and by the time we had reached the little hotel on the lake shore at Mwanza, I was just about ready to throw in the towel.

As luck would have it, I got a couple of days off from them, and after a bath and a bit of a snooze, I went out onto the hotel veranda for a drink. Sitting there was a very good-looking woman. We talked together for quite a while and had a couple of drinks. She was the wife of a diamond expert.

"My dear girl," I finally said, "can't you come along with us on safari for a few days?" I asked the question completely as a joke, but as soon as the words had slipped off my tongue, I knew I meant it, every word. Diana, much to my surprise, and to my delight, replied, "Yes." As Diana bade us all good night, she told the hotel owner that she would leave a letter for her husband at the desk: "I know he won't be along for at least three days."

We set up a very attractive camp beside the swampy river. I handed my tent over to Diana and quickly had a spare dining tent erected for myself, before one of my "friends" could invite me to share with him.

Still the two childish men would not talk directly to one another, but now, with Diana, there was at least another go-between for their conversations. While we awaited news of the elusive sitatunga, which I desired to find, we went out for buffalo and elephant. We contacted buffalo the very first morning out, in a well-wooded valley. I judged that a drive was called for, and I wanted to give Rudolf the best chance. Alfred had already gotten a good specimen, whereas Rudolf's was rather poor.

Having instructed Kikunyu and Tabei for the drive, I then placed Alfred on the far side of the valley while I took Rudolf to the near side. This I judged was the most likely side for the buffalo to break. How wrong I was! Within a very few minutes four really good bulls broke cover and went up the slope, straight for Alfred. Poor old Rudolf's mouth drooled as he watched them going along to give his hated rival the chance of a lifetime. Shortly thereafter, two quick shots echoed up and down the valley, and one buffalo slowed a bit behind the others as they entered the bush once more.

I went into the foul bush with Tabei. There was a clear blood spoor. It was so thick in there you could barely find a place to peer through. However, I spotted a climbable tree and went up it. From about twenty feet up I spotted the buffalo, as clear as could be, standing very alert under a bush. It was very quiet, swishing its tail and looking in all directions. Once again I recalled the words of wisdom of Piramus: "Few of God's creatures ever look up." This wounded buffalo, keeping a very urgent guard on itself, not once looked more than five feet off the ground. As I slid silently down the tree, I signed to Tabei to hand me my .470. Having slung the rifle on my shoulder, I regained my previous position and was able to draw a steady bead on the buffalo's heart. I squeezed the trigger. With a bellow of rage, the bull dashed out toward Alfred. Another shot rang out there, and then all was silent. A few moments later we were examining the buffalo. I pointed to Alfred's last shot: "That was a good one, smack in the brain."

On our arrival back in camp, there, much to everyone's surprise, was Diana's husband, Nick Vanderscut. Later in the day Nick asked me if it would be possible for the two of them to stay on in camp for a day or so: "We'll pay our 'wack,' of course." I jumped at the idea and would not hear of him paying anything. To me, Nick and Diana constituted a most wonderful lifeline for this perilous voyage, and I intended to hang onto them for as long as possible.

Later, I led the whole party along the edge of the bush, and, after we'd gone about a mile, a very good bull presented itself at fifty yards. Rudolf made a first-class shot, straight in the heart. The bull ran forty yards and then tumbled over—a very fine trophy. Everyone congratulated Rudolf except Alfred, who stood about looking bored.

As we went on, another bull came out of the dense bush at fifteen yards from us, lowered its head, and came straight at us. I had to move over a couple of yards to get a tree out of line and then brained the buff, which came crashing on with its own weight to within eight feet of us.

The reaction of everyone was really quite extraordinary. Kikunyu, as always, opened his great mouth in an enormous grin. Tabei opened his eyes wider than ever. All the men came up, one by one, and grasped my hand. Not one soul offered a word. Finally, Diana came up to me, and took my one free hand in both of hers in a caress full of feeling. Still in this magic silence, I went to look at that buffalo. It was a huge animal but as thin as a rake. Its nose was discharging freely. "Rinderpest," I curtly remarked.

In front of the campfire that night the men complimented me for the way in which I had coped with the situation in the bush. Diana kept very quiet. One by one, they drifted off to bed, finally leaving just Diana and me. After spending a few more minutes staring into the fire, she got up. I too got to my feet, and there in the deep shadows, yet close to the fire, Diana came into my arms and we kissed long and deeply. Just as suddenly, she left me and walked to her tent, without looking back. Neither of us said a word.

Nick and Diana stayed in the camp four days, and on the last evening, after everyone else had gone off to bed, I, as was my custom, remained on at the campfire. I sat there with my thoughts going privately through my mind to the accompaniment of the nearby crackle of the fire and the far-off roaring of a lion down near the Kagera River. Almost without the slightest sound, I found that Diana was sitting in the chair beside me. Softly I spoke to her. "How wonderful. Here I am quietly communing with nature, and you suddenly are beside me, as silently as an angel from heaven."

She smiled into the firelight. I took her hand and caressed it. Then I pointed up to the moon and said: "Oliver is in town tonight, in fine style." Diana nodded her head and pressed my hand a little urgently, saying: "The whole thing is very beautiful."

We got up together and walked into the shadows, where we kissed deeply, as she curved into me wondrously. I was very aware of her. She clung to me as I shepherded her toward my tent. Then she stopped me, saying softly, yet firmly: "No, Bunny." She kissed me once again, claiming my mouth entirely. Then she turned from me quickly and went to her own tent.

The next morning Diana and Nick left camp for Nairobi, having made arrangements to meet me there at the end of the safari.

After the Vanderscuts left, my task became difficult once again. Alfred was still not saying one word to Rudolf, and Rudolf was looking longer and more poisonous daggers at Alfred as each day went by. The final two weeks were absolute hell and seemed never to end. To make matters worse, the sitatunga hunt made a screaming anticlimax. Alfred was the one who chiefly wanted one of these rare and very hard to hunt, almost waterborne, antelope, and it was Rudolf who got one!

Three days later the long drive back to Nairobi was over. Having put my clients into their hotels—one at the Norfolk, the other at the Stanley—I contacted the Vanderscuts. I then arranged a dinner party at Muthaiga Club for us all. We had a very enjoyable party, despite my two hunting companions. Nick and Diana were very good and kept them somewhat divided in the conversations. Before Diana left, she asked me to join her for lunch the next day: "Nick has to fly back to Williamson's mine tomorrow. Will you comfort me?" My answer was, "Of course."

We had a delightful lunch together, and as I dropped her back at the New Stanley Hotel, she asked: "Are you taking me out tonight? Nick will not be back till tomorrow, just in time for our plane."

"Diana, I'd love to take you out. We'll have a nice dinner, maybe dance a little, and—" Diana laughed her way in at this point: "And then, my dear Bunny, I'll go to my lonely couch. I'm being fair to you. I do not intend to go to bed with you." She was very forthright, in a typically American way.

"All right, Diana," I replied. "I'd still very much like to take you out for the evening."

"Well, as long as we understand each other." She gave her hand to me as she added: "Bunny dear, that is not saying that I wouldn't like to, but I just do not intend to. See you at seven-thirty." She blew a pretty kiss to me and was away.

East Africa Campaign during World War II. These men were in the 5th Kings African Rifles. (Photo courtesy of Carla and Anton Allen)

Maurie Randal and Baba (David, Anton, and Lavina's mother) with Maurie Randal's younger brother.

A very young Bunny with a trophy Cape buffalo.

Bunny's first wife Babs with their son David; to the right is Denis's wife Paddy and their daughter Shirley.

Head of Donald Dickey's rhino at Makindu. 1904.

These tusks were shot in control work and probably came from Shamba *raiders— leaning against a very old minor hunting car.*

Bunny's brother Ba Allen is in the middle.

(left to right) John, Bunny, and Anton Allen. (Photo courtesy of David Allen)

Bunny and daughter Lavinia. (Photo courtesy of Carla and Anton Allen)

Anton, David, and Dingle the Dalmation.

Bunny with Satu, one of his favorite Rhodesian ridgebacks.

East Africa goes on alert during World War II. Here is a typical mounted patrol. This was taken during the Abyssinian campaign.

This armored car was part of the vast armored divisions in East Africa during World War II.

Notice the unpaved ground in this picture of typical army transport.

Bunny and David Street are in the back. Dave (left) and Anton are in front.

We were held captive in Ethiopia until the ras recognized my name. Fortunately, the ras was a good friend of my brother's, so he let us go.

Kikunyu, sitting atop a mogambo, *was Bunny Allen's gunbearer for many years.*

Dave and Anton with their Daisy air gun. (Photo courtesy of Carla and Anton Allen)

Bunny at Olechugu Farm. (Photo courtesy of Carla and Anton Allen)

Tanganyikan rains always produced lots of mud. Here Puffing Billy, the car, sinks. 1930s.

Italian prisoners of war, taken during the Abyssinian campaign. 1944. (Photo courtesy of Carla and Anton Allen)

Anton, Mathui, and Kieol help client get a good buffalo. 1960s.

Carting canoes for hunting sitatunga in the Moyowasi Swamp.

A smiling Kikunyu next to a hundred pounder.

Carrisa Farm, Kenya. August 1976. (left to right) Bunny Allen, Ben Carpenter, Dan C. Williams, and David Allen.

Celebrating at the New Stanley Hotel in Nairobi following 30 days of highly successful hunting. Left to right: Front Row: Bunny Allen, David Allen, Jens Hessel. 2nd Row: Ben H. Carpenter, Dr. L. S. Thompson, Jr., 3rd Row: John W. Carpenter, III, Sandy Thompson, Anton Allen.

Bunny with Cy and Madelaine Nelson. 1960s. (Photo courtesy of Carla and Anton Allen)

Carla and Anton in 1975.

H. CLAASSENS.

Chapter 8

Good Safaris and Bad

S afaris come and safaris go, and some appear to go on forever. There are good safaris and bad safaris. And every now and then you have one that you might term a positive stinker. Such a one was my next safari.

When the two men arrived from a small town in Illinois, they looked all right. Myles Turner, who was hunting with me on this safari, remarked: "Well, Bunny, they look decent enough." I concurred. How wrong we were, and it did not take long for us to find that out. Their names were Krosovitch and Camifold.

We set off to Ngorongoro Crater before going across the Serengeti Plains. I asked them if they wanted to go down into the crater for one day.

"What can we shoot in there?" asked Camifold.

"That's reserve in there. You can't shoot a thing, but you can get wonderful photographs."

"Say, son," broke in Krosovitch, "the only good photo to me is a dead animal that I just have shot. Get it?"

"Yep, you're sure right," added Cami. Myles and I exchanged glances. We pushed on across the Serengeti.

We camped near Ikoma, where the disgusting Krosovitch decided to grow a beard. "Look, Cami," he said through his foul cigar smoke, "I intends to grow this beard. When I shoots me a lion, I'll take half of it off, and when I gets me an elephant, why, the other half will come off."

"Sounds good to me," encouraged Cami.

The pair intimated that if they got "the stuff," as they called it, the safari could end earlier but they would pay in full. That sounded good to me. Both Myles and I wanted to "get shot" of them just as soon as possible. Therefore, we put on the pressure. We got them up early and back to camp late. "The stuff" was coming in well, and the dirty black-cum-ginger beard was growing fast.

After four days, the revolting Krosovitch had the amazing "bad" luck to shoot a very beautiful lion. He had the audacity to shoot this lion wearing a double-breasted, city-slicker type of greatcoat and pointed black shoes, and with a stinking cigar between his black teeth. After we got back to camp Myles remarked to me, "Did you see that ill-begotten bastard? I felt like crowning him."

"Yes, I saw him all right," I answered. "Look here, Myles. Make him wait for his elephant. I want to see that one side of his face growing hair like a baboon—until he looks like an arsehole, which, of course, he is."

He did have to wait for his elephant. And he did finish up looking like a somewhat untidy arsehole. Fate decreed it that way. They both had to wait until two days before the end of the safari to get their elephants. We had given up trying to rush the hunt. Earlier, in the hope of finishing the safari quickly, Myles had gone all out to get trophies for them. He shot a leopard for each of them off one bait.

However, as the days went on, it became too obvious to me that these two characters were out for their full pound of flesh. They were not going to cut the safari short. That story was just a line of bull to try to get trophies. They wanted to get back to their hometown to tell their troop of girlfriends what good chaps they were, what good shots they were, and—"Was I scared when the lion charged? What, me?"

We spent the last few days of the safari at Babati. The idea was to make our brave men climb up and down Fiume Mountain looking for an elephant. It was almost certain to be a small tusker. As soon as we arrived at the camp, I noticed the clients eyeing the local beauties, and I knew I'd have to be on my guard. Sure enough, later in the day Krosovitch sidled up to me and said: "Say, can you get me one of those dames?"

I tried to pass it off as a joke and laughingly said: "If I did, the medicine man would stop you from getting an elephant."

"See here, I ain't kidding! I want one o' them babes, see?"

I "saw" all right, and I quickly worked out my plan of action. "I'll see what I can do." I did not intend to pimp for this revolting creature, but at the same time I wanted to keep the peace until the two remaining days of the safari had passed. As I left our goggle-eyed, half-bearded barbarian, I said: "It will probably cost you a spear in your belly." I thought that was a nicely pointed last comment on the subject.

Later that evening I heard the two men discussing the "local babes."

"Oh, don't you worry, Kroso, I noticed them, you bet. Nicely made, eh?"

"Damn right. That babe I was looking at through my glasses had the most lovely pair of handfuls that I've ever clapped my goddamned eyes on."

They then looked at me, and Cami spoke first: "See what you can do for us. We each want one of 'em, bad. Yep, real bad."

Then the bearded clown: "We'll make it worth your while."

I wanted to ram those filthy words down his filthy throat. However, I kept my temper, as I clenched my fists. "The last man that fooled with these women got a spear in his guts for his trouble." This fabrication I put forward in the hope of putting the pair of swine off. But it was not going to be so easy. Cami came back with: "Wal, we sure don't want any trouble. Just fix the babes. They all have a price."

Before going to my tent that night, I had a few words with Myles. "These sods"—here I threw a thumb over my shoulder toward the clients' tent—"are on the rampage after the local girls."

"Yes, I noticed that."

"Any old elephant will do. I intend to move tomorrow evening, with or without elephant tusks."

Accordingly, the following morning, well before dawn, I had the pleasure of getting the filthy Krosovitch out of his bed and off round the back of the mountain. Here we shot a very large bull elephant with tusks like toothpicks. It was a famous victory! Myles took Master Cami high up onto Fiume. After much climbing they too got an elephant, with tusks not quite so small. Yet small. While Myles organized the extraction of the tusks, I started to arrange the "babes" party with the local headman; he, in turn, got a small company of well-armed tribesmen to perform an extremely warlike dance on the approach to the camp. Then, according to plan, they advanced the dance toward the clients' tent. In the meantime, I made for my tent and lay down on the bed. Everything then went exactly according to plan. Almost immediately, two very frightened faces arrived at my tent flaps.

"Hey, Bunny what goes on? What are these goddamn savages?" I pretended to be aroused out of a deep sleep and slowly got to my feet, listened, and then looked extremely worried, or that was my intent. I glanced at the two cravens, as

I responded to their questions: "It sounds to me as though those 'goddamn savages' are after you." I pointed at Cami, who shuddered. Then I pointed at Kroso: "And you." At this Kroso's jaws fell about two inches and he actually trembled as he got round behind me for protection.

"Lie low here, you two. I'll go out to see how bad the situation is." I didn't have to say more. As one man, the two heroes slunk away to take refuge in the bathroom portion of my tent. On going outside I saw Myles, who had just returned. I enlightened him as to what was going on. He remarked, "Well done, Chief, rub their noses in it."

I saw the leader of the dancers and paid them for their performance—further, I asked them to do some rather special bloodcurdling screams and shouts before they finally went off down the hill from the camp. I intimated to Kikunyu that he could encourage them in this. His grin told me that he had gotten the message. However, the merry bunch of dancers hardly needed any encouragement. As I made my way back to the tent, the dancers were beginning to emit the most terrifying noises. The most comical of sights greeted me as I went into my tent. There were the two terrified men, literally fighting to get under the bed in order to hide from the "savages." I smothered my laughter as I said: "Well, I've had a word with them. They are in a very bad and dangerous mood."

Two very green-white, frightened faces began to appear from under the bed. I continued, "I told them that you must have two of their best-made young virgins."

"Look here, Bunny," whined Kroso, "all we want is to get out of here, safe."

"What goes on now?" asked Cami. "Sounds as if they are going away."

"My God, it does sound so," came hopefully from Kroso.

At this point I shouted, from the tent, to Myles: "What's going on, Myles?"

The reply came in a loud voice, so that the customers could not fail to hear: "They have posted their bowmen beyond the fires, and they are going now for the torture bars."

Kroso almost fell to his knees as he pleaded with me: "Oh, Jesus Christ, get us out of here. Please get us out of here."

"Torture bars," moaned Kroso. "Oh, dear God in Heaven, torture bars." His teeth chattered beautifully. I smiled into the starlit sky.

"Look, you two, there is just one chance." I then proceeded to unfold my plan. They were to wait in my tent, befouling it, until I brought the car right in the doorway. "As you hear the car coming along, put the tent light out; got that?"

"Yep, yep," they answered in unison. "Dear God, please get us out of here," added the gallant Kroso.

"Well then, as I get the car right to the tent, you two jump in the back and cover yourselves with the sacks you'll find there. You must hide. They'll probably search for you as we leave."

I then went off and instructed Tabei to fill my car with gasoline and get it ready for the trip to Arusha. As Tabei went to do those chores, I added: "Oh, Tabei, put in the back six empty sacks. Dirty sacks that the skinner has been using will do."

When the stinking men climbed out of my car a few hours later, they were a very sorry sight. The blood and the salt and the muck had done its work.

That was the end of my worst-ever safari.

✗ ✗ ✗ ✗ ✗

It was just about at this stage that four-wheel-drives really began to hit the front rank as hunting vehicles. During 1946, I had acquired a former American army Jeep. However, it was rather small to use as a regular hunting car. I had used it just as a scout car, and for that purpose it was intensely useful. Then came the rather larger Land Rover, and that had become my regular hunting car.

When Diana and Nick Vanderscut arrived for their safari, I had just acquired my first Land Rover. I also took the Jeep along. It was always a fully employed workhorse.

It was wonderful to see Diana and Nick again, and they appeared very happy at the thought of the days to come. Diana looked more beautiful than ever. Before we left Nairobi, Nick asked me if he could be contacted while on safari.

"You know, the diamond mine might have a big query," he said.

"Yes, Nick, they can send a message by Nairobi Radio station. They send out safari messages each evening. Tell them to send it after the nine o'clock news."

We drove to the already set-up camp. It was on a lovely bend of the Uaso Nyiro River. The cover of thorn trees looked like delicate lace, and, as they were all in flower, there was a sweet smell in the air. Doom palms surrounded the camp like sentinels.

After a quick cup of tea for me, a whiskey for Nick, and a special vitamin drink for Diana, we set off to try out the guns and maybe get some camp meat. Nick did not prove a very great shot, but he managed, after a miss or two, to get himself an impala. That made him very happy, and he was content to rest on his laurels awhile. "You take Diana for something next," he suggested. In a few minutes we sighted some waterbuck, in among anthills and bushes. I took Diana for a stalk, and after a little distance I pointed out a nice buck to her. She made a neat shot. I ran up to find it in the long grass, where Diana joined me. I complimented her and gave her a gentle kiss. I was surprised to find that she responded so warmly; she said: "Bunny, it's so good to see you." That was a very quick start, or should one say restart, to things.

Diana was very different in her reaction to my approaches than she had been twelve months before. This time there was no doubt in her mind that she was going to have an affair with me, and very soon she left no doubt in my mind. That first night she came and spent a little time with me before the campfire. She said that Nick was asleep, but she added: "He is sleeping fitfully. I must go back to him." She kissed me a sweet, clinging good night. "Tomorrow, Bunny, I will come to you."

While elephant hunting the next day, Nick collected an eighty-pounder. That evening, as Diana and I sat before the campfire and before I was properly aware of it, Diana was on her feet and behind my chair. Her arms came over my shoulders and she turned my head to meet her lips. Then she said: "I'll come to see you in a little while." She pointed to my tent as she quietly went her way.

An hour or so afterward, as Diana left my tent, she said: "I'd like to stay longer, but after that first deep sleep, Nick wakes and sleeps lightly." Then with a mischievous giggle: "I must try one of my sleeping pills on him. Good night, darling."

"Good night, darling." The gorgeous smell of her remained with me.

The next morning, much to my surprise, Nick was up almost as soon as I was. Obviously, he had something on his mind. I only hoped it was no overlap from the previous night. It had been wonderful, but I felt a little guilty. However, I need not have worried. He was full of cheer and happy. Business was on his mind: "Bunny, I'd like you to send me in to Isiolo. I want to get on the phone to the Nairobi office on a matter that I just sheer forgot. It's pretty important."

So, there and then, I organized an early breakfast and laid a car on ready for Isiolo, about eighty miles away. I asked: "Is Diana going with you?"

"No, I'll be better without her. She'll only get dusty going, and hot waiting in Isiolo. Can you entertain her?"

"But of course. We'll go over to Buffalo Springs for a swim and see what the buff situation is there."

We all arranged to be back in camp for lunch. Diana and I had a lovely swim, while I sent Kikunyu and Tabei on a buffalo recce. Yes, there were plenty of buffalo about. We would come to hunt them in a day or so, probably the next day.

Nick had arrived back in camp just before we did. He was sipping a cool beer. "It's lovely, Bunny, but not cold enough." That proved to be Nick's theme tune throughout the safari—"More ice!" He had been successful with his phone call, apparently. All was well,

but they might have to call him down to the mine. Something was going on—wrong!

95

After dinner the expected radio call came in for Nick from Nairobi: "And now we have a safari message for Nick Vanderscut, on safari with Bunny Allen. You are urgently needed at the mine. An aircraft will be awaiting you, Wilson Airport 2 P.M. tomorrow. That ends the safari message."

Diana and I looked at Nick. Nick looked at us. Then he said: "Wal, I guess that is it." He took a deep drink of whiskey. "Bunny, what do I do? How do I get there? I must go."

I thought for a moment. "You had better take the Land Rover. I'll send a driver with you to bring it back. When you return, fly to Isiolo. We'll meet you there."

"Fine and dandy," Nick answered. Then he looked across at Diana, to query her: "You'll be all right, honey?"

"I guess I'll be fine. Maybe Bunny can take me on a camel-donkey safari for a couple of days, and scoop me out a hollow in the sand to sleep in." She said this with laughter in her eyes, yet we could tell she meant it.

Nick retorted: "Swell, yep, get that over and done with before I come back. I certainly don't need any of that." He looked at me, expecting me to concur or whatever. It took me exactly two seconds to jump at the idea: "If Diana is really serious, we could run up in the Jeep to the Merilli *lugga* and there organize a foot safari to look for your second elephant, and see what the leopard chances are there."

Quickly from Diana: "I am really serious." So there and then it was decided. Nick would leave at the crack of dawn in the Land Rover to drive to Nairobi. He would be back in Isiolo on the third day, unless he let us know by radio message that his return would be further delayed. In the meantime, Diana and I would do our safari.

Everything went according to plan, and by midday the following morning Diana and I were set up in a pretty little camp at the Merilli sand river. We took the Jeep only, and so we had but the barest necessities. As dusky night became dawny morning, I walked Diana slowly round the first bend in the sand river and pointed to a pool of crystal-clear water. I handed her soap and towel: "There is your morning bath." She almost breathlessly answered, "What heaven," and in another moment she was briefless and in the pool. As I divested myself, I watched her, admiring her, with thoughts of the night.

She looked up and caught me conning her. "What is it, Bunny? Is that love in your eyes?"

"Yes, it is." I glanced her all over. "I am just marveling at the love in your thighs."

She threw two handfuls of water at me. "Lover, you are horrible. Come in the pool."

I must say she was a very game girl. We walked and stalked and we talked. By early evening we had arrived back in our "hip hollow" camp. Mwangi, the cook, had prepared another delicious meal, to which Diana and I did full justice. To finalize the meal Mwangi brought us each a glass of milk. He had a slight grin on his face as he served this to us, and I gleaned what it was all about. I sipped mine and had the answer. Diana ogled hers a bit, then said: "Wal, Bunny, I don't usually take milk." She patted her wonderful curves. "It's bad for all this, but when on safari, do what they do on safari, I suppose." She then took a little drink, looked somewhat surprised, and added an inquiry: "Has he put salt in it, or something?"

I enlightened her: "No, Diana, it is camel's milk. It is excellent stuff to march on." She took another little swig: "Say, Bunny, you drink mine. You've got quite a 'route march' ahead of you. It's time for bed!" However, I was, in fact, not allowed to finish all her camel's milk. She reached over to reclaim her glass: "Hi, let me have another little go. On second thought, it's good."

"Watch the aftereffects, too. It's very strengthening."

"OK, Sonny, let's drink it down and hit the hay."

✕ ✕ ✕ ✕ ✕

The next morning, at a decent hour, the camels and four donkeys arrived as ordered. They were quickly loaded up, and we set off on our fly-fly safari. We had a great day together. As the moon rose into the heavens, at about 8:30 P.M., and the stars twinkled in the clear sky, Diana declared herself more than ready for bed. "Bunny, it's been a wonderful day, but I am dead tired."

"Yes, I'm sure you are. You were very brave." I looked at her, thought for a moment, then: "I think it best if I went to my own hollow tonight."

She answered quickly, softly: "No, stay with me." Then, with a light laugh: "But no nonsense. Just keep me warm. It's cold tonight. We can spoon ourselves to sleep." So, in the cool breeze, we settled down in the "double hollow" and played "sleeping spoons" all night.

The following day I sent a message back to the main camp with instructions to meet Nick in Isiolo, unless they had heard by radio message to the contrary. On his arrival, they would bring him up to our base fly-camp with further supplies—and an ice-making box!

By the time Nick did arrive, the camp was in apple-pie order, with cream on it, by way of an ice chest full of ice. "That'll please him," commented Diana. And it did. Nick was as pleased as punch.

The next day Nick got another elephant. He did splendidly. I got him up to within thirty yards of the bull. Then, with a shot almost broadside, Nick took it in the heart.

Nick went off to bed, slightly glassy-eyed and happy. Diana escorted him to the tent door, then came back to me: "Thank you for a wonderful few days, Bunny. I can't tell you what it has meant to me." She waved her head from side to side, and the firelight reflected from her eyes as she went on: "But now, my sweet lover, I'm off to the sack. I'm really dead beat. It is as much sheer excitement as being physically exhausted. Good night, dear Bunny." She kissed me quite lightly and almost ran off to her tent.

The next day we put up a couple of leopard baits, and on the third day a good-sized leopard visited one of them. In the evening I took Nick along to sit over the bait. Tabei was with us, and Kikunyu took Diana to restock our supply of sand grouse. We had been sitting at the bait for about half an hour and then, suddenly, our leopard was up in the fork of the tree. The light was still quite good, and Nick should not have fuddled the shot, but he did. The leopard was off the tree like a flash and into thick bush in two bounds.

We picked up a blood spoor at once and followed for a short distance, but we had to give it up for the night. A very worried Diana greeted us on our arrival in camp, and she did not like hearing that the wounded leopard had gotten away. I spoke up as I laid a hand on Nick's shoulder: "Perhaps I ought not to have let Nick shoot, Diana. The light was getting a bit poor."

"Pooh!" came her reply. "I guess you're always ready to make excuses for people."

First thing in the morning, leaving a nervous Diana waving to us from her tent, we set off back to the leopard spoor. There was the blood again, freshened up by the night dew and gleaming once more. Tabei led the way with a blanket wrapped around his left arm, a heavy club in his right hand, and a sharp knife on his belt. I carried a shotgun, and I, too, had a good knife in my belt. Nick brought up the end of the Indian file, carrying a .300 rifle.

I had given him his instructions: "If you see it, take a shot quick. Tabei and I will get out of your way, but, to be quite frank, I don't think you will get a shot." I pointed to my shotgun: "It will be this." Nick nodded.

The very slight blood spoor led into thicker and thicker bush. At this point, just as I was wondering what to do next, and when I thought it was high time to send Nick out of this thicket, wise words from the past came to me: "Few of God's creatures, including the human, ever look up."

As I looked up, the leopard sprang from a rock ledge just above. I lifted the shotgun a foot and fired from the hip as the cat was in midair. Then the leopard, the shotgun, and I fell in a heap on a hard, black rock, hidden in the undergrowth. Tabei leapt into immediate action with a club in one hand and a knife in the other. In a very few moments there was a dead leopard, a broken-stocked shotgun, and a rather bruised and slightly scratched me.

Nick had been able to do nothing other than gaze in quickened wonder. As I got to my feet, Nick was there to help, but before he had time to get a worried look on his face the broad grin on mine assured him that all was well.

We collected and carried back a very handsome leopard. Diana greeted us with a kiss each, and the balance of the day was declared a "public holiday." After dinner that night all three of us had a drink or two, and Nick took rather generous "slugs," as he called them. Lighthearted and happy chatter followed until Nick's head nodded several times, and then his chin finally settled down for the night. Diana walked over to him and gave him a gentle shake: "Come on, Nick, better make for the hay. You've had a busy day."

Off they went to the tent. In a very few minutes the light went out, and shortly afterward a shadowy Diana came to join me at the fireside. She sat down close to me, and we talked softly of the morning's events.

"I was relieved to see you coming back all safe and sound. My imagination was giving me all sorts of dreadful ideas." Diana looked at me for a moment or so, and then tenderly said: "You were lucky not to have got more hurt than you did."

"I just got a few scratches and one large bruise from Mother Earth," I said, laughing.

"Bunny, what made you look up? Nick said it was quite astonishing."

"Oh, that's a very long story, my love. A mentor of mine, many, many years ago, taught me to look up."

"I'd like to hear about him."

Diana, for her part, was thrilled as she heard of one exploit after another, and of the great wisdom of Piramus Berners. With a depth of feeling in her, Diana remarked: "Do you know, Bunny, I don't think there are many men in the world today like your Piramus."

"Diana, there never have been many men like him in this world. Piramus was a man apart, and wise beyond his years. He was only twenty-one when he died, at Mons in 1914."

I looked at her and waited for her to raise her eyes to me. "Have you enjoyed the safari, Diana, as much as you thought you were going to when you planned it last year?"

"Bunny—Bunny dear, much, much more."

I put my hand to her chin for a moment, and said: "Will you tell me something? Why all the difference, this year to last?"

"You mean between us?"

"Yes."

She thought for a moment or so: "Bunny, my dear—all I can say is that a lot of water has passed under the bridge." Then she enlarged on the situation. "Haven't you noticed him with me?"

"Yes, I've noticed. There is no warmth."

"No warmth!" she emphasized. "God, he's like an iceberg! Bunny, he gives me everything, everything, that I want—except the one thing I so crave—affection. Just a little, precious, fond affection."

Diana had gotten quite carried away by her tirade. Her eyes were a little misty in the firelight, until the softest, sweetest, elfin smile crept into her pretty face: "And then I met you. The complete opposite. So full of affection, to the point where it is exhausting. Your affection could kill me—but what a wonderful death!"

We got to our feet. "Let's go for a little affection."

"Yes, all right. This will be the last time, this time. Will you meet me in Europe next year?"

"Yes, next year we'll meet in Europe."

Chapter 9

Hollywood Goes on Safari

B y 1947, the four-wheel-drive vehicle was well established for hunting. Not only were the actual hunting cars four-wheel drive, but also the load carriers were beginning to be four-wheel drive as well. This meant that there were more and more areas that we could get into to hunt, more quickly and more often. One did not have to allow so much for the weather. Everything speeded up. A business-minded American could have a satisfactory hunt in two weeks, whereas before the war it would have taken him two months.

And, mark you, the American "safari invasion" of East Africa really got started in 1947. Inquiries were coming in hot and strong. Some clients who had been out before the war came back for the second time, very often bringing friends. Thus the safaris tended to include more people in the camp, very often a family group. This happened several times for me at the tail end of 1947, and from it I built up a pleasant reputation for running such safaris.

For this I probably owed a great deal to my old friend Doctor Kurt von Wedel, from Oklahoma City, for he was the one who came out again and again, bringing a party of friends. Some of these were wealthy friends and relations, and my name went back and into the homes of more than a few very wealthy and very charming Texans, who brought their families out on safari with me.

However, during this period, I did take out one safari that had no touch of four-wheel drive in it. Rather, it was flat feet, hooves, and an automatic-drive Oldsmobile. The client was Jenny Rucks, an old friend, and Jenny's trip was quite sudden and unplanned. She had a few days to spare, met me in Nairobi, and wanted to hunt while she awaited the arrival of her husband.

I was lucky enough to get ahold of my younger son, Anton. He went up to Mount Kenya to lay on a buffalo for Jenny while I fixed up odds and ends of business. Also we had to await Jenny's daughter Marilyn.

It was while we waited for her that Jenny discussed the business aspect of the safari with me. She wanted to give a boost to the agents of the Oldsmobile car. Therefore she needed to have the car in the forefront of the safari. She did not want to take a regular hunting car. "The Oldsmobile can do the job," she declared. Since she was a nice, very attractive woman, I agreed to do what I could, but on one condition.

"Jenny, if it's necessary, will you jump aboard a mule, or even a camel?"

"Bunny, I'll jump aboard anything as long as you keep my little Olds in the forefront whenever possible."

So it was agreed. When Marilyn arrived, there was another very good reason for doing what they wished. She was quietly surprising.

Anton had a nice mountain camp set up in a pretty glade adjacent to a good track. We had no trouble at all in getting the Olds right into camp. The weather was fair, and the track was dry; that helped.

With the assistance of Raymond Hook, we got close to a herd of buffalo. Anton took over to help Jenny get her handsome bull, while I held Marilyn's hand to keep her and me from getting nervous. She was a sweet girl, and truly delighted at her mother's success. In fact, it was she who suggested another hunt, for elephant this time. And then for a lion. And so it went, over several years, each hunt no more than a week's duration. However, on this first hunt we were unable to get the Oldsmobile right up to the dead buffalo. It was just too rough going. We had to settle for carting the mountain to Mohammed. The whole buff head and skin were laid out in front of the car, with Jenny and Anton, looking fairly warlike, alongside. I do hope it did the car agent some good!

One day, Anton and I took Marilyn to swim in one of the icy mountain streams, and mama came too. She laughed and giggled at us while we gasped and snorted. Anton and I ogled with open amazement Marilyn's beautiful, sylphlike figure. We exchanged "father-and-son" glances as Marilyn dived in at one end of the little mountain pool and jumped out the other end. I, for one, was glad for the icy water! In any event, the safari came and went, and we had to wait a full year for the continuation of our "eye-contact" affair. For that is all it was—Marilyn spoke not a word of her feelings, though her eyes spoke whole chapters, of which some sentences touched on desire.

After Jenny's hunt, there began a whole string of film safaris. One after the other came *King Solomon's Mines*, *Where No Vultures Fly*, and *Nor the Moon by Night*, to mention a few. I took some interest in all of these projects, in one way or another, but for the most part it was to finish up their elephant sequences. That usually involved elephants charging smack at the camera.

For some reason unknown to me, I had built up the reputation that every time an elephant saw me, smelled me, or whatever, it charged. And so it appeared that if any film outfit needed an irate charging elephant, they came looking for me. In fact, on one occasion, for the film *Nor Moon by Night*, the cameramen, who had started in South Africa, came all the way up through Rhodesia,

Mozambique, Tanganyika, and finally to me to find their charging elephant. My son and I got them what they wanted within two days. We also got some very good crowd scenes of elephant, and a herd of thirty-five cows charging flat out, straight at the camera. That last scene was not required, and I don't really think I would like a repeat of it! The film company was pleased, and they paid well. The mistake they had made was trying to get the elephant charge in thick bush country: Either the elephant was on them before they could get a picture of it, or it didn't charge at all. They had spent two months repeating this same mistake.

We took them up into the more open Isiolo country, though in the background there was forest and thick bush aplenty. The very first evening out we very nearly got the elephant charge. Anton went into the bush to spook the lone bull out toward me and the cameras. The bull came out, all right, as speedily and as bravely as could be. Yet it cut off its charge just before it was due to go down. However, they got a splendid shot of a charging elephant, and they used it in the film.

The next day we continued the hunt for the perfect bull charge. The elephant was supposed to come to within about twenty feet of the cameras before it went down. With luck, we located two bulls in nice open country, walking slowly toward us, browsing the while. We quickly picked the spot to set up two cameras. The wind was perfect for us, and the excellent camera crews got everything ready with no noise at all. In fact, all one could hear was the breath of wind and the rumblings of the jumbos' stomachs, which drowned out the slight whirr of the battery-driven cameras. All we wanted now was for only one elephant to come directly toward us—there was only one in the script!

Luckily, fate befriended the film company that day. Just as the two elephants were really getting close, the tinkle of some camel bells disturbed them and they came on in a rush. Sheer luck divided them, for they went to either side of a thick thornbush. The one coming head on for us came harder and faster; I shouted to the camera crew to run back to some cover behind rocks. The cameras rolled on automatically. Anton was more or less sitting down to my right. I was in a trembling, erect position. The splendid bull came roaring on, head and trunk held high. The next moment I shouted, "Now!" Anton's shot was a fraction ahead of mine, and the fine old bull was already on its way down as my bullet struck it. The cameramen came out of their hide with a sort of hushed cheer as they hastened to switch off their cameras.

"First class!" said cameraman number one. "Fantastic. It could not have been any better." And I must say that when I saw the film several months later, our charging bull looked pretty good!

The next day, our last with *Nor the Moon by Night*, at various times either Anton or I put on the hero's hat and hunting jacket. Then a few feet of film were rolled on us as we moved in the bush, with elephants in the background. To start with, all worked according to plan, and they got several good shots. The director was pleased. Then he wanted a herd of thirty-five elephants a few hundred yards away driven toward us.

Anton, Kikunyu, and I went into action. The herd moved beautifully, and the cameras ground away. Then the elephants abruptly stopped; they may have seen a reflection from one of the cameras. They fanned out to face us. They muttered together for a few words, then they came, in the shape of a gently opening fan, straight at the cameras, the crew, the director, and poor me. They came on and on until I shouted over my shoulder to the cameramen behind me, "Scram, you chaps!" The cameramen ran, and their cameras went grinding faithfully on.

At twenty yards I knocked down the leader. The rest of the herd pulled up in their tracks, looked at their fallen leader, muttered again, and then an enormous cow elephant filled up the rank and on they came again. At this stage I was aware of the shouts and yelling of Anton and his men. With thirty-odd elephants rapidly closing the gap on me, I lifted my beloved and trusted Rigby and fired a shot inches over the new leader's head. The herd once again pulled up, muttered some more, and then, to my great relief, turned and went away.

At this moment a very worried Anton arrived on the scene with his gun at the ready. He had thought, perhaps, to see the mangled remains of his patriarch and find himself eligible for his share of the Bunny Allen millions! In actual fact, he was very relieved to see me all in one piece, albeit with a somewhat damp smile on my face. He put his arm around me. I was very touched.

As we all sat around the campfire that evening, I had to explain why I had shot over the elephant's head. I turned from the red embers in the fire to the sandy-headed questioner. "Well, for one good reason, because we had run out of licenses." Then, as an afterthought, I added, "Have you ever had a bullet half an inch over your head? It is very frightening. Elephants are sensitive creatures."

That, I judged, was a sufficient explanation. For myself, I knew there were other telling reasons to take the risk and not shoot to kill. I had just shot and killed one elephant. The remainder had seen it tumble. Furthermore, the yells and screams coming from Anton and his men were upsetting for the elephants. And lastly, I had turned elephants before with a shot over the leader's head.

When, several months later in Nairobi, my two sons and I saw the completed film, we were amazed at how well it had all turned out. The elephant sequences were nothing short of remarkable. The Isiolo elephant had turned up trumps!

While we are dealing with the subject of elephant charges for films, it is worth recording the extraordinary incident that occurred on the *King Solomon's Mines* set. I did not take an active part in that film, but I did tender my advice for it when asked, which was on several occasions.

Stan Lawrence-Brown was the hunter in charge. Old Stan was a very able hunter and knew exactly what he was doing. However, one never knows exactly what the elephant is doing, or what it is going to be doing. There was Stewart Granger—or rather, his stand-in—all set up in the foreground, with the enormous jumbo ready to charge. And there were the cameras, grinding away. The elephant charged, a rifle or two cracked, and down went the bull in a great cloud of dust and leaves. The next action was quite uncalled for, and not in the script. Eight huge lady elephants leaped into the scene, coming straight for anyone and anything. Stan, being a sensible chap, took to his speedy heels, advising everyone else to do likewise. They all complied with amazing willingness. Meantime, the cameras rolled on. When finally there was a hush, Stan poked his nose around the corner to see what was what. He was a little surprised. There was not an elephant in sight! No, not even a dead one. Stan and his merry men came back onto the set to scratch their heads and speculate as to what had happened.

Stan rightly presumed that the cow elephants had lifted their bull from the ground and carried him away. In this he was proved right when the film was developed. We searched for that elephant high and low for a full week, with a spotter aircraft helping for most of the time. Not a sign was ever found. His gallant wives got him clear away from the mines of King Solomon.

✕ ✕ ✕ ✕ ✕

Soon came the time for Jenny Rucks to return for her elephant hunt. Much to my disappointment, Marilyn did not accompany her.

"She just couldn't come, Bunny. It's no use—she must complete her studies."

"It's a shame," I answered. "I was looking forward to seeing her again."

Jenny quizzed me with her piercing eyes. "Yes, I bet you were. You liked her a lot—I saw that. It won't hurt her to be away from you."

She said all this rather hesitantly, but with emphasis. For a woman who joked a lot, she was now in deadly earnest. However, when she saw me looking somewhat crestfallen, she relented and added, "But, Bunny, she sent her love to you and said you could go and see her in New York."

"Thank you, Jenny. I will at the first opportunity." With a little bit of luck, I wouldn't have to wait long!

As fate would have it, a film company had invited me over to the States to discuss plans for the making of a big film in Africa. They sent me a ticket with the first stop New York for one night, then on to Hollywood. Jenny and Marilyn met me on my arrival in New York and whisked me off to their very nice sixth-floor apartment, just off East 65th Street and Park Avenue. Jenny dropped us off at the doorway, excusing herself.

"Bunny, I have a very important appointment. I'll be back in about two hours, and then we'll go out to lunch. Marilyn will look after you."

And she certainly did! She tucked her arm in mine and practically ran me into the elevator. Its door had hardly closed on us before her lips met mine. There was a splendid urgency about them. They gave an uplift to everything except the elevator, which came to a shuddering halt somewhere between the third and fourth floors. The shuddering unfastened our lips, but we did not lose contact. She was close to me. I was very aware of her. With the first shudder of the lift the lights failed, but she held my hand and pressed hard and soft against me. After a moment or two I got my voice going again.

"Well, and what do we do now?" Her only answer was to unfasten her camel's hair coat and take me inside its folds to her body, covered only by a very thin silk dress. It was astonishing. She appeared to envelop me completely and I reacted in the only possible way. I was aware of every lovely part of her—her ups, her downs, her vales, her rounds, with taut little promontories teasing me. I longed for two mouths and four hands, the better to do her bidding. But then, at that moment, the lights went on, the lift went up, and I came back down to earth.

Marilyn murmured, "Damn and blast."

The doors opened. We swept through them and on through the apartment door, which opened as if by magic. Then about five steps took us to an open door behind which was an inviting bed. Marilyn sank down onto it, with her camel's hair coat and one or two sundries collapsing in a heap on the floor. We then proceeded to complete what had been started in the lift. It was all shamefully hurried—but marvelous.

Marilyn was off the bed in no time flat, shook herself rather like a hen coming from a dust bath, and pointed to a door.

"Run yourself a bath. I'll be right back."

She ran down the passageway to the kitchen. I was making my slow, thoughtful way to the bathroom when I heard a loud *plopph*. A few moments later Marilyn came in, bearing two glasses of champagne. "One for you—one for me. Welcome to New York," she said.

"You are an incredible girl," I answered. We drank. Then we bathed and played a little. "Now you make yourself smart to go for lunch with Ma." I did all that, I think. I had a nice lunch with my two girls—Ma and daughter—and then I was put to bed to get over jet lag and fag, the better to be ready later for our game of tag!

The next day, I climbed on board the aircraft to Hollywood, where I spent three days. For the most part I was discussing with a very pleasant, diamond-studded Mr. Goldstein the ways and means of making a rather large-size film, as yet unnamed. It would star Clark Gable, Ava Gardner, and Grace Kelly. I was to find the job both exhilarating and exasperating. The demands made upon me were at times perfectly ridiculous, but the results were nothing short of remarkable.

It was about that time, back in Mombasa, that I got myself married again. This was a strange stroke of fate, because, in retrospect, I could never have done this great film, *Mogambo*—they now had a name for it—without the help of my wife Murielle. We had several comparatively happy years together, although much of her time was spent in Nairobi looking after business interests. Well, Murielle took to the job of getting the great *Mogambo* show on the road as a duck takes to water. And, having gotten the show on the road and under canvas, it was she who saw that the supplies came in. She was all business, to the fingertips. I had more the mentality of a "strolling player" than that of the manager of a supermarket. Mind you, Murielle helped very much on all my safaris during the time we were together, but *Mogambo* was her great work.

Clark Gable proved to be a very nice man and was charming to talk to. Even when under strain after too much work, too much drink, or whatever, he was always easy going and reasonable. In *Mogambo*, the script called for Clark to be making up to and falling in love with Grace Kelly. This he did well and truly, on and off the set. He was everywhere with her. It was so delightfully obvious at all times. I especially noticed it when we all sat watching the lions, when we were in and about the elephants, or in and near the snorting buffalo. He held her hand, put an arm around her, exchanged nice eye messages. As the film proceeded, the plot called for Clark to switch his attention to Ava Gardner. This he did as quickly and easily as if by the press of a button!

Chapter 10

The Strange Case of a Rhino Aphrodisiac

J enny arrived at the film set one day, and it was lovely to see her again. She twinkled at me as she said, "Come and meet Jane Ayre."

Jane was a good-looking girl—tallish, with sandy red hair, piercing amber eyes, and a generous mouth. She had a lovely voice, deep, rich, and melodious.

"Bunny, Jenny has told me all about you." She said this with great emphasis. It was almost like a warning signal. In fact, I felt a little flattered.

I retorted, "Jenny says you want to shoot a rhino. Now, why do you want to shoot a rhino?"

"D'you know, Bunny, I really can't give you an answer to that right now." She took a little kick at nothing in particular. "Maybe I'll be able to explain as we go along."

I looked at her much as a doctor would look at a patient. "It sounds to me as though you have a problem, maybe?"

"Yes, maybe."

Next morning at dawn, leaving Jenny asleep in bed, we climbed on horseback and rode the two miles to a large forest glade. At one end of it was a small herd of grazing buffalo. At the other end was a fine-looking rhino. It was heading slowly for the forest edge, cropping succulent plants and branches en route. Suddenly it stopped, snorted, threw its head in the air, and whipped around. Tabei passed Jane her rifle. The rhino did two more whistling, watery snorts and came at us.

Jane shot straight and true. The old rhino collapsed in an armor-plated heap, fifteen feet away. Up to this moment, Jane had been wonderful, but now with the quarry down and out before her, she quite went to bits. She trembled and shook and had dew-lit eyes as she came to stand close to me. She gave her rifle to Tabei and reached for my hand. She wanted comfort. Her eyes were glued to the rhino all the time. More than that, they were in fact glued to the rhino horns. Her trembling abated after a minute or so. She left my shelter and walked over to the rhino, studied the horns, then felt them. She felt them well and truly, then slipped her fingers down to feel the prickly hair bits at the base of the horns. I walked around to study her. Her eyes were positively searing.

In the meantime, Tabei had gone for the horses. These now arrived, and the plan was for us to go back for breakfast and come along afterward in the hunting car with the skinners to collect the trophy. I explained all this to Jane. With a deeply wild look in her eyes, she let me know that she did not want to go for the car—she wanted to stay.

"Please, Bunny, let them go. They can bring the car up here."

She walked back to her horse. She was behaving quite oddly. To pacify her, I fell in with her wishes and sent the gunbearers off. Jane felt the horns once more, looked across the rhino at me, and now I noticed that her eyes, though still staring, were quite dry. Instead, she was slightly drooling from the mouth. It was most peculiar. She was genuinely affected, and I was positively puzzled. I did not know what to do.

As it happened it did not matter, because at this stage Jane rather took over. She came around to me and sort of led me over to an old, large, spread-out rhino dung pile over which a bed of forest moss had grown. From then on nature took its course. It must have been the aphrodisiacal charms of Old Father Rhino!

We moved down to the Tana River almost the same time as the film party. I set the camp for *Mogambo* at a little watering place called Korokoro, while Jenny and Jane accompanied me another twenty miles downstream to Bura. Here we had a nice, lazy time. Every afternoon I packed the girls off to their tents for a beauty sleep, while I amused myself punting a dugout canoe along in the shallows, fishing, and generally mucking around in the river.

Jenny had been watching me from her tent verandah. As I climbed up the riverbank she called to

me: "Hi, Bunny." I walked over to her, and she went on, "You just love this, don't you?"

The next day Jenny got an elephant. It fell right down on its tusks, swayed there momentarily, and then stayed in that upright position. Jane had gotten it all beautifully recorded with her camera. This time there was absolutely no reaction from her. She caressed the beauty of the ivory, but there was no headlong rush for the "hay." It was only the aphrodisiacal quality of the old rhino that seemed to have that effect. The Oldsmobile figured in the foreground of the jumbo picture, with my fine chap Tabei at the wheel.

Jenny was happy and ready to rejoin her husband, and the nice but bewildering Jane Ayre left me with barely a good-bye kiss. I reckoned myself to be just another guinea pig.

After the camp in the Masai, the *Mogambo* safari folded up, as far as I was concerned. All that remained was to sell off the equipment, and I did not feel like acting as a tout for the auctioneer! Therefore I made my way to Nairobi and to the offices of the film company in the New Stanley Hotel. I continued upstairs to see Goldstein and Company. I paid my respects to Goldy, and he was pleasant, as always. He said, "Thanks a million, Bunny. We couldn't have done it without you. Oh, by the way, I reckon we'd like you to come over to the States and help us publicize the film." He cocked his head to one side. "Can you manage it?"

"Yes, of course. Give me a little notice." And so we arranged it.

Just after my interview with Goldy, I had news, bad news, of my old friend and mentor, Jack Soames, who was in the Nairobi Hospital. I immediately went to see him. He was ill, indeed. He had been living down at the coast for some time, the doctor having told him that the altitude at his farm was too much for him. Within three days Jack was dead. He had been a most splendid help and friend to me over the years—always ready with that little bit of help and encouragement at the right time. I was to miss him a great deal.

I crowded in one very interesting safari between the end of *Mogambo* and my departure for the States. That was for a very nice man and his mother from San Francisco. Donald Dickey's father apparently had planned a safari quite a few years before. He had laid on the guns and had the other equipment ready, and then, sadly, he had died. So Florence Dickey, his widow, had suggested in the fullness of time that the son should do the safari in the father's stead. The father had been a well-known naturalist, and Florence was fairly cued up as well, especially on birds. This I was to find out very shortly after the start of the safari, and as a result I felt somewhat stupid.

We were proceeding to our campsite beyond Narok. I could see Florence industriously studying the birds and flowers en route. When she asked me what one particular bird was, I answered foolishly, "Oh, that's a cockioli bird." She looked at me quite severely and proceeded to tell me exactly what it was, including its Latin name. Florence put me very firmly in my place, and for the rest of the safari I did not cross swords with her again. She was not a girl; she was not a woman—she was a lovely lady. Right from the beginning she acted splendidly and bravely.

The very first night out tested her mettle. As we headed for our campsite deep in Masailand, the heavens opened up on us. We could not go forward; we could not go back. We had to camp exactly where we were. The wretched camp crew had to erect a tent for Florence in the pouring rain. There the dear soul sat, on her bed, her feet on a wooden box weighted down with rocks, while six inches of water ran through her tent. With all this, she had a big smile on her face and appeared to be enjoying it!

One day when out hunting for buffalo, we had a most remarkable experience. It was very early, and the sun was only a thought in the eastern sky. We were walking through one of the beautiful glades that abound in that part of Masai. The wind was perfect for us to approach a fine-looking herd of buffalo. There was a tailor-made fold in the ground to get us up to within two hundred yards of the herd. We wanted to view them from there to see if there was a suitable bull for Donald.

Several of the herd were looking in our direction, but with the rising sun smack in their eyes and us deep in the shadows, they were clearly puzzled. There followed a snort or two, and more and more heads rose in the meantime. Donald's movie camera was doing its best to imitate a skylark! One after another, the buffalo threw their heads about, snorted, and took a few steps in our direction. They were gradually forming into a semicircle. It was a herd of about two hundred strong that now faced us looking magnificent—heads in the air, tails swishing, and feet stamping to the accompaniment of snorts and bellows.

They were now barely fifty yards away. The sun was higher in the heavens, and we were becoming more visible. I could stand the suspense no longer and slowly rose to my feet. Then a considerable portion of "all hell" let loose. If ever there was a buffalo cacophony, here it was. As the great animals turned and fled, the pounding of their hooves receded. Soon only the mooing of the calves was left behind in the mad scamper.

After covering about three hundred yards the herd pulled up, and while the cows milled around in the background, gathering up their calves, a dozen or more large bulls come out to face us, with heads held high. It was the sight of a lifetime.

Donald turned to me. "Bunny, that was worth the whole trip. . . . Wonderful!"

He did not realize just how privileged he had been. Ever since then I have been looking for a repeat performance, without success.

Chapter 11

An All-Girl Safari

The time had arrived for me to cross the Atlantic once more to the New World. Again that surprising girl, Marilyn, met me in New York. She had altered little since I had last seen her—that is, in looks. Yet, she had matured somewhat and was, in fact, all the better for that.

She had moved into her own apartment. Her mother and father were away, and therefore she had arranged for me to stay with her. Thinking back on my last episode with her, I became slightly weak at the knees, wondering if I could "last the course," as the saying goes. Yet I need not have worried. She had steadied down. She was a charming young hostess to me, for those three long days while I worked and three short nights while I played.

This time there was no headlong rush for the bed. We went gently through the first day and finished up gently in bed. I had various phone calls to make, and also had to get my schedule from the New York office of MGM for my stay there. I can tell you I was busy: radio shows, TV shows, interviews all day—hardly was there time left to dally with Marilyn! I found a little time, but when I got home to the apartment, it was usually fairly late and I was ready to sleep. Marilyn positively surprised me. She slept with me, gently.

Before I left New York for the West Coast, I had an unusual inquiry. A girl named Beverly Putnam phoned me up asking if I were interested in taking out what she termed "an all-girl safari." I was a little noncommittal in my reply.

"Look, I'm off to Los Angeles tomorrow. I suggest you see me at the Warwick Hotel on my return."

"Right. I bet I persuade you." From that moment I liked the idea. I love to be persuaded.

It was a great whirl of events when I got to filmland for the premiere of *Mogambo*, where I met all the young stars lined up for my meeting. I must say they were a sweet lot of people, or so they seemed to me. Then there was the film, which I certainly enjoyed a lot.

The publicity tour for the film took me all over the States. One stop that left nice memories was Charleston, South Carolina. There I gave a talk to several hundred of the sweetest girls, all about seventeen to eighteen years old. After my talk, I asked if they had any questions for me. At once there were several bright questions, which I did my best to answer. Then a lovely voice from way back in the hall said, "Say, Mr. Allen, let me ask you a question. Why do you shoot those beautiful animals?"

I realized I was on difficult ground, and I did not answer immediately. In fact, I put on a slight act. I let her suppose I hadn't heard her question adequately. Therefore, the lovely thing was encouraged by others, and certainly by me, to come right up on stage. There she repeated, "I can't understand why you shoot those beautiful animals, Mr. Allen."

"Well, I'll tell you what. It happens to be my business to hunt animals, and, what is so much more, it is inherent in man to hunt."

At this last statement, one or two of the audience actually clapped their hands, sweet and helpful young people that they were! Being encouraged, I went on. "And mark you, and remember for the future, it is the same hunting instinct in man that urges him to go hunt for a girlfriend, and for a wife. If it were not for this h u n t i n g instinct, many more young ladies would be left on the shelf."

This caused quite a lot of laughter, in- cluding some from my pretty girl on stage. Then a voice from far back said, "I reckon women do a bit of hunting, too!" That caused masses of laughter.

I agreed with this. "How right you are, and in the animal kingdom, the females do the greater part of the hunting."

Before the pretty girl left the stage, I promised her I'd not shoot too many animals. I kissed her on her fine, full red lips, and she tripped down the stairs! Many years later, that same girl came out on safari with her charming husband

and two daughters. They were a great joy. And she still had fine, full red lips.

Ultimately, I found myself in New York City once again. There I kept my date with Beverly Putman, the "all-girl safari" girl. We made our arrangements, and in due course "all my lovely girls" arrived. When the safari got going, suffice it to say that they were a grand bunch of girls. 'Tis true that some of them were getting on a bit, and one rather unkind nitwit called it the "old girls' safari." It did not deserve that judgment. Their ages ranged from nineteen to forty-nine.

I quickly discovered that it was far more restful to take two or even three girls out than just one. With just one person, you are having to "give" every minute of the way—be it talking, showing, doing, or whatever. With two or three they more or less take care of themselves. They talk to one another, show one another, do with one another. All the paid hunter has to do is the occasional pointing of a finger, nod of agreement, or shake of the head. Oh yes, one alone is full-time work, especially if it's a girl. They ask the most extraordinary questions and make the weirdest, if not wildest, demands.

At the end of the safari we had a farewell party in Nairobi The party was put together by Jeri, a very attractive girl I had passed on the New Stanley Hotel steps months earlier. I remembered very well the day when the good-looking, very smartly dressed girl had gotten into an open blue Buick. I had often thought of her.

At the party, as soon as I could get near enough to Jeri for a few words, I said, "Do you know, ever since I first saw you I've wanted to meet you."

"And now that you've met me, I'm going away. Why did you delay so long? I'm off tomorrow."

"Off?" I answered. "Off where?"

"Back to the States."

"Well, actually I am . . . but . . . oh, I'll tell you some other time."

I had to wait a little while for that "some other time."

The very next day, while I was bemoaning the fact that having just found Jeri I had immediately lost her, I had the most pleasant compensation. I received a lovely letter from Diana Vanderscut telling me she was in England. Nick would be out of town. "Why not come and join me?" she wrote.

I did, and we put up at the Skindles Hotel in Maidenhead, smack on the cold Thames. As we went up the creaking stairs and along the creaky passage, I remembered that I was in good company. Didn't that jolly King Edward VII escort his beautiful Lillie Langtry up those selfsame, creaking stairs and along this selfsame creaking passage?

I looked out through the window while Diana was doing some unpacking. I watched two brave swans swimming against the strong, storm-filled Thames. They were making slight progress. At that moment a beam of sunlight came down through a slit in the gray sky, and the swans, with a background of wintry willows, looked to all intents and purposes like part of a stage set. It was quite beautiful . . . but only for a few moments. Then the sunbeam vanished, just as an explosion occurred from the hands of Diana. I turned and beheld her. There she was in a little short nightie with an open bottle of champagne in her hands.

"Come on, Bunny, let's drink to our reunion. We'll phone Sibyl to tell her you'll be with her in one hour."

And you know, I was. Diana is a very strong character. We had a good tea party with my lovely mother, Sibyl, and she and Diana got on well. That was an achievement, because while Sibyl was a sweet, lovable woman, she was tricky and jealous of her sons.

We went on to Rome for a final two days, where we expected to meet Nick. However, a letter awaited us at the Hotel Flora.

Nick couldn't get away. He wrote, "Discuss with Bunny a safari for the summer of 1957. I think that the Stewarts will join us." This Diana and I did as we toured Rome, wined, dined, and slept. Finally, she accompanied me to the airport to see me away.

"Well, Bunny dear, see you in about eighteen months."

"Thank you, Diana, for all your help. You've been sweet to me. I love you."

"I guess I kinda like you," she retorted. She blew me a kiss as I went through the doors.

Chapter 12

An Ethiopian Ras Offers Marriage

I did not pause long in Nairobi, for I wanted to see my new riverside cottage. It was upstream about a mile from Murielle's house, which was built on ivory foundations as a result of an elephant hunt. My house had been completed for me while I was away, and as I drove down the rough track I experienced a fine, heart-pounding feeling of happy contentment. Not long after, the sun set prettily and a couple of young Rhodesian ridgebacks came to sit beside me in front of the cracking fire. I smiled into the firelight as I settled down to enjoy the African night. All was quiet except for the gurgle of the swift-running trout stream.

Then the cough of a leopard came from across the river in the bosky undergrowth. I lifted my head. The two dogs pricked up their ears. I requested silence by laying a hand on each of their heads. The dogs looked up, and kept silent. They understood. There was one more series of coughs as the leopard made its way downstream. A bushbuck barked in alarm. The stream gurgled on. Life was very sweet.

I had imagined that I'd stay in solitude and peace for a while, enjoying my new cottage and getting the garden started. That was not to be. The very first morning, two four-wheel-drive vehicles came rolling down my track. In them were a bevy of beauties and three men. Monsieur Talou introduced himself, his wife, two daughters, the husband of the older daughter, Mariamme, and the boyfriend of the younger daughter, Danielle. They were on their way up to Ethiopia and wanted me to escort them, doing a little game watching en route. They had been advised by the Nairobi game warden to contact me.

They had a quick look around my cottage, and then Monsieur Talou said, "Mr. Bunny Allen, we would so like you to come with us. With you, my girls"—he swept his arm around, indicating his beauties, which they certainly were—"with you my girls will feel quite safe—safe from the lions, the elephants, and safe from the bandits."

Mama kept the flame going. "Bunny, come with us. We have heard about you from your friends, from several also in America. They said we must get you." The two girls nodded their heads in unison. The husband and boyfriend smiled.

I found that I fit into the team very well, and they really proved a most delightful lot. And if that first evening meal was any indication, I was going to be very well fed. I provided the larder with birds from the shotgun. We had a good variety, and the French girls did a splendid job. I remember well how they contrived a magnificent pigeon pie, with birds from a Marsabit forest and beautiful pastry over the top. I helped them to build a camp oven. Pierre Talou always managed to produce a bottle of wine for special occasions. After Marsabit we descended to the plains and sped toward the Huri Hills, and on to the great escarpment marking the boundary of Ethiopia. As usual, we saw quite a few greater kudu. The French fairly marveled at the sight of them. Mother and the two daughters looked at them as they sped by and said, "Beautiful, very beautiful." And I looked at Mother and the two daughters and said, "Beautiful, very beautiful." Mama Suzanne wagged her finger at me, and we all laughed. Beautiful, very beautiful!

At last we were camped at the foot of the Mega escarpment. At the top was Ethiopia. We had a nice little trickle of a clear spring to camp beside while the young men examined the two cars and serviced them for the rough climb. Luckily, both were able mechanics, and we carried an adequate supply of spares. That last night on Kenya soil we had a happy time, with the usual delicious meal and several extra glasses of wine. The three girls escorted me under a little cedar tree, where they kissed me good night. That did not make me sleep any better! Later in the night I blamed the leopards, but it was those kisses.

As I gazed at the stars from my bed, I thought how good life is, and how many lovely people there are in this world of ours. There I was with six people, all of whom had been complete strangers when I met them eight or ten days before. They were so thoughtful, so kind, so attractive. I was very content.

The following morning we rose with the sun and had a good, big breakfast. It was going to be a long day. I had last been on this alleged road in 1942, during the war. Then it was pretty bad, but with a hundred vehicles, a company of engineers, and hundreds of willing hands, moving downhill, the passage was not too bad. Now this was a different kettle of fish. And, of course, fourteen or fifteen years had passed without any repair work having been carried out. We knew we had a problem ahead of us, but none of us realized its immensity. We learned. It was to take us thirty-six hours to make the climb of four miles.

After breakfast, we packed up and started the ascent. From the start it was twists and turns and washouts, with here and there a fallen tree across the track. There was one lucky factor: It was quite dry. It took us three hours to do about the first mile. Then the real trouble started. We came on a very big washout that we misjudged and tried to cross without filling it in and building it up. The result was dismal failure and a broken shaft on the rear drive of the leading Willys. Our mechanics had a spare, all right, but the position of the car made it a most awkward repair to carry out. It took some hours, and there were additional trials.

While the repair was in progress, Suzanne and Mariamme wandered off into the cedar forest to answer the call of nature. They waved to me as they went. As a precaution I called out, "Don't go too far."

Suzanne's quick reply was, "Don't worry, we won't. We're French, you know." They laughingly disappeared into the thick cedar forest.

The work on the car continued, and we had forgotten the two girls until suddenly screams of fear came from them. Then, "Bunny! Bunny! A leopard!" This was followed by the noise of metal on a stone, more screams, and some ugly growls. It was a leopard, all right.

I seized my gun and a few shells and quickly followed in the girls' path. I had rounded but two large cedars when I found Suzanne trying to pull Mariamme out of a washout covered with sticks and twigs. Just beyond her was a leopard, trying to strike at her with its paws. Then I saw that the leopard was caught by one foot in a spring trap attached to a heavy chain. I took two or three steps forward and then, firing over Mariamme's body, I put two barrels straight into the leopard's face. I turned back at once to poor Mariamme, and with a little more assistance she was back on her feet. She had quite a lot of blood on one leg and one nasty gash. Suzanne also had a scratch or two.

Papa Pierre appeared to be a fairly qualified doctor, and he had the girls feeling better very quickly. The one bad gash on Mariamme's leg was certainly from a sharp stick. She had just one leopard scratch, above the ankle.

We finally reached the little town of Mega, at the top, about 6 P.M. the following day. There, Bromley, the British resident, made us most welcome, and a doctor pronounced Mariamme's wounds in good order. When Bromley heard of our leopard experience, he remarked, "Oh, that forest is bang full of leopard. The locals trap a lot of them, but even so they don't seem to diminish."

"Is trapping legal?" asked Pierre Talou.

"Certainly not," responded John Bromley, "but who's to stop 'em? At the moment, laws don't count for much here."

By and large, we found that John Bromley led a pleasant enough life as British consul at Mega—a good climate, all supplies sent to him by air, together with an adequate supply of alcohol. What more could a man nearing retirement ask for?

Our next port of call of importance was Negele, a big center I knew of from my war years. Now, according to John Bromley, rather a bigshot ras was in charge there who could help us on our way. We spent two days getting to Negele, what with some rain and mud problems and the continual search for fuel. We carried a lot extra, yet there was always the threat of a shortage. We hoped to alleviate this when we got to the ras of Negele. In the meantime, birds found by the roadside and the wild vegetables and fruits we picked in odd nooks and crannies en route kept us supplied with food. The clever girls did the rest. Their culinary skills were quite stupendous. I fell in love with the cooking. I fell in love with the girls, perhaps with Suzanne, the mother, most of all!

Fifteen days after leaving Isiolo we reached Negele. Here the ras was firmly ensconced in a heavily guarded thorn fortress. His guards ushered us inside and instructed us to pitch our tents. Later, they summoned us to appear before the great man. Consequently, Pierre and I made ready to obey, but we immediately learned that the whole party was required to attend—"men, women, and children." Consequently, we all trooped over to the office of the ras. He was a good-looking, middle-aged man—tall, with a very smart little beard. He was well turned out, in typical Habesha dress. He spoke fair to good English.

"Good day to you, ladies and gentleman." He shook everyone by the hand, with a slight bow to each of the girls. Then he sent for another chair so that the three girls could be seated, while we four men were left standing. That was fair enough. He very civilly asked us where we had come from, what we were doing, and where we were going. He pointed out that there were armed gangs operating on the roads and that sometimes in certain places they were not safe to travel on.

To make his point, he spoke again. "You see how I live? I am in a fortress. I have guards—well-armed guards." His hands indicated the heavy zareba around his headquarters, and he pointed to the armed guards in his office.

Just at this moment, a rather young Habesha man came rushing into the office carrying, of all things, Mariamme's leopard skin. This had been salted every day, and we had left it out in the shade to dry. Obviously this zealous youth had seen it and was trying to cause trouble. He chattered away in Habesha at about ninety to the dozen, and our ras looked rather gave. He immediately said to Pierre, "This is a matter that is serious. How did you come by this skin?"

I thought it better to take over at this point, and I started to explain the situation, but the young man broke in with more rapid Habesha. Said the ras, after this last fluent flow, "How can we tell you speak truth? The negus demands all leopard skins. This is serious."

The better to make my point, I said, "Please allow me to show you." And I walked over to Mariamme, who fortunately wore a khaki skirt. I showed the gash on her leg and the leopard scratch on her ankle, both of which were healing well. In so doing, I exposed her truly lovely leg to just above the knee. I heard an intake of breath from the young man. He apparently had spotted the two dimples behind her knee, a sign of great beauty much treasured by the Habesha. He spoke to the ras (who proved to be his father), and then the latter held up his hand to me while the two of them had a short discussion.

Finally, he said, "You may go back to your tents. I will call you later." And as we turned to go, he added, "It is forbidden for you to go out of the compound."

I knew it was futile to argue at this stage, so all I said was, "You can substantiate the leopard facts from Bwana Bromley at Mega."

"Yes," he briefly answered. "I'll do that."

We were dismissed. That was the position. What the ras said was the law, which we had, perforce, to obey. There was nothing to be done. We had to wait and see.

I must say that the ras saw to it that we had the necessities of life. We received plenty of pasta and tomato paste and other leftovers from the Italian days. Firewood and water came to us, and, best of all, lots of freshly roasted coffee beans all the way from Jima, a couple of hills away. However, what we lacked and chiefly felt the need of were toilet arrangements. We had one little camp-type, hole-in-the-ground toilet. It just did not go around for seven keen stomachs consuming Italian food. We protested to no avail.

Thus, the suffering went on for two days and nights. On the third day, Pierre and I received a summons and marched before the ras. He coughed a couple of times and swept the papers from his desk, scattering them about the floor. I could not help but think that he'd seen some irate British officer do the like. Then, looking through beetling brows, he proclaimed, "You are in very serious trouble. The negus demands that you stay here until he can send a judge of the Supreme Court to deal with you."

Of course, it stood out a mile that the rascally ras was trying to scare us into falling in with his wishes, whatever they might be. Knowing something about the Habesha from my wartime days, I had a shrewd suspicion as to what the ras was after, and I was correct in my deduction. He was seeking the hand of Mariamme for his son. The young man was infatuated with her.

"If you can agree," the ras said, "you can go free, where you will, at once. Furthermore, after six months you can come and visit your daughter, to see how happy she is. After that she can go with you to her mother to have her baby. Her first baby will be a boy. The sign under the knee says so."

At this halt in his harangue I spoke up quickly, before Pierre could possibly say the wrong thing. A firm negative answer to the request at this time would have been a definite mistake. Now was the time for a little delicate diplomacy.

"Pierre, the ras is making an honest request. I suggest you return to our camp and talk the matter over with Mariamme herself, and her mother. You will have to bear in mind the promises already made, and the assurances given to Mariamme's grandparents."

I got up, turned to face Pierre as he rose to his feet, and knowingly, yet secretly, winked an eye at him. He immediately excused himself to the ras and made his exit. Now I sensed was the moment for diplomacy, and not of the gunboat variety. I'm sure the ras grasped what was going through my mind. He gave me a look and, with a slight smile lighting his face, ordered his two aides to quit his office, leaving the two of us alone.

He turned to me and said very gently, "I know what I ask is difficult for Mr. Talou. I know I ask a lot."

He paused, looked up to the ceiling for inspiration, and continued, "My son, he is a young man, strange in his ways. He has never liked a girl. Then he sees Mariamme; he sees the sign behind her knees. He hears her name, Mariamme. His name is Mariann. It was all too much for him . . . and for me."

I answered, "Yes, I understand, and so, I am sure, does Pierre. And I can assure you that he does not disapprove of the idea— your idea—in principle. It is something quite different."

I then went on to explain, with a story right out of thin air, on the spur of the moment.

I told him about Mariamme's arranged marriage with Bud, that there were all sorts of complications—promises made to grandparents, and so on. I could see I was making a little headway with the ras, but precious little. Then, suddenly, like a bolt from of the blue, we were saved!

He had been looking at the list of names of our party on the desk before him. "Allen," he said, "Allen." His piercing eyes looked hard at me. "Could you be any relation, a brother, of Ras Allen in Addis Ababa?"

"Yes, of course. I am his younger brother."

"Well, forever, why didn't you tell me? He is a great friend of mine. We played polo together."

I could have kicked myself for not thinking of my brother, Ba, earlier. What a bloody fool I had been! His name solved all our problems. During the war years, Ba had been commissioner of police to the emperor. After that he had taken various government posts, and at present was in charge of desert locust control in Addis. It turned out that our troublesome ras had worked a lot with Ba and held him in great esteem. The key to the door was ours immediately. In return, Pierre offered to have his son over to

New York to visit when they had returned there. Pierre was the American agent for Coty, the *parfumiers*.

Pierre ended up by saying, "And your son, Mariann, can learn English with us, and maybe a little French." He said this last with a knowing laugh.

The next morning we were on our way, with almost a tearful farewell. The ras could not do enough. We had full tanks of gasoline, full boxes of food, and hearts full of gratitude. It was altogether an amazing turnaround.

The family wanted me to accompany them on to Cairo, but I knew I had to get back home. The next day, just before my French friends left to continue their journey, Mariamme found me alone for a moment and slipped a little folded note into my hand. She hurriedly said, "Please don't read this until we have gone." She briefly kissed me and went on her way. Then we all said our farewells, a little sadly, I think, for all of us. I certainly had become very fond of them. They were a sincerely genuine lot. Pierre paid me very generously for the pleasure I had had with them. I felt as though I should have been in the paying seat!

After they had disappeared from the hotel, I went into a quiet corner to read my billet-doux. It was the sweetest love letter, as if written by a girl of fifteen or sixteen, rather than by a girl of Mariamme's age. She had fallen in love with me as the safari progressed. She just wanted me to know—nothing more, nothing less.

H CLAASSENS.

Chapter 13

Stuck in the Mud

I t was just as well that I returned to the farm when I did because, unknown to me, a close friend, Jo Bruce, had collected a couple of very nice men for me to take on safari. Here and now I should put Jo Bruce into the picture. She'd been a good friend of Murielle's, and on odd days and nights I had taken her out for a hunt or two, though never for more than two or three days at a time. She was a delightful woman, and we had some most enjoyable safaris together. She had always said that she would be sending some of her friends on safari with me. Now here were the Holbrook brothers as a proof.

They were a complete contrast, these two brothers—in looks, in manners, in speech, in everything. Bob was a city man from the East, and Dar was a country man from the West. Their work too couldn't have been more different: Bob, an advertising man from New York; Dar, a geologist from San Marino, California. Nevertheless, they were a most splendid team to take on safari, and great companions. They took everything as it came, be it good or bad. (And, believe me, on this safari we had them both.)

Bob and Dar came well provided with guns and ammunition and, to my delight, with a very small Jeep. This they intended to take on safari to augment my normal safari car. The fact was that these two brothers intended to drink quite a bit on their trip. They judged they needed another vehicle just to carry the whiskey!

We started the six-week safari in northern Tanganyika. I camped them under the Great Rift Wall, and there we had a good mixed-bag hunt for the first two weeks. The two brothers indulged in a lot of fun in camp, and neither of them wanted to work too hard to get trophies. Mark you, if a good head came into camp, they were delighted. Considering the amount they drank, they were amazingly good shots. I especially noticed the way Bob's rifle shook on its way to his shoulders, yet he seldom missed his mark.

One night in camp as we sat around the fire after dinner, we discussed their shooting. Said Bob, "Well, Dar, that was a fine shot you put in on that running buffalo today."

"Yes, Bob, I must say I pleased myself. I guess I wanted to keep up the standard that you have been setting. You haven't missed a thing."

At this stage I butted into the conversation. "You both astonish me. You are both hard drinkers. Look at your hands—always very unsteady, yet you both shoot straight! I can't make it out."

Bob looked across the fire at me. "Bunny, it's just years of practice. I've always drunk. I've hunted whenever the opportunity occurred. Maybe if I didn't drink I couldn't shoot as straight as I do."

And I think he was right about that.

Since those days with Bob and Dar, I have taken out many hard drinkers of hard spirits from Texas and other hard-drinking states. I found the great majority of them really very fine shots.

Not very often was there a dangerous wounded animal to follow up. It was a matter of getting to know yourself and your capabilities. Mind you, while these two brothers were most delightful men, they, too, had their snags. There were times when I had to play them carefully. Bob, the city man, was quick-thinking and impatient. Dar, the country boy, was rather slow and a little too easy going. There were times when I felt I had to protect him from his more forceful brother. Also, Bob rather liked to keep moving. After two weeks in our camp under the Great Rift, I could see Bob wanted to get going.

One morning, right out of the blue, he said, "Bunny, what about a move?"

"Right, where do you want to go? What do you want to try for?"

"Well, I'll tell you. I was talking the matter over with Dar when we went to bed last night. A pal of ours talks about a regular Shangri-la for game, somewhere near a place called Iringa. Do you know it?"

"Yes, I know it. It's way south of here. I haven't been there for years."

We went hunting in Iringa but didn't have much success. We stopped for a few nights at Kondoa Irangi in a government rest house, at the hotel in Dodoma, and at the Iringa Hotel. One evening at the Iringa I noticed a couple of other guests, two girls and a man. The girls were sisters; the elder, Rachel, was married to the man, Bernard Cohen. The younger, Leila, was traveling free, and possibly easy. They had motored up from Johannesburg and were going to Nairobi by easy stages, with one or two commitments en route. From there they were possibly going to motor on to visit Israel, if it were not too difficult. Both girls were very attractive and well turned out. Rachel was perhaps the prettier, but Leila was so amazingly vivacious that she stole the show. Before we parted that night we tried to work out if it would be possible to meet up again along the road in Nairobi. It appeared that we might do so at Dodoma, where Bernard, being a wine expert, was offering the Tanganyika government some advice on growing grapes.

First thing next morning, I checked on my safari staff. They were getting bored with the inactivity. I wanted to get my gunbearers' ideas of what to do, and also those of dear old Mwangi, my ancient cook. Sometimes they picked up some useful information as we traveled along, but now their minds were barren of suggestions. When I got back to the dining room for breakfast, I found Bob in earnest conversation with a Roman Catholic priest.

"Hi, Bunny," was Bob's greeting. "Father Patrick says they have whole heaps of sable and roan down near their mission." On the strength of this encouraging information, on top of what I had gleaned from the friendly hostess of the hotel the previous night, we decided there and then to visit the mission, a mere thirty miles away.

I must say that the fathers and brothers made us very much at home. They gave us their best shade tree to camp under and some fresh vegetables from their garden. There, however, the hospitality ceased. They had nothing in the way of meat or drink. So we invited them—we had met about four or five—to come to our camp for evening drinks. Then we set out to look for sable and roan but did not see any.

We returned to camp, and after we had bathed and dressed, the inmates of the mission started their invasion. The four or five we had met were only the advance guard. We produced the whiskey, and down it went. A few minutes later a few more Irishmen trickled in, followed by the arrival of a car full to the brim with jolly Irish monks. They may have been Irishmen, but they didn't mind knocking back Scotch whiskey!

While we chatted and drank in front of a good campfire, I noticed that there was a continual flow of new arrivals to the gathering. The Irishmen had sent the news far and wide. In the end there must have been twenty-five or thirty downing the Holbrooks' Scotch. The two Holbrook brothers began to look as bewildered as I felt.

By about 10:30 P.M. we managed to eject the last of the missionaries and their followers. In the time at their disposal, they had polished off ten bottles of Scotch and all the beer we had—about a dozen bottles. To the end, they pointed onto the tsetse-ridden bush, saying, "Sure, there be plenty of sable and roan in there—always." We took that now with a large pint of salt. Wasn't their larder empty? My guess was that between the hammerings of the jolly monks and the guileful ways of the poachers, all the game had gone off to kinder climes.

The next morning we pulled out for Dodoma, and I hoped for the best. It was a safe hope, for nothing could be worse than the predicament we had just left: no sable, no roan, no Scotch—just masses and masses of tsetse.

We arrived in Dodoma to find the wine conference in full swing, our friends from Jo'burg duly installed, and but one room for the brothers Holbrook. It looked as if I would have to sleep out. In fact, my safari staff was about to erect a tent for me in the open space between the hotel and the railway track when a pretty shadow fell across my path. It was Rachel, approaching in the light of the setting sun.

"Bunny, you don't have to go to all this bother," she said, pointing at the tent coming off the truck. "Just come in with us. We have two rooms. You can share with Bernard, and Leila can come in with me." She looked ready for my reply, but added, "Unless you have some better idea."

I grinned back at her, then made my reply. "That's really sweet of you all, and I'll very happily accept the kind invitation. I certainly do have an idea. Let's just see if it bears fruit."

She got the message all right. "OK," she said. "I'll tell Leila and Bernard. See you on the veranda for a drink in a while."

On the veranda, I noticed that Leila had slipped away, returning a few minutes later. As she handed me a drink, she said, "Oh, Bunny, I guessed you'd like to take a bath. I've run one for you in my room, sixty-nine, just around the corner." She pointed up the passageway.

"Thanks, Leila," I replied with a smile. Room sixty-nine, of course, had to be just around the corner! We all had a good laugh, and everyone started to trickle off to bed. As Leila went with her sister, she said to me, "Bunny, give me fifteen minutes, and then go to room sixty-nine."

Finally, I headed for sixty-nine, not really knowing what awaited me there, but I must admit I hoped.

It was. The sweet Leila was just completing her toilet. She was putting up her hair very prettily in preparation for the night. She pointed to the bed.

"Jump in," she said. I was extremely tired, and I just wondered if I might drop off to sleep before Leila joined me. As if to read my thought, Leila said quietly, "Don't worry, Bunny, I won't let you drop off to sleep." Next moment she was there, and what followed made for a very interesting night.

✕ ✕ ✕ ✕ ✕

Having reached, once again, my brand-new little cottage on the trout stream, I found a letter awaiting me that meant a bit of a change in my plans.

Henry and Ewell Stewart wanted to come out fairly shortly instead of waiting until next year. They were acquaintances of my sweet friend, Jo Bruce, and were originally going to come on safari with Nick and Diana Vanderscut. Now, owing to some big business coming up, Henry wanted to advance his hunt and come out as soon as possible. Consequently I sent him a cable: "Come immediately if you don't mind slight gamble on rainy weather." They decided to come immediately.

The Stewarts had, by their letter, sounded like an agreeable couple. They certainly were. He was slightly slow in thought, yet a very wise thinker. She was as quick as a ball of fire, and shrewd. They were a handsome pair—both tall—Henry sandy-haired, Ewell with tresses black as a raven and a complexion of peaches and cream. As Henry was keen to get a sable and roan, that precluded a hunt in Kenya, and we set off for Tanganyika. Knowing that we'd get along all right if we stuck to the main road south to Dodoma, no matter what the weather was like, we set off.

We did a little shooting around and about Lake Manyara. This enabled me to sum up the shooting ability of my customers. I found that he was a good but somewhat excitable shot. She was very steady. The camp did not go hungry. In actual fact, Ewell soon decided that she did not want to shoot much. She loved taking photographs, which she did with professional skill.

After a day or so in our camp and the usual chatter around the campfire, I gathered that both Jo Bruce and Diana Vanderscut had talked of me. In fact, Henry stated, "Yes, Bunny, Jo said you were hell with the girls. She said I'd have to watch you with Ewell." He leaned over to pat her hand.

I laughed as I answered, "Ah, she flatters me." I hesitated before I added, "Anyway, Henry, look at the record. They've all gone back home."

"That's good news. I need Ewell at home; the children are still rather young."

I looked at Ewell. "They'd need to be."

She said, "Thank you, Bunny." Then, "OK, Hank, I'm safe. I'll come home. But I don't say that for ten years hence!"

We all laughed and went to bed.

The Wheel of Life

The Stewarts were a grand pair. Yet the warning light had flashed. I knew I had to play this safari in a very cool style. I did not intend to fall in love and upset this very pleasant applecart.

While in our first camp, both Henry and Ewell shot a buffalo. She took the first one, and it all passed off without incident. Then Henry had a go, and we had excitement. He had a perfect heart shot at about fifty yards, but he pulled his aim over to the right by several inches. We had a stomach wound to follow and quite a long chase. Night came on before we came up with the buff. By now it was in the thickest bush, and in any case we could not follow the sparse blood trail.

The next morning, as we approached the area where we had left the wounded bull the previous evening, a buffalo charged out at us from thick bush. We were walking in the open, and I downed it with a brain shot. The buff fell about eight feet from us. Kikunyu and Tabei, carrying the customers' rifles, had jumped aside, allowing me to take my shot. Naturally at first we thought it was our wounded bull, but not a bit of it. This was a brand new bull, large but young. The reaction by Hank and Ewell was immediate. He seized my hand and meant it, and she kissed me warmly. I quickly entreated them to silence, pointing into the bush ahead. I then whispered into Ewell's ear, which was nearer and smelled sweeter, that Hank's bull was still ahead. She passed the message on. Hank nodded.

Hank and I went to join Kikunyu. We at once heard the labored breathing of the buffalo. I put my finger between Hank's eyes. His big baby face lit up as he nodded his head in understanding. We went in on a narrow game track for only about ten yards. Then the bull came, luckily from our left. We were both able to swing around and give it one. The animal collapsed in a heap almost at our feet, with an exhalation of breath nearly equal to the roar of a lion. God, that was a gallant old bull!

Next we packed up camp at Manyara and headed south as the heavens opened to let the rain down. The main road stood up, however, and we reached Dodoma, en route for Tabora, without great difficulty. But here I had to change my plans. I knew that the road west, alongside the railway track, would be impassable. I arranged with the stationmaster at Dodoma to get me an open freight truck to carry the two safari vehicles. We loaded them and piled into the guard's van to Chaya. Here we offloaded and pitched our camp alongside the railway line, allowing us to hunt the whole Lake Chaya area. It was a pleasant enough camp, and we much enjoyed it for three nights. The first night there, after our splendid dinner and while we nursed a "go-to-bed" whiskey, we talked of the exciting buffalo hunt.

Hank asked, "Heh, Bunny, that buffalo hunt. Can you explain it to us? We left one wounded buff. We come back in the morning and find two. What gives?"

"I reckon the wounded one, who was a real old boy, had a scout who accompanied him and guarded him. That is just as the elephants do. In fact, much of the game have this habit."

Hank and Ewell nodded their heads and waited for me to go on.

"Somehow or other the old boy mislaid the young man for a while. During the night the scout caught up with his senior, and now wounded, companion. I think that explains it. When the scout charged us, it was trying to make up for its past failings in guarding the patriarch."

The next morning, we bumped the hunting car across the railway tracks and made our slow way through the mud and slush to Lake Chaya. Two days passed without our seeing the elusive roan bull we wanted. Then, on the third day, there was the perfect roan standing under a tree in the *miombo* forest at a range of 250 yards. Hank had a perfect rest over a fallen tree, but he made a nonsense of the shot, pulling over to the right again. The roan was off like a stolen horse heading for home. I seized Hank's rifle, took after the roan, and shot it. Having gotten the roan behind us, we were now after sable and elephant.

The next morning we put the safari vehicles back up on the wagon and waited for the Tabora express to chug its way into the little Chaya station. Around 2:30 in the afternoon our railway safari was on its way once more, and by evening we reached Tabora.

The Stewarts were good walkers, and now they needed to be. On the fourth day of our walking hunt, Kikunyu and Tabei, Ewell, Hank, and I walked at a good steady pace, and within twenty minutes we found ourselves face to face with a good-looking elephant. It was a hundred yards away, coming in our direction with the wind in our favor. The animal was walking and cropping, cropping and walking. Tabei handed Hank my second Rigby .470.

I whispered to Hank, "If it stops, or as soon as I say—straight at its brain."

Hank nodded his understanding. He leaned over to me. "Back me up." I nodded back.

The old bull continued its advance on us until it was seventy-five yards away. There it abruptly stopped and threw its head up a bit higher.

"Now," I said to Hank. Our two rifles rang out as one. The elephant dropped in the same moment.

"Bravo," came happily from Ewell.

Yet I had observed a twitch of one leg on the downed animal. I was watching carefully as we advanced. Sure enough, when we were fifty yards off, it was up on all fours and away, with its tail pointing straight to the heavens.

I shouted to Hank, "Right up his arsehole." This is precisely what Hank did, and the old bull collapsed into a great heap.

Just for safety's sake, I asked Hank to walk around and put another in the brain.

All's well that ends well. Of course, Hank and Ewell asked me what had gone wrong with our first two shots. They both missed the brain.

"Even yours missed," stated Ewell, looking at me as if I were not allowed to fail.

"Yes," I agreed, "mine missed. We misjudged the height of its head a bit. We should have been one wrinkle on the trunk lower."

Then Ewell looked with pride at her husband. "But, Hank, darling, that second shot you really put"—and here she imitated my English voice to perfection—"right up his arsehole!"

All we needed was to comb out a sable from that *miombo* bushland. The following day we made our way by car over to a rocky hill. Nearing the hill and within a half-mile of the elephant hunt, we saw a lone sable bull. Shooting at 250 yards, Hank certainly hit the sable, but not in the right spot. In a moment, I had made my decision and took off at a run with Tabei. I took a steady aim off Tabei's steady shoulder and the trophy was Hank's.

Hank, as usual, was childishly, delightfully happy, and he complimented me once more on my running ability. Ewell gave me the sweatiest, saltiest kiss I've ever had and reminded me once more that she was all woman.

And that completed our trip. All that remained was to get aboard the Central Line train and go back to Dodoma. I did suggest to Hank and Ewell that instead of getting off the train at Dodoma we should really go the "whole hog" on our Central Line safari by traveling all the way to the terminus at Dar es Salaam. However, I made the stipulation that if we did that, it would be only fair that Ewell accompany me to Dar's honeymoon island for the weekend. Hank laughingly declined this fair offer, and Ewell said, "Not this time, Bunny. Maybe when I come next time."

The Wheel of Life

When I got back to my lovely cottage, the rain was still about and the flowers were a sight for sore eyes. The dogs and I had a hunt or two, and, of course, there was mail to attend to.

Directly after the rains, about two weeks later, some friends of Diana and Nick Vanderscut were coming along for a three-week hunt. There were three of them—Harry Welker, his son, and a close friend, Andy Boyler. They were from Williamsport, Pennsylvania. They sounded, and proved to be, a first-class trio. Harry was a well-to-do dentist, his son was at college, and Andy was a heavy haulage contractor. What a splendid chap he was. It was a pleasure to get stuck in the mud with Andy around!

As I awaited my safari people at Nairobi Airport, I bumped into a beautiful girl. This, I thought—when I had time to think—I richly deserve. I had been starving for consumable beauty for more than long enough. The girl was my lovely Joy, whom I had not seen for over a year. She was at the airport to meet her twin sons, coming out from school in England.

Before Joy left me she said, "Bunny, do come and see me when you can. I've got a house at Karen." And, so that I would make no mistake, she added, "I'll leave a little map at Muthaiga for you."

"Lovely," I replied. "I'll be there at first opportunity." I kissed her, and she left me with a wave.

Shortly afterward, Messrs. Welker and Boyler arrived, and my mind was swept away from dreaming. They were nice, very nice. I could tell at once that we were in for a pleasant safari. I took them to the Norfolk, where we all dined and they slept.

I am a great believer in adages. For instance, the "ill wind" is bound to touch someone for the good. That particular wind swept around the corner of the Loita Hills in Masailand, some twelve days after the start of the Welker safari. It brought with it torrents of rain, which caused masses of mud in which we got stuck more than several times. Yet we were able to hunt pretty well. Buffalo, rhino, and all the plains game came our way. Apart from that, we saw a nice big slice of the annual migration of game to the Serengeti. We saw thousands upon thousands of wildebeest on their great trek, as well as thousands of zebra and *kongoni*. It was a great sight. The clients completely forgot about their guns! I must say I found that was the usual way of things. If the clients who had come on safari to shoot saw some strange happening or phenomenon, then they were more interested in it than in going on with their shooting. They would want to study what was going on and take pictures of the proceedings. They would forget all about shooting.

It was while returning from one of our migration-studying forages that I was able to see Andy Boyler in action. The rain had poured, and I had gotten us really and truly stuck in the mud. And much of the Masailand is real mud—the best!

Andy got out of the car, walked around it, looked

H.CLAASSENS.

147

under it, looked under it again, and then looked up at an overhanging tree. He then blinked through his thick glasses at me and, pointing to a certain limb in the tree, said, "Say, Bunny, will you have your man cut that for me?"

While the limb was coming down from the tree, he walked over a few yards and picked up a pretty heavy balk and threw it down on the car's rear end. He then indicated several more such timbers. These we lined up under the car. Then he cunningly laid two flattish logs on top of the first lot. Finally, he wedged in the limb cut from the tree by some special Andy formula, leaving it protruding from the rear. Then, by what appeared quite light pressure from Andy and one helper, the safari car rose in the air, clear of the mud. Logs and timbers were quickly in place under the wheels—and the car was ready to roll.

So Andy and I left the camp just as it was getting dark. We had a driver and one other helper, and we had Andy's special "jacker-upper." We expected some rain and mud, and as far as Narok we had rain and mud. It took us four hours to do the seventy miles to Narok with no real trouble—just a slow grind, and all the time nursing the sore clutch. After that, it was thick powder dust almost all the way.

As we approached Nairobi, it was just after 2 A.M. We paused on the side of the road for a few minutes, and to once again check on the clutch. We looked at each other in the light of the truck and both roared with laughter. Andy looked incredible to me, and I must have looked the same. For the first half of the journey we had gotten covered in rain and mud, and for the second half in clouds of volcanic ash. The effect was grotesque!

I had another good look at Andy, then said, "You look like a piece of badly cured Gorgonzola cheese."

He quickly retorted, "And you look like an undercooked long French loaf that has fallen into a dirty corner."

We laughed ourselves up the rest of the hill into Nairobi. I think we were still tittering as we drove up the drive to Joy's house at Karen.

From the moment of the Nairobi trip's being on, that lovely girl had been on my mind. I knew we were going to arrive at a very awkward hour, but I knew that Joy would not mind. I knew, also, that my two men would be taken care of by her servants. In town, at that time of night, they would have been rather lost.

As I stopped the car outside the house, Andy asked, "Bunny, where are we? Aren't we going to a hotel?"

"No, Andy, we'll stay with this good friend."

"He must be a good friend for you to call on him at this time of night."

"Yes, she is a very good friend of many years' standing. She won't mind me knocking her up at this time."

I picked up a small pebble from the driveway and threw it gently at what I judged to be one of Joy's bedroom windows, as Andy, pondering my last remark, said, "Oh, that's it, is it?"

Right at that moment I did not understand his question. The difference between the English and American idioms did not strike me until later.

We had a bath and then ate splendid eggs and bacon with toast made golden in the bacon fat. Then more toast with yellow farm butter and homemade strawberry jam. As I ate, I quaffed several cups of Earl Grey tea. Andy downed two huge Scotch whiskies. Then I was very firmly put to bed and very gently kept there until morning.

We returned to camp the next day, with a repaired truck, in time for drinks, a bath, and dinner. Just before turning in for bed,

The Wheel of Life

I overheard Andy telling Harry of our trip and our stay with Joy. I heard him use the expression "knocking her up" and the laughter that followed, and I remembered. Then and there I hastened to enlighten them concerning the usual English meaning of the expression "to knock up."

Chapter 14

Texas Invades East Africa

S oon began the gentle and pleasant Texas invasion of East Africa. As it happened, I had been totaling up my time in Kenya, and much to my astonishment, it came to more than thirty years! I had arrived in 1927; it was now 1958. The years—most wonderful years—had gone like a flash. Quite some time ago, now, Doctor Kurt von Wedel of Oklahoma City had come out on safari with me. Then some years later, Charles F. Urschel, who had lived in Oklahoma City and knew the doctor, came on safari. They, in turn, knew the Seeligsons, also originally from Oklahoma. All these families had moved, through the interests of ranching and oil, to the wilder miles of Texas.

Now, right out of the blue, came a safari inquiry from San Antonio. It was from one Frates Seeligson. He had gotten in contact with me through my doctor friend and Charles Urschel, who was a married relation of Frates's. Frates sounded like an amusing chap, which he certainly was. He was to be accompanied by Tom Slick, also of San Antonio. They were to arrive six months hence, and I decided to take them to hunt in Masailand.

Frates sounded as if he wanted to shoot a lot. In fact, he sounded like a real "killer." He did not prove to be that at all, but he did like to shoot his gun. He liked the *bang, bang, bang!* If he had been old enough to serve in the war, his place would have been in charge of a machine gun battalion!

For Frates's safari I needed one other professional hunter. I got Fred Poolman, a very good hunter and a pleasant fellow. I looked forward to meeting Frates immensely. His letters were really encouraging. I could tell that he had a good sense of humor—and that certainly helps a safari along. I did not hear from Tom Slick prior to his arrival, so I had no preconceptions about him.

Well, they arrived, and I must say that Frates was much as I expected him to be. Tom also seemed very nice. They both were in their mid-thirties, and both were of medium height. But there the likeness ended. While Frates had a dark, ruddy complexion with black hair and large brown eyes, Tom had a light, graying complexion with gray-white hair and large, steel-blue eyes.

Frates was well and truly sun-browned and looked as if he had been constantly caressed by the open air of the Texas plains. Tom was inclined to be rather pink and gray, along with several other orchid shades, and he gave the appearance of being rather over-air-conditioned. They were both nice men. Fred Poolman and I decided we'd have an enjoyable safari with them.

We started off in Masai, west of Narok. There was a mass of game about, and the weather was fairly good—that is, no rain. As was my habit, I had arranged for the visitors to switch with Fred and me from time to time, when it did not upset a planned hunt. So, in the course of a week's hunting, it turned out that we usually had at least one change.

Frates and Tom turned out much as we expected them to be; one could not have had easier clients. Yet they continued to be so different. For instance, if there were some delay in the course of a morning's hunt, Frates would just pull out a book and be content. Tom was not so. He would be impatient, walk around, fidget, and generally be a slight "blind." Tom had to keep busy, keep employed. Frates always carried three or four books in the hunting car, some of them most unlikely tomes! If there were the slightest stop or delay, out came a book.

The hunting went well. They each got a good enough bag out of the Masai. In most cases Tom got the better trophies, but Frates had a lot more fun. For instance, when he got a rather poor leopard, he positively "yeaked" to the high heavens in happiness. Yet Tom, who got a far bigger and better one, barely made a slight purring sound. Frates got a very large lion, but without much of a mane. (I must say, I rather misjudged it with the early morning light in my eyes.) However, Frates was as happy as a Santa Gertrudis bull in clover, and pointed out what large feet his lion had!

Luckily, Tom was not keen on getting a lion, in which opinion I encouraged him, as did Fred Poolman. I overheard one very sage remark Fred made to Tom: "The only lion worth shooting is a cattle-killer." And then as an afterthought, "Or a man-eater."

Each got a good buffalo with, again, Frates fairly "whooping" with delight. Tom was pleased—but not enthusiastic. It was one long, great pleasure to hunt with Frates. With Tom it was a little unrewarding.

I never saw Tom again, but Frates was back on safari time and time again. When he left he said, "Bunny, you can bet I'll be back here again within two years. And after that, I'll come every two years until I marry."

He did that, and after four years he married Martita. Afterward, both Martita and Frates came every two years until the closing of Kenya. And they have recently come to visit me with their three lovely children. There is, indeed, a lot of joy in life!

The Wheel of Life

About this time, my right-hand man for many years went back to his native land, and thus I lost his valuable services. I speak of Kikunyu, the "caterpillar." He had been a wonderful, stalwart help for a long time—brave as a lion, cunning as a buffalo, quick as a cheetah, stealthy as a leopard, and with the eyes of a vulture. He was a great man. His own people wanted him as a leader. He must have done well for them.

As soon as the rains ceased, I had a really enjoyable safari with two friends of Jo Bruce. They were Bob and Mary Abrahamson from Minneapolis, and they were very good value indeed. He was thin and funny; she was plump and jolly. They both had hearts of gold. I went

H.CLAASSENS.

154

to meet them at the Norfolk Hotel. I had left my car out front and walked through the inner courtyard. There I saw a man eyeing me from the bottom block. He advanced a few paces, stopped, tilted his head to one side, and eyed me again, slantwise. He then marched directly up to me, held out his hand, and said, "You're Bunny Allen."

"Yes," I replied, "but how did you know?"

"Wal, yer know, I make an opinion of a person before I meet him. I study his letters. I listen to what people say. Jo Bruce said a lot about you. And, of course, she showed me a picture—I suppose that helped."

By now he had a twinkle in his close-set eyes and a big smile on his tight-lipped mouth. I was able to recover my hand and shook it, somewhat surreptitiously, to get the circulation back.

"Come and meet Mary," he said, and off we trundled to the bottom block. There Mary was waiting, bright as a London bun direct from the oven. She was as round as a perfect chump chop, and he as lean as a sparerib.

I found that Bob Abrahamson very often called Mary "Baby." So very quickly in my own mind I named them "Abie and Baby." In fact, to me it was the "Abie and Baby safari."

I took them first to Lake Manyara in Tanganyika. Then we headed south to the country around Kondoa Irangi to look for greater kudu and an elephant. And while down there in that beautiful country we had quite a fantastic experience.

We were wandering around slowly in the hunting car, looking down little side tracks, game tracks, anywhere to get the very beaten track. There were rock-laden hills of every shape and size. Now and again we would climb up a hill to scout the countryside. Suddenly we saw the biggest of all hills, covered in great white, marblelike rocks. I looked at Abie and said, "We must climb that."

He nodded his head emphatically as he answered, "Yep, I reckon you're right—we must climb that."

The path followed a fairly easy gradient. It turned out to be a very well-worn elephant track. In fact, after going a few hundred yards, we came on the fresh tracks of one big bull; then, in turn, a nice warm "drop." This was exciting. Abie's piercing little eyes were popping out of his head. The gradient was very gentle, taking advantage of every little roll in the ground.

About halfway up the hill, the cloud evaporated and we had glorious sunshine. We noticed that the old bull had gone steadily on and up. Then came a spot where the elephant had had to squeeze between two enormous boulders. They were so close set that you could see where the great flanks of the animal had polished the rocks on either side.

All of a magnificent sudden, we found ourselves at the summit of the hill with the elephant. There it was, twenty-five feet ahead of us, with its head poking out between two monstrous boulders, looking at Africa. That is exactly what it appeared to be doing, and while so doing it was keeping cool in the pleasant breeze. No doubt it was also dreaming of its fine days gone by and, maybe, cogitating on the possibilities still to come. Abie and I exchanged fairly big smiles. We knew we had been privileged to witness something, to say the least, a little unusual.

We watched for quite a few more minutes, and then we took ourselves gently, silently away. We backtracked some fifty yards before cutting over to the left of the elephant lookout where, more by luck than judgment, we found ourselves on a slight shelf of protruding rock below and in front of the grand old beast. Thus we were in a position to look up at it and see its tusks and trunk. The elephant had shortish yet very thick tusks. Each one must have been around a hundred pounds. I noticed that they were set very close to the trunk, which they had had to be for it to negotiate between the two boulders. We were only about fifty feet below.

At this point it is fitting to recall that we had set out that morning to hunt an elephant if we saw one—and to shoot it for the ivory, if the ivory was worthwhile. This elephant was very worthwhile. Even so, we did not, from the start, look to our rifles. We were too intrigued even once to contemplate taking up arms.

We withdrew and made our way back to the patient Baby. She protested slightly and looked at her watch. "Now, Bab, you said one hour. D'you know you bin gone more'n three?"

It was unbelievable that we had been making our study at the top of the hill for almost three hours. That time had passed like ten minutes!

Later she said to me, "Bab says it was a fine big-tusker. Why didn't Bab shoot it?"

"I reckon we just got too fond of it," I replied. And that was about it. From the moment we had seen the magnificent backside, we had not thought of shooting.

Three or four days later, Abie shot an elephant with tusks about twenty pounds lighter than those of "Old Hilltop." Abie was delighted with his tusks and still talks of our fun up on the hill.

Very soon after this I bade farewell to Abie and Baby. They said they would return in a year or two.

Back home, I had to rest myself up and think about the Dorn safari, coming along soon. The question of whom to get to help me on that safari was very pleasantly resolved for me, without any effort on my part. Out of the clear blue sky my two sons arrived. David was fed up working in the game department and had decided to start hunting professionally, and Anton was fed up with hunting with a firm from Tanganyika.

Frates had told me that I would enjoy the Dorns, and I certainly did. They were true, blue-blooded Texans, and you can go the world wide and you won't find better than that. They shared a marvelous sense of humor. They enjoyed their drink—no, I'll go further than that—they enjoyed their drink very much. Always in the safari car, Dale and Jean carried their little canteen. They called it their "survival kit." They also appreciated our good camp food, especially all the good wild meats.

Chapter 15

A Close Call

After leading another safari, I retired to Chestnut Cottage for a while, having met up again with Jeri, my lovely girl of the open blue Buick, accompanied by her Yorkshire terrier, Kitoria. There I planted fruit trees, various berries, and vegetables; Jeri planted roses and lovely flowers. The rain came down well and truly, and the cottage became a place of love and beauty. The trout continued to jump over the falls in the pretty stream, and the leopards continued their strange cacophony in the forest beyond. Nature was in command. Nothing could be more agreeable. We passed the time in sublime happiness.

In time, the rain ceased and safari work started again. I decided to take Frates and the Murchesons down into the Masai country. The Murchesons were a very nice couple. She, bubbling over with life, was most attractive. She had the sweetest smile, and her laughter was infectious. He was a very nice man, though a little dour perhaps. The contrast between John Murcheson and Frates was remarkable. Frates, of course, was so full of life, always ready for a laugh, even in the darkest hour, while John Murcheson was always steeling himself against that darkest hour, sure that it lurked just around the corner.

I think the finest example of the typical John action, or rather inaction, was after he shot his lion. Once we were back in camp, Frates and Henry Poolman, my other hunter, came to admire our King.

"My, my, what a beauty," said Frates.

"It certainly is the best," said Henry.

Frates admired the magnificent beast, then looked at John, whose face was almost expressionless.

"John! John!" he screamed, "what's the matter with you? Why don't you jump up and down—or something?"

A mild grin creased his face—nothing more. It takes all sorts to make a world.

✕ ✕ ✕ ✕ ✕

My next safari of note and consequence with Texans—two delightful couples, the Nelsons and the Woffords. Four more charming people you could not meet. All of them wanted to hunt, and we were out for a month. I got Henry Poolman to help me, as both of my sons were otherwise employed.

We went down into the Kimana country, northeast of Mount Kenya. It was a great place for a mixed-bag hunt and fine bird shooting. Also, we enjoyed attractive campsites with an abundance of good, clear water. We had to do a great deal of the hunting by foot, as the countryside was heavily strewn with large, black volcanic boulders, which very often barred the area to safari-car travel. This forced our customers to really earn their trophies. These came in well and truly—and quickly. The whole party were good shots.

Being true Texans, they were very fond of their drink around the campfire. I joined them, while dear Henry Poolman drank Pepsi. Henry was a splendid fellow and a great favorite with all my clients. It was a real tragedy when he was killed on a lion hunt some years later. He was one of the best of the new generation of white hunters. Actually, it has always been a matter of wonder to me that there are not more accidents among professional hunters on safari. Over all the years of hunting in East Africa, there have been only about fifty fatal accidents to white hunters in the course of their duties. The golden rule is, and always will be, Look after the client! He or she—and I say especially she—must not get hurt. One fatality of that sort on a safari, and you are finished as a professional hunter. On this very safari, in fact, I had a close shave.

I had taken Cy and Madeline Nelson on an early morning run in the safari car. We were on one of the better tracks in among the black boulders where we could make steady progress. Out of a curtain of lacy thorn trees, all in bloom and filling the air with their precious scent, strode a lion. I could tell that it was a pretty good trophy, and I hastened Cy out of the car. The lion disappeared into another batch of thornbush. We followed its tracks for a short while, and then it presented itself for a reasonable shot.

However, Cy did not make one of his best efforts.

He hit the lion pretty firmly, but the

shot was not a killer. The lion was away like a flash and appeared to be going well.

I made the mistake of giving chase immediately, without enough thought. I knew that Tabei would bring Cy along behind me. We were in open thornbush terrain with thick bush patches here and there. I had run about a hundred yards when caution, almost too tardily, stopped me. I looked around to see our lion advance out of tall grass at a fast trot toward Cy and Tabei. Cy appeared transfixed, and as the lion leaped, I swung my .470 Rigby like a shotgun and brought it down from midair. As it fell, quite dead, its claws dug into Cy's leather boots! Cy's face was as white as a sheet, and I felt mine was about the same. When Cy was able to speak, he said, "That was a little too close, wasn't it?"

"Yes, Cy, that was far too close." I was trembling. Madeline, who had watched part of the performance from the not-too-distant car, was relieved to see her husband return safely. She was not as relieved as I!

The other outstanding event of this safari was Rollins Wofford's elephant hunt. Henry and I had gone out on an early-morning recce, leaving the clients abed. From a slight rise in the ground, we had spotted a good-looking bull in among some tall swamp grass. We could see only one elephant, even though we watched for some time.

I sent Henry back for Rollins, only a mile or so away, while I continued to watch. The animal was several hundred yards away and was keeping very quiet as it grazed on the thick grass. Every now and again I'd see its great head sweep round in a semicircle as its trunk gathered up the grass, preparatory to tucking it into its mouth. On several occasions I caught a glimpse of two fine-looking, sunburnt tusks.

Very soon an excited Rollins arrived, all agog and ready to do battle. We advanced slowly on the elephant, for the going was thick and tricky; from time to time we could hear the beast scything away on the grass. At last we could see it in a little opening in the swamp. Rollins made a perfect brain shot, and we had two hundred pounds of ivory on the ground, as quick as that.

Then the fun started! From nowhere at all, suddenly a great trumpeting broke out. Almost immediately four very black elephant heads, about twenty-five feet off, poked their way through the tall reeds to look at us. It was like a stage set, and I for one felt very much like the "wicked uncle"! The heads wagged from side to side in a horribly menacing manner. I must say I expected them to charge at any moment. I am sure they were debating just that among themselves. Yet the splendid Henry forestalled them. He cupped his hands to his generous mouth and made the rhino "love call." A most astonishing change of demeanor at once appeared on the elephants' faces. Their eyes opened wide, and their trumpeting ceased. Their trunks reached up to the heavens as they sought for the smell of the hated rhino. Then they turned and fled into the silence of the swampland. It was just too much for them. Of course, they usually see rhino "off," but in this case, when they could neither see nor smell their rivals yet thought they could hear them, they fell into submission. I really think that Henry's quick cunning and knowledge of bush lore saved our bacon that day.

Rollins's tusks weighed 106 and 104 pounds, respectively. They now reside in a museum in San Antonio, Texas. The last time I was there I saw them, looking very handsome. I also saw Cy's snarling lion in his ranch house. He smiled as he took a playful kick at it!

Now it was back to Chestnut Cottage for a week or two—or three! Jeri had made it a place of beauty and a haven of peace. Roses were standing up and climbing and clinging, and doing everything a rose should do. Fruit and berries were thrusting their faces in profusion to the warm sun, and mushrooms poked their noses out to the cold night air.

Often Jeri and I would take a ride up into the forest of Mount Kenya. On these rides the dogs, ridgebacks and Faux Pas, would follow us, and Kitoria came too, riding up on the crupper of my saddle. When the others gave chase after a bushbuck or something, Kitoria gave tongue from her secure position. They were great, though short, days.

More and more safari work was claiming my time. Often now I would have two safaris out at the same time, using my two very able sons as well as others when necessary, usually close friends. When I felt like loafing at the lovely cottage, I often had to go out on safari. Safari was never a drudge to me, but the quiet life at home was increasingly a draw. Nevertheless, here I was about to take out three charming ladies—two from the DuPont country, Floma Ladelly and her sister Anita Wiesbrod, and their friend from New York City, Janet Jacobson. It was going to be a restful safari for me, because they did not want to shoot anything, except with the camera.

After spending a week at the ranch, my ladies and I moved on to one or two of the national park lodges. There we got very good photographs. It was interesting to see how each of the ladies chose her own favorite animal, her own favorite tree and flower. For instance, Floma liked the little dik-dik. And that choice suited her well: She was short, like a dik-dik, and very pretty, like a dik-dik. For her part, Anita's favorite was the giraffe. She was taller and had long, lovely legs that went on forever. In turn, Janet's favorite was the splendid, brave warthog, and, do you know, when she laughed, which she did a lot, she snorted!

I must say I found this nonshooting safari a pleasant change. Apart from the film safari, this was the first purely photographic safari I had conducted. I liked it. I am not suggesting that I was willing to give up genuine hunting for taking pictures, but I could see that picture taking was a great thing. I could see that more and more people would come just to take pictures, with a little meat for the pot thrown in! I am not one of those who say that hunting will always go on. It is inherent in man to hunt, though, just as it is to fight and to make love. In fact, these qualities in a man often go hand in hand as he proves his manhood. It is only when these things get out of control that the trouble starts—when science takes over from nature, when speed gives no time for balanced thought, and when jealousy crowds out the beauty of love.

The three charming girls had come, and now it was time for them to go. They had grown to love the African outdoors—all our beautiful animals, swift mountain streams, sluggish muddy rivers, the giant forest trees, the sweet-smelling bushes laden with blooms, and the rest: The wondrous campfire and the smell of wood smoke and, when the time was right, the enticing moon doing its best to encourage romance, even though it might be only the holding of a hand!—all of that is part of a safari, and by no means a small part.

✗ ✗ ✗ ✗ ✗

In no time at all, it was again my pleasure to take my good friend Frates Seeligson on safari. He was accompanied this time by his brother, Arthur, and Arthur's wife, Linda. Also to swell the party were Bill and Adelaide Fuller and their daughter, Marcia. It was a fine, big party of fine, big-hearted people. We had six weeks of good hunting and happiness. My two sons and Jens Hessel helped on this trip, and it worked out fine. We did a lot of traveling, starting on the Tana River, then on to Ngorongoro Crater and across the Serengeti to Ikoma, and finally we hunted on the Grumeti. Frates was his usual wonderful self. His brother was also very nice, though not so exuberant. His wife, Linda, was a most lovely girl with a heart of twenty-four-karat gold and as gentle as a lovebird.

Bill and Adelaide Fuller were a handsome pair, and their daughter was pretty as a picture. Naturally, during this safari little romances took place, none of which amounted to anything much and no harm was done. It just kept one or two people in practice and several others on their toes.

As a direct result of this safari, a few months later the Fullers came out again, this time with Harry Tennison and his lovely wife, Gloria, whom I had first met in 1947, when she was a very young person.

Jeri and I selected the new campsite with the help of a friendly Indian employee on a local sisal plantation. I found the way and selected a truly beautiful site right on the river. All we wanted now was a big full moon, and that was due in three nights.

The Indian was quite a comedian. As we drove the four or five miles down through the dense bush, being bitten by tsetse flies all the while, his conversation was, more or less, thus: "Ah-ha, here right, here left—and around—a-ha, elephant bullshit—you see—I tell you so, yes? Plenty bullshit here! Ah-ha, right here—no, no, not right, it isn't—I am meaning left here—or big tree hit. Ah-ha, under big tree plenty buffalo bullshit! You see, Bwana Mkubwa, plenty bullshit here!"

And there certainly was. It was his every second word! However, he was a goodly wight and showed us a splendid camp. Yet, getting the large, load-carrying truck in was another business. The bush was so thick and the bends in the track so many and some so acute that we almost had to hack out a new route. It took five hours of hard labor to complete the job.

On the very first day after everyone had gone out hunting, leaving just Jeri and me in camp, a large herd of elephant cows and calves came down to the river, only a couple of hundred yards downstream from the camp. There must have been at least two hundred animals altogether. For an hour or more they played in the water. It was a most wonderful sight. Then they crossed the river and slowly disappeared. I hoped there would be a repeat performance for the customers, for it was the sight of the century! As it happened, they repeated the show every day we were in that camp, so that all our people saw them at one time or another. Luckily, there was no big bull among the herd, so no one was tempted to hunt this prize camp herd.

The elephants behaved in the same manner each day, crossing the river between 8:00 and 9:00 A.M. each morning and returning between 5:00 and 6:00 P.M. each evening. One thing I noticed was that there were quite a few very young calves among them, and on the second day there were one or two that were literally only a few hours old. I decided to look into the strange phenomenon and, together with Tabei, backtracked the herd after they had crossed the river. We went through the dense bush for about two miles on the very distinct tracks used by the elephants. Then we sighted a big patch of large baobab trees. That was the home of the herd, and it proved to be a maternity ward! There, among the baobabs, were about a dozen mother jumbos. There were three calves still wet from birth, and the balance of the cows were about to produce at any moment—or so it appeared. The wind was perfect for us, but even so, we were extremely wary. We studied this most magnificent sight for a few minutes and then took our leave. Tabei and I felt extremely privileged. All the way back to the river and camp, Tabei was clucking his tongue and shaking his head in astonishment.

The next day, everyone stayed in camp to see the elephant safari cross the river, and some of us saw quite a fantastic sight. One cow and small calf had wandered off a few yards from the rest of the herd, and the calf in turn went a few too many paces from mama, putting its trunk into the river. A large crocodile immediately seized the trunk and pulled the calf toward the depths. The calf screamed, the mother screamed, and four large cows came rushing up to the rescue, trumpeting at the top of their voices. Mother and the other four made straight for the stricken calf, thrashing the water with their trunks and beating a tattoo on the riverbed with their feet. This was altogether too much for the croc. The calf went free, to go whimpering off with its mother. The other four cows stood their ground for a moment or two, and then they, too, retired, glancing over their shoulders as they went. It was a fine piece of work—fine elephant teamwork. It was another example of the group family life of elephants.

In the meantime, Jeri had been a very good girl, doing a trip to Mombasa and back just to bring us monster prawns and sweet lobster. We now had a delightful change of diet. The clients appreciated that, and our stock of Pouilly-Fuissé shortened smartly.

Then Jeri headed for home. She was missing her sweet little Kitoria, and, what is more, she knew the form. She knew that clients do not really want the wives or girlfriends (call them what you will!) of the white hunters in camp. They want 100 percent attention.

Chapter 16

Bad Luck
and Some
Unpleasantness

M y next safari was in the Voi area, with yet another family of Texans. I had met them in San Antonio a year or so earlier, and in fact had had a dove shoot on their ranch. The family consisted of Lou and Betty Mormon, their two sons and the wife of one, and their very sweet daughter, Susan. Betty was the sister of Romona Seelingson, mother of my friend Frates. So, to some extent, it was like taking out old friends.

The day after I had finished setting up the camp, in came the Mormons. We served them oysters—beautifully. None of them liked oysters! The second course was prawns in an Arab sauce. None of them liked prawns! Not wishing to risk a third failure, I asked, "Don't any of you like seafood?"

Lou replied, "That's right. We don't. San Antonio is so far from seafood that we don't risk it. We like beef."

In ten minutes the cook had rustled up some good underdone steaks—eland, of course, but for the customers they were beef. Then, to make matters worse, my assistant on the safari, "Coley" Coles, announced that he also did not like seafood! So what could

I do? Of course, I ate it. I had such a surfeit of those aphrodisiacal foods that I was almost climbing the walls. I longed for some of my old flames to appear. I judged that, as attractive as Betty was, I should not chance my arm with her; Lou would certainly have taken umbrage. And while I cast an eye to dear Susan, she settled that matter for me by falling in love with Coley! Thus, poor old Bunny was left out on an aphrodisiacal limb.

I plunged myself into work—all day, as much as possible. I ate a lot (of seafood) and drank my share, told fireside tales, and went to bed all tired out—but I was always up early, dying for that lifesaving several cups of tea. The safari went well enough, and the Mormons loved the game meat.

After a few days, my two sons and Freddie Seed came to join the safari. With six customers, Coley and I were a bit overstretched. On every safari some things go wrong—that is, not according to plan. The Mormon safari was no exception. Usually they are minor points, but on this occasion it was an unlucky business that turned out rather badly.

Everyone was very keen for Susan to get her elephant. Coley, who for the most part was hunting for her, had located a respectable animal; the only snag was that it was rather close to the national park boundary. Coley had invited me along this time to give a hand, and I had been out scouting and was about to meet up again with them when I heard a shot, followed by the sound of something crashing through the trees in my direction. Then the very next moment I was presented with a perfect brain shot, but only for a moment.

There was a plain blood spoor from what was quite obviously a lung shot. The elephant might go five or ten miles—or forever, if the lung was only just touched. Coley had failed to get a backup shot in, and I had missed my golden opportunity. It was a pileup of misfortunes, but I must say that I found myself as the chief failure.

We knew we were very near the park boundary. The elephant was probably already in the park. That being the case, Coley would not follow it up; he would just report it. He was a purist and always went by the letter of the law. Coley reported the matter to the local warden, and two days later the dead elephant turned up in the park and Susan lost her pair of tusks. She was very sporting about it and accepted it as just bad luck, which it certainly was.

$$\times \times \times \times \times$$

At this stage I eased up a little in the safari business. I knew that in the following year I had a rather tight schedule, with several more Texas safaris taking me quite far afield. With the luck of the draw, I was next able to run several safaris within a stone's throw of Chestnut Cottage. In fact, quite a lot of the hunting was on my ranch land; we overflowed onto the hunting block right next door.

Among those hunts there are three that I remember really well, because of the delightful people that came on them. As was usual with my safaris, all three of them came by way of recommendation from previous clients: They were the Dorrances, the Fentresses, and the Noltes. The advantage of this sort of introduction is that both sides have some sort of previous knowledge of each other. Thus, when you start a safari you are not complete strangers.

One evening, I believe it was on the Fentresses' safari, a very tall Mukogodo tribesman arrived in the camp. He was very upset. A lion had just taken his favorite girlfriend. He said that it would not have been so bad had the lion taken his favorite wife, but his favorite girlfriend was too much!

He was a fine-looking old man, well over six feet tall, with enormous cutout earlobes reaching down to his chin. He climbed into the back of the hunting car, carefully guarding his equipment as he did so, for he was indeed well-endowed!

Within twenty minutes we were at the scene of the crime. There were the remains of the young maiden, with honeycombs strewn and wild bees buzzing in all directions. Apparently the old man and his favorite girlfriend were gathering wild honey as a sweetener for the favorite wife when the lion had set upon them. The gruesome, half-eaten body was in a little thicket. In my judgment, the old lion (for indeed its pug marks showed it was an old one) had gone off for a drink. It would return.

There was a convenient thicket nearby, from which we carved out a hide. Then, telling the old warrior that we'd do our best to take revenge on the lion, we returned to our camp to get the necessary gear. In an hour we were back and in position, armed with two rifles, a shotgun, and a powerful spotlight. I intended to use every method, fair or foul, to get that lion.

We sat in the hide, heard the birds sing their various lullabies, and saw the sun turn from yellow to golden to red. Venus followed the sun, and a small crescent moon appeared as if suspending the evening star. There was beauty everywhere—if one forgot the favorite girlfriend.

The yowl of a hyena brought us back to reality. The lion kept quiet. However, I knew it was coming; the Piramus in me told me that for a certainty. Also, from the look in Tabei's eyes, I knew that his sixth sense was working, too.

The night settled in. Maybe an hour passed, then Tabei touched my hand and motioned toward the remains. Soon I heard the heavy breathing of the lion as it fed. I fail now to remember who actually was in the hide with us. It was many years ago, and I wanted the whole thing out of my mind as quickly as possible. However, I believe it was Jamie Fentress. Whoever it was, I alerted him to the fact that our lion was on the spot. He knew what he had to do. As soon as I switched the spotlight onto the lion, three shots crashed out as one. With a sighing grunt the wretched lion collapsed in a heap. We wasted a minimum of time on it and headed for camp.

Next morning, at the very crack of dawn, we were back at the awful scene. However, as early as we were, the lonely lover had beat us to it. There was the old man, bent in the task of burying his favorite girlfriend. We helped him erect a cairnlike pile of large stones above the shallow grave. The killer lion was a real mess. It had hardly a tooth in its head, just two long black hairs feigning a mane, and it was scratched all over from fighting. Its claws were all but worn out, and its feet were as large as pudding plates. We abandoned it as it was, but as we left, the old man buried his spear in the lion's belly, emitting as he did so a dreadful oath. We saw the old boy make his way back to his nearby *manyatta*. As he left he once more mumbled, "But why couldn't it have been my favorite wife?"

✕ ✕ ✕ ✕ ✕

My good friend Frates soon came once again. He brought a most charming couple, Tobin and Ann Armstrong. As a rather complicating factor, I had another safari out at the same time. This was for four other Texans, Dan Auld and his wife, Pat, and John Moore and his wife. The white hunters were my son David and Henry Poolman, with Frates and company, and my son Anton and Jens Hessel with the other couple. We set up their camps for the start of the safari only about thirty miles from each other: Frates in the Kipsing sand *lugga* and the Aulds quite adjacent to my ranch. Thus I, in overall charge of both safaris, could get from one to the other quite easily. As I recall, the men's chief desire was to get elephant, while the girls wanted leopard. We were in good country for both. The weather was wonderful and everyone was happy.

Having gotten Frates's party settled in, and after spending a couple of days with them, during which time I set up a very likely leopard possibility, I went over to the Dan Auld camp. There also, they had a good, big leopard feeding on a bait. That was to be for Pat, and Jens Hessel was in charge of the hunt for her leopard. The rest of their hunting had gone along well enough, but as yet, there was no sign of a big enough elephant for the two men. They each wanted one for the *Guinness Book of Records*! We judged we'd satisfy the girls' needs (regarding elephants!) from this camp. I certainly thought we could get a good enough elephant for Tobin Armstrong from the Kipsing *lugga*. That was the one elephant wanted out of that camp.

However, let me get back to that famous day when the beautiful Pat Auld got her leopard. I remember so well her setting out from camp that evening. She was dressed in exotically cut jeans tucked into the smartest type of cowgirl boots. She wore a Mexican-type shirt, albeit of natural colors, and a long, red Indian shawl over her shoulders. Her raven black hair was hanging down her back in a long plait, tied with a neat brown ribbon. On her fine, round head she wore a black Stetson hat, at just the right angle. As I wished her good hunting, I looked into, and noted the determination in, her eyes. I thought that if this girl got into a tussle with a leopard, the leopard would come off second-best.

Dan was on his fourth Scotch when we heard them returning. Golly, she was happy! She positively tumbled out of the hunting car, seized her big husband in her strong arms, and kissed him urgently. We all drank several glasses of champagne, more than we meant to. We eventually went to bed feeling no pain whatsoever.

Things were not so happy at the Frates's camp, however. Apparently Frates, out with Henry, had driven up a sand *lugga*, gotten stuck in very loose fine sand, and broken an axle. There was no option but to walk back to camp, about eight miles.

When he arrived back, he was tired, sweaty, and very thirsty, and he blew his top somewhat! Four whiskies, a bath, a good solid meal of eland steaks, and a bottle of burgundy later, he was back to normal.

On the morrow the rescue team went out for Henry's car, together with David and Tobin to do battle with elephant. In the meantime, I decided to take a stroll to check the leopard bait and see if the evening breeze was correct for the blind. Much to my astonishment and joy, I found a leopard already there. It had Ann's name written all over it. Quietly I eased my way back to camp to send David and Ann along. I escorted them back, having explained to David the situation. At that I left them and made my way back to camp.

It must have been two hours later, with not much light left in the sky, when we heard the shot from Ann—only one shot. I immediately hied myself off to see what was going on, hoping to see a dead leopard. Instead I found a nervous little Ann and a worried David.

Tabei had joined me by now, and at once I felt better. Here was my right-hand man. We had to call the hunt off for the night; the next morning at first light we'd carry on. Ann was very upset. We reassured her, however, and told her that we'd find her leopard in the morning, probably dead.

We found him, true enough, in the morning, in a hole in the riverbank, but still very much alive. As he came out at us, Ann had the satisfaction of nailing him with a brain shot. David, to make doubly sure, sent in a load of buckshot.

Something unpleasant happened later that same day. David took Tobin to look for the big-footed elephant. They were away all morning and came back for a late lunch. I saw that Tobin's forehead was cut, and he had some blood on his face.

"God," I said, "what happened to you?"

"It's your damn gun," he replied. "It blew up in my face!"

Without knowing it, he had rammed the rifle barrels into the sandbank of one of the riverbeds while climbing it. The second barrel had gotten well loaded with sand and had burst open upon firing. It might have been worse. It could have whipped his eye out. However, his wound healed quickly, and he realized that the accident was no fault of my double Rigby. Incidentally, Tobin got his elephant, all right. His first-barrel shot had proved a good one.

✕ ✕ ✕ ✕ ✕

The next safari that came my way was a real pleasure from beginning to end. It was with the wonderful Dorn family. This time Dale Dorn brought along his entire family, consisting of himself and his beautiful wife, Jean; his elder son, Tucker; his younger son, Johnny; and two very pretty daughters, Clayton and Sharon. We had a splendid camp set up in the Rift Valley near Lake Magadi. The game warden, Denys Zaphiro, helped us on this safari in that he had some very troublesome lions, which he wanted to get rid of. These lions were in a very inaccessible spot, halfway up the Great Rift Wall. They had been killing and eating Masai cattle.

Directly after breakfast, Denys started the aircraft trek to the ledge camp. By noon the camp was all set up, and Dale, Jean, and staff were there. A nice fat zebra was the bait, installed at a good spot near the Masai *manyatta*. To me, the whole setup smelled of success.

The next day, just before dark, we distinctly heard a shot up on the ledge. Jean had gotten her lion, and it was a beauty.

✕ ✕ ✕ ✕ ✕

I had met a woman named Una in San Antonio some time before she came out on safari. At that time, she was about to marry John Cox, a very nice man, and they were going to come very soon to Kenya. I remember almost her first words to me.

"Bunny, do you know, I want to get me a leopard. That is my first wish. Can you do that for me?"

I put my tongue in my cheek as I answered, "I don't see why not, Una. We'll certainly try."

And try we did. And get it we did. However, the getting of it was a little painful for me.

After a not-too-early breakfast, I took the car up near a very good spotting hill. Leaving Una in the car with a book and a gunbearer, I took my leave.

"I won't be long, Una. I just want to spot from the top. Maybe I'll see a nice big buff for you."

"OK," she replied, "but don't call me unless you see a real good 'un. You know, I already got me a fair buffalo. I'd like one like John's."

So up the rocky hill I went with Tabei. Even before I could get the glasses out for a look around we saw a sleeping leopard, curled up like a great pussycat. It was less than fifteen feet from us. I dispatched Tabei by sign to bring Una, with a finger to the lips for silence. It seemed at least an hour before they returned; actually, I suppose it was the longest fifteen minutes I have ever endured. In the meantime, the leopard stirred not one hair.

At last Tabei and Una climbed onto the flat rock, still thirty yards from me. With another touch to the lips, I commanded her to silence. At last she was beside me with her rifle in her hands. When I pointed out the leopard, she could not see it. Then, like an answer to a lady's prayer, it raised its head slightly. Una at once was all action. She fired. The leopard, certainly hit, swung around and round several times.

I firmly said to Una, "Shoot again!" She did, and missed. The leopard moved out of sight between two rocks.

I said to Tabei, "Quickly run to the car and bring me the shotgun."

I then took the rifle from Una's hand and followed after the leopard. I found myself in a type of half cave, but completely open at one end. As I searched for the leopard, it came for me. It was almost a repetition of Nick Vanderscut's wounded leopard, but coming from a greater height and throwing me down onto much more solid black rock.

As it came off the ledge, I fired. I certainly hit it somewhere, yet this was an unaimed shot from the hip that probably went into the guts. As the cat landed on me, it gave my prominent nose a swipe with one great paw. Then it just lay on me and started to chew my arm, its huge amber eyes locked with mine, not more than ten inches distant. I felt no pain. I felt no fear. At such times I am sure one's senses are dulled. In fact, all I can remember vividly is the beauty of that leopard's eyes.

After a few moments of arm-chewing, my leopard went to other pastures. It rather appeared to slip its mouth around to the back of my head and neck, and I felt one paw on the top of my head. Before I could even think of what to do next, the leopard left. I was up on my feet pretty fast—aware of no pain—and then, much to my relief, Tabei appeared around the corner of a rock with my shotgun.

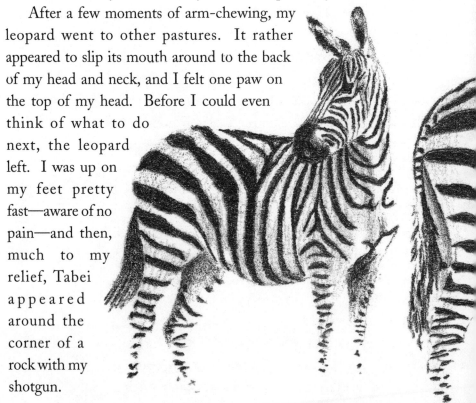

"*Tiari*," he said, as he pointed out where the leopard had gone. I handed him the now-empty rifle and, taking the shotgun, followed the leopard. It had made very little ground, and I finished it off immediately.

By now the facial scratch wounds were bleeding profusely, and so, by the time I got back to Una, I must have looked quite a mess. She shuddered slightly, and she is not the shuddering kind! I saw my face in a camp mirror about an hour later: It looked like a raspberry tart that had been dropped onto the floor.

After we had settled Una back in camp and we both had had a drink, I got Tabei to run me over to the local hospital for Africans. There they did a pretty good job on me—tidied me up, put plasters on my nose, and treated my chewed-up fore-arm. I did not let them sew it up, though, because I thought it best to have that done in Mombasa, which we had to pass through on the morrow.

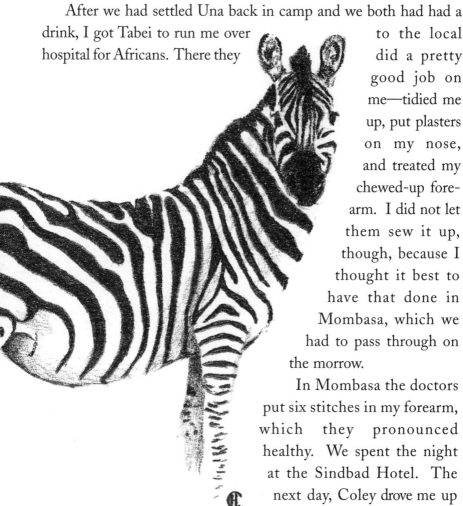

In Mombasa the doctors put six stitches in my forearm, which they pronounced healthy. We spent the night at the Sindbad Hotel. The next day, Coley drove me up to Nairobi while I lay on the back seat. I went into the hospital, where I stayed for two weeks, in great pain all over my body. I was bruised from head to foot, and my head was a mass of scratches. However, the main damage I was not really to feel until some years later. As well as breaking the coccyx when I fell, I had also mashed up the whole of my lumbar region. So now, in what should be my Indian summer days, I am stiffening up in the wrong places and feeling somewhat wintry.

Chapter 17

An Adventure in Somalia

y the time of the mid-1960s, the safari business was fairly booming. As a result we were going farther and wider. For my part, I continued to use only Kenya and Tanganyika, bar one sally into Somalia. That one Somalia safari, which was merely a recce, was quite an adventure and not unamusing. About half the Somalia police force was after me at one stage!

Jeri (whom later I married) took a run up into Somalia to see what the possibilities were there. She had a lot of contacts from the time she'd lived there. Like a complete fool, which I am at times, I went without my passport. After all, the last time I had gone through the frontier, there was a war on; I didn't need a passport. Just stupid thinking, or rather, lack of thinking.

Thus, at the border I was refused entry by a young Somali askari. He of course was acting within his rights, but I deemed him somewhat unnecessarily rude and took umbrage. I asked him to telegraph his headquarters, explain the situation, and ask for permission for me to proceed to Mogadishu and put the matter right. This he agreed, in an unsatisfactory manner, to do. In fact, he did nothing.

The fact that I was going to go short of petrol if I didn't take steps in the right direction clinched my decision—I would run for it. Therefore, late in the evening, as dear Jeri made up a fabulous guinea fowl stew in our camp, back about half a mile from the frontier gate, Tabei and I planned our route. Then, having had a real good heavyweight meal, and having seen the frontier guards douse their lights, we took off in half moonlight. All went well— apart from our disturbing a few elephant—and we went in the right direction, as luck would have it. We made good progress— and circled back onto the main road about a mile beyond the gate. The going was flat and very easy. I judged that my troublesome askari at the frontier would discover we had gone by around 9 A.M.—and the fact that I had made off in the Kenya direction for several hundred yards might well fox him for a while.

Anyway, for the nonce we were free and away. We enjoyed the drive after light had properly arrived and saw quite a lot of game. One splendid sight was all the Hunter antelope. Whereas in Kenya, between the Tana and the Somali boundary, one saw dozens, here we were seeing hundreds. We also saw a few elephant, but signs of hundreds; a few lesser kudu; a family of cheetah on the stalk; gerenuk; dik-dik; and giraffe by the score.

Apart from a few nomadic herdsmen, we saw no humans: nobody to bar our passage. In fact, we slept the first night at a district commissioner's rest house about halfway to Margarita, made very welcome by the Somali in charge, who cooked for us splendidly. The next day on to Margarita, where we spent the night with an Italian who was managing a farm owned by an acquaintance of ours in Nairobi. He and his beautiful Somali wife were kind and very good to us. However, they gave us a mild warning, having seen the Kenyan registration number on my Land

Rover. Apparently the local police, that very morning, had come around looking for a car with my number.

By now, the chase had become a game for me. I was keen to do all I could to achieve my purpose, which was to reach Mogadishu without being apprehended. However, I did not wish to embarrass our hosts. I need not have worried. They joined in the game wholeheartedly.

I gathered that the police post was situated near, but not on, the Juba River. That was the danger spot. Was there a way round? Sadi Hana, the beautiful Somali girl, said, "Of course there is. Let Abdi show them the way, past my father's village. Then on to the camel track to the bridge."

Thus it was settled. We left very early the next morning, before any patrol could reach the farm. We needed the extra petrol, which was so kindly provided by Gelentini Gelato at the farm. We crossed the river as the sun rose. Luckily we had briefed Abdi as to what he should say if questioned about us: We were cattle traders returning to Merka, having concluded our purchases. I say luckily, because as we reached the far side of the bridge two Somali policemen came running down toward the river whence we had come, gesticulating and shouting. They were too far away from the car to see who was in it, or to see the number plate.

All they could do was to shout and gesticulate, and all we did was to shout and gesticulate back, just as though we were saying good-bye to friends. We went at top speed through sand, dust, and ruts, stopping only near Merka to top up with petrol.

Once on the main road, the sweet Land Rover sprouted wings, and we were in the air some of the time. Jeri and Tabei hung on to everything they could; I had the wheel. My driving mirror had been lopped off ages before, so I asked Tabei to keep a weather eye open behind us to see if anyone followed. We progressed quite a few miles at a good "bat" before Tabei suddenly exclaimed, "*Ahh, bwana, iko vumbi.*" (There is dust.) That could only be the enemy! "*Lakini, mbali. Kwenda tu-kwenda!*" (But it is far. Just go for it!) Alarmed, yet at the same time encouraged because our pursuers were still far off, I stepped on it.

In the distance I could make out a railway level crossing. This had to be the line to Afgoi, which was the railhead from Mogadishu. I remembered it from the war years. And, believe it or not, my friend Piramus must have been watching from the heavens, for a goods train was slowly puffing its way toward the crossing. Words tumbled out of my mouth: "Tabei, run to the engine driver. Give him this money. Say we are being pursued by robbers, disguised as police. Say anything. Hand him the money. Tell him he will be a great man, *insha'a Allah.*" And then, as a last thought: "Tell him I was in the 5th K.A.R. Tell him my platoon sergeant was Sergeant Dagane Absie, M.M."

As it proved, these last words were the magic ones. The stoker of the train had been in the 5th K.A.R., which was full of Somalis. The train held up my pursuers so long that I was in the capital, home and dry, before they were over the level crossing.

Once in Mogadishu, we headed straight to Jeri's house, where we at once told her husband, Randall, the position. He laughed and joined in the game immediately. By luck, there was an inside courtyard behind a tall outside wall. My car was safely stowed in there, away from any prying eyes. After the excitement of the chase, I believe I slept for two days (between bouts of eating and drinking).

Randall arranged a very nice party at the house on the third evening, and I was able to meet people who could enlighten me as to the hunting possibilities in Somalia. These were both governmentals and actual hunters. Among those at the party were Laddie Winza, who ran safaris out of Nairobi, and his sweet wife, Ada. They had some Americans arriving there for a hunt. I was able to tell them what I had seen and gathered on the way up. I also had the chance to make my number with one or two government officers—against the time when my car and I were caught!

On the fourth day, I decided to run the gauntlet. Accompanied by Jeri and Tabei (Randall felt his position in Mogadishu ruled him out), I drove down to the Croce del Sud Hotel, parked outside, and went in for a noonday drink on the patio. Jeri and I sat ourselves at a table for two, while Tabei took his beer, with money for a second, and sat on the low wall near the car. He said he wanted to watch. We all watched as we drank. Before we were on our second drinks, a corporal of the Somalia gendarmerie took notice of our car. He walked around it twice. He checked on the number. He took another turn around the car, his eyes getting wider and wider the while. He looked at Tabei, walked up to him, questioned him, but to no avail. Tabei just shook his head slowly and raised his hands to the sky. The then somewhat puzzled gendarme walked away to the corner of the street, maybe looking for a brother officer.

Now, I thought, was the moment to make our getaway. We were in the car in no time flat and off before our policeman could flick a fly off his nose. Then followed a real comic opera scene. Or was it more like an old slapstick movie? All we lacked were Fatty Arbuckle and Buster Keaton. The keystone cops we had. As the K.A.R. 69 sprang into action, the "copper corporal" spotted us. His heroic flourish on his whistle died in the blue smoke of my gallant exhaust together with accompanying backfire of seeming derision.

We made good progress at a smart city speed until reaching a sort of small square. Here a traffic cop making all sorts of very precise signs with his white-gloved hands almost fell off his rostrum as he saw us approaching. He pointed to us, pointed to our number plate, raised his hand in the air, pointed to the side of the road, and blew his whistle as it had never been blown before! Taking no notice, I hurtled old *soixante-neuf* across the square, narrowly missing the copper's rostrum and a barrow load of watermelons. In fact, the pusher of the barrow let go his charge, and watermelons scattered in all directions, some bursting open and others running on forever. From then on, for about five minutes, I went from street to street via one corner or another.

By now the general public was in on the game, and I noticed that when I had gone down one street for perhaps the second, or even third, time, people on the pavement were actually clapping their hands in applause. However, all fine times have to end. Two gendarmes on motorbikes had come in close behind us, and I found myself cornered in a cul-de-sac with a fruit and vegetable market at its end. I pulled up our brave car just before it sent a stall full of tomatoes flying. A further mounted gendarme had joined the terror squad, and so now three Beretta pistols were pointing at us. I raised my hands in submission and a rather damp smile lit up my face. No answering smile, not even a glint of lightness, came into the threatening eyes of our captors, and their pistols continued to wave around in menace.

Therefore it was with relief that I noticed several more policemen step out of a car as it arrived. One had quite a lot of gold braid on his coat. He had to be an officer. He was, and he was also an ally. I knew him. He had been at the cocktail party. We were saved. He smiled broadly at me and shook me by the hand. He bowed very cordially to Jeri and kissed her hand. He did not forget Tabei. He shook his hand and smiled with a friendly *jambo*. He was a splendid gentleman and a friend in need, indeed.

He then smilingly looked at the car and said, "And this is the elusive car. Now I do need you to put that right. If you follow me to the main police station, we can do it in five minutes."

So then started the final performance. The officer gave his instructions and we got lined up for the run through the streets to police headquarters. By the time we got into the main street, quite a lot of passersby had become bystanders and cheered us as we went. Jeri at once responded in warm style, standing up, waving, and once in a while, as the cheering grew, blowing kisses. Tabei also responded well and waved madly. I, driving now at a more sedate speed, blew the hooter from time to time. Our cavalcade consisted of the police car up ahead, followed by three motorcyclists, then our now-famous "69," with three more motorcyclists behind. It resembled a junior ticker-tape parade going up Fifth Avenue.

We soon put right the matter of my illegal entry with the payment of a small fee. The illegal car called for another small fee. Then, to my surprise, the nice officer asked us to accompany him to the mayor's parlor, which was right next door. There the mayor and his very pretty wife made us most welcome and fed us Coco-Cola. Furthermore, he then presented me with the "freedom of the city of Mogadishu." This was a gesture, the mayor said, in case I thought the city had treated me badly. He added that I had greatly thrilled the citizens by my wild drive through the streets. "It was entertainment such as we seldom get," he said. Naturally, I thanked him for his great kindness.

The Wheel of Life

As I was saying my good-byes, I noticed a down-at-heel Somali talking to my nice officer friend. I turned to say *ciao* and the officer said to me, "Oh, this is just one other thing." He indicated the down-at-heel. "He says you owe him 1,000 lira for the watermelons."

Having got to Mogadishu and sorted everything out, we had to think about the long trek back. Once more Randall was most helpful. He arranged a lovely farewell party for us. At this party he did not have to think of useful people for us to meet or talk to. He merely thought of nice and beautiful people. Most of the girls were truly out of the top drawer for loveliness. Some were pure white, some were pure Somali, and some were betwixt and between.

I remember one girl in particular. She stood out with half a dozen others as something very, very special. She had honey-gold hair, honey-gold skin, large green-gold eyes, the nose of a goddess, the mouth of a very ready cherry, and a chin of desire. Her bosoms were an absolute invitation to the dance, and if perchance she was ready for a prance, they were comfort from first glance. I dared not look any lower. She was beautiful. She was wonderful. I made my way to her. I took her by the hand, and then put my arm around her wondrous waist. My other arm caressed her shoulder and the hand aroused a breast. I was wondering what my next move should be when I heard Jeri's voice from just behind me, "Don't you wish you were an octopus, Bunny?" At that, the sweet beautiful girl, my target, laughed very prettily and long. I disentangled myself from her with covering laughter, and spent the rest of the evening in the rich company of Jeri.

One other quite astonishing thing happened the day before we left Mogadishu. Jeri and I had taken a stroll down near the little harbor. A coastal boat had just come in and was discharging its passengers. Some of these were walking along the small jetty. Suddenly Jeri seized my arm and said as she raised a hand and pointed, "Isn't that Ba?" And it was my brother Ba. Now Jeri had never met Ba. She knew him just by my description of him, and her acute perception. Ba was living at Lamu and had, apparently, just sailed up to Somalia to see friends and relations. Ba was a law unto himself. He lived off the land in more ways than one! He was as surprised as we were. We had a great reunion, before Jeri and I departed.

We were keen to get back to Kenya, but we intended to enjoy the journey and not rush. As we left the outskirts of Mog, I inquired for the camp of Caccitori Grande, an Italian hunter whom I had met at one of the parties. Eventually, we got to him in time for a good lunch. Caccitori was a very nice chap, and he had a pleasant American client. They had, that very morning, collected a good lion and so were celebrating. What luck, we were there for the "fizz."

Caccitori kept a good camp. Over my many years of experience I found that you could measure how well a man ran a safari by his personal appearance. If he were scruffy and unshaven, you could bet your bottom dollar that his camp was likewise, and his whole safari, more than likely, not top class. We enjoyed our three hours in the Caccitori camp and then left. As we proceeded along the main road to the Juba River, I was able to point out the very patch of thorn trees where I had camped with my platoon of the 5th K.A.R. during the mad rush on the Marda Pass in 1941. It was still a sand road, as it had been and as it forever will be.

As evening approached, we looked for a pleasant place to spend the night. We eventually came to one and took off to the left. If it was possible to find a country land in that arid region, this was it. After going two to three miles, we came out onto a nice open space letting out through some large rocks to the sea. Away to the left were a few buildings of what appeared to be a fishing village. Without knowing it, we had arrived at Brava.

I noticed a pretty group of date palms in the middle of the open space, made for it, and decided to pass the night there. Within ten minutes of getting the car offloaded and a small fire started, I noticed a short, stocky man approaching us from the village. I gave him a wave, which he answered gaily as he greeted me from a slight distance.

"*Jambo, effendi. Habari gani.*"

"*Mzuri, tu?*" (And how are you?) I answered.

"We are well. Brava is glad to see you."

"Oh, so this is Brava? It is very pretty."

"Yes, *effendi*. It is a nice place. *Maradadi.*"

Jeri was busy the while, making our bed and preparing the evening meal—that is, she had got as far as unwrapping a guinea fowl. "*Jambo, memsabu,*" said our new man (for that is what he proved to be). He shook us all by the hand. "Call me Haji-Haji Wanjiko."

At that, Wanjiko, Tabei, and I looked up and at each other. What was that typical Kikuyu girl's name doing down here at Brava?

"Wanjiko?" Tabei said in an inquiring tone.

"Yes," replied little Haji. He was pleased that he had puzzled us. "Let me explain," he said.

He then went on to tell us his story. Many years ago some Arab slave traders captured his mother and her husband and brought them to the coast. The husband died, and his mother, Wanjiko, passed into the hands of a Swahili gentleman. Haji was produced, and he took his mother's name as his family name.

It was a nice little story, which he told well. Before he left, he shinned up a palm and brought down some yellow dates. They formed our delicious pudding that night. "Tomorrow I bring you *oisterri*," he said.

"*Asanti sana*, Haji," I replied, having not yet zeroed in on the word *oisterri*.

"See you, Kesho." Haji waved himself away.

We spent a pleasant night under the whisper of the palms and the murmur of the distant sea. Dawn found Tabei brewing an excellent dish of tea. While we were consuming this, our new man, Haji, came waddling up. *"Oisterri, effendi,"* he said and displayed a fine bowl of oysters, all ready to eat. They just needed a lemon. Believe it or not, the splendid Haji produced a nice juicy lime out of his pocket the very next moment.

He was an absolute godsend for the whole of our stay in Brava. He took us shopping; he produced bottles of Chianti from the ancient *aubergo*; delivered fish to us, fruit, milk, and even a scanty supply of vegetables. Haji was the wonder of Brava.

We thoroughly enjoyed our stay there. It was the loveliest spot we found in Somalia. It was with regret that we had to pack up and caravan on. I can still picture the very worthy Haji waving to us as we left. He was a fine fellow. Of course, I always intended to go back and look for him, but it was a daydream that never saw light.

Our trip back into Kenya was uneventful. No trouble at the border, no trouble at Chestnut Cottage, just a whole heap of letters and bills to contend with. Among other things there were eight safari inquiries. Now, with my having fixed a base at Lamu, and David and Anton established at Nanyuki, we were able to arrange the safaris to suit us all. For the most part, they took on the highland hunts and I did the lowland. We very often combined, however, and made special arrangements for old clients who wanted one, two, or three of us. Long-distance hunts we often made a family effort.

At this time also, we were starting to use aircraft quite a lot more to get from one place to another. My sons had not, as yet, got hold of their own plane. That was to come a year or so later. In the meantime, a good friend of mine, Chico Basto, a Portuguese ally who waved the Union Jack, stepped in to help. He loved a safari of any sort, and he could usually get in some bird shooting, at which he excelled.

John Alexander, employed behind the camera for my next safari, went down with my daughter, Lavinia, to make the camp ready on the Tana River, a few miles out of Garissa. Jeri and Chico's wife, Beryl, went the following day with some friends, en route to Lamu. They stayed the night in camp and left more provisions. While there Jeri checked on everything, for at that stage I did not know how reliable John Alexander was. He was very thorough.

Jeri and her party set off early next morning for their long run to Lamu Island. The party consisted of Jeri (plus five Yorkshire terriers), Beryl, Peter Bruckmann and his wife, Jack Pearson and his wife, and a rascally Kamba driver. Up to Bura, on a nice sandy road, all went well. Beyond that point the clouds gaped open, and down came the rain, to join rains of some four or five previous days. The countryside became a quagmire. It took them until almost dusk to reach Baragoi, still forty-five miles from Lamu, with the worst ahead. There they struggled in to see my eldest brother, Denys, who had a house of the veterinary department, right on the roadside. Denys offered them drinks to help them on their way.

Meanwhile, my host at Petley's Inn at Lamu was expecting Jeri and her guests as of 5 P.M. Eleven o'clock arrived, and Colonel Gerry Pink battened down the hatches, took his pink gins onto the upstairs veranda, and surveyed the moonlit sky. No rain in Lamu. Three pink gins later Gerry noticed a boat approaching the government jetty. And what is more, it made fast there. "Damn sauce," he said a little explosively.

He called to his servant, Abdullah, to go and tell the boatman to take his boat to the other jetty, three hundred yards farther along the seawall. So the offloaded suitcases, boxes of fruit, and vegetables for the inn had to be reloaded onto the boat. It then chugged off to the farther jetty and offloaded once more. Twenty minutes, or three gins, later, the baggage arrived at the bottom of the stairs leading to the inn's bedrooms.

Two stalwarts had arrived at the top of these stairs, each carrying two boxes of fruit and vegetables, when an extremely irate Colonel Pink confronted them. He was incapable of unspluttered speech, but he was full of action. In no time flat the four boxes were hurtling down the stairs, spilling ripe tomatoes, ripe papaws, and dozens of eggs in all directions. This was too much for Jeri's and Beryl's five Yorkshire terriers. They broke loose and were instantly up those stairs to attack the fiend above. They seized him at any point available.

Jeri, hearing Gerry's yelp for help, slipped on the fruity, eggy mess to rescue him. For a moment there was a golden silence. Then a drunken, misunderstanding Gerry became the complete gentlemen that he was. He said, "Oh, Jeri, I'm so sorry. How dreadful. My god, how dreadful. I'm sorry, what can I say?"

Jeri kissed him, introduced him, and everyone had a drink. They recovered some eggs from the spillage, and within a short while clever Jeri had given them all a fine vegetable omelet, using, of course, the staired tomatoes, followed by papaw purée l'escalier.

When I got over to the mainland the following day, I was lucky enough to find a Somali who, by the greatest of good fortune, had been in my old K.A.R. battalion with the fighting 5th. "*Effendi*," he said, "you want to get to Bura. I want to get to Bura. Maybe I can find a track to get us there." For a certainty we were not going to make any progress on the main track. Thus I decided to let Mohamed Farah show me his way. I was not short of gasoline. I would need quite a bit. I had it.

After about two miles, he led me off a track to the right, going onto slightly rising ground and sand. This was encouraging. We went through bushland, with sparse trees, into forest with big trees, some huge trees. Here and there we passed groups of native huts with the inhabitants sitting around. We got into deeper and deeper forest. We were well into the Boni Forest, and here were the Wa-boni tribesmen: great elephant hunters and, of course, poachers. I noticed that there were also some Somalian men in among the Wa-boni tribesmen: great elephant hunters and, of course, poachers.

We had progressed fairly well, and the rain had eased off. Only now and then did we have a holdup because of water. I must say that my 5th K.A.R. pal knew his country. In another half-hour we were out in bright sunshine. In the meantime, we had picked up another couple of Somalian gentlemen who desired a lift in our direction.

Within half an hour we came to a slight glade in the forest, and in it were two dead elephant. Now, this was a sudden and surprising development. I knew at once that I was in with poachers. And, what was more, I was carrying two poachers with me in the car! They disembarked with an *"Asante sana, effendi."* (Thank you very much, sir.) I smiled at them in reply. I felt that it was rather a damp squib of a smile, for I was very uncertain of myself. Only three things I knew I had to do, and as quickly as possible: Say nothing, notice nothing, and get the hell out of there.

As I drove out of the glade, two shots rang out in my direction. In a few seconds, I was behind large trees, driving on in thankfulness.

Within a few minutes we had left the forest and were in thick bush country. It was a very indistinct track, but we were throwing dust up now and past all fear of getting stuck in the mud. I judged that we were quite near the Somalian border.

Within half an hour we struck another large track at right angles. This had to be the Bura-Ngala Ngalama Road. I turned left, and in an hour and a half was held up at the gate into Bura. I was back at the Tana River.

At once I wanted to report the matter of the elephant poaching, but instead I had to spend almost half an hour explaining to a stupid gate guard, and a more stupid gate guard corporal, exactly who I was and where I'd come from and why.

Then, when I was feeling completely exasperated, they permitted me to see the game department man in charge. He was even more stupid! He had no transport to take him to the scene of the crime. He had no radio contact with Garissa, and, who was I, anyway? What was I doing in Bura? In fact, he asked me all the same questions that the gate police had, plus a few more. Eventually, without anything accomplished, I left Bura to go on to Garissa. There I told the same story about the poached elephant and got a more sympathetic hearing. They said they would send out a patrol the next day. That was the last I heard of the matter, bar the fact that I was informed that my hunting party could not move anywhere north of the Garissa-Burma-Lamu Road. That news I imparted to all in camp as soon as I arrived there. It was going to curtail our movements quite a bit and probably wreck our hopes of getting Hunter antelope.

In Garissa with the Land Rover and the big truck, I was at a shop getting a few supplies. The rascally Kamba driver who had driven Jeri and company to Lamu was at the gasoline station. I noticed several Somalis eyeing my car and muttering amongst themselves. You can always tell when Somalis are displeased or angry; these were. As I came out of the shop, the Somalis marched up on me, muttering, grimacing, and wagging a fist or two.

Being the brave chap that I am, I jumped into the car, where I judged myself to be safer. Then three or four of them stood in front of the car to block my passage and the rest came to the car door. They continued their gesticulations and excited chatter. I asked one of them what was the *shauri*. He handed out a Swahili speaker to me, and then I got the whole story.

Apparently, my Kamba driver, when he returned from Lamu, gave a Somali at the little hamlet of Ijara a lift to Bura. The agreed-upon price was forty shillings. The simple Somali handed over a one-undred-shilling note. The Kamba said he would get change at Bura. In got the Somali, out got the clutch, and off they went.

About five miles along the road the Kamba asked the Somali to open his door and look at the rear wheel—this while the car was still bumping along. The Somali, unwittingly, did the Kamba's bidding, thus presenting a *shuka*-covered Somali backside to the ready Kamba foot. The next moment, the Somali flew through the air while a delighted Kamba chuckle came from the car. He was now sitting pretty, with one hundred Somali shillings.

Before the Somalis could wreak their revenge, I explained that the "very bad man" was just around the corner: "Let's go to get him." So in they piled—spears, *simis*, clubs, and all. My car was full to overflowing. At the gasoline station my Kamba driver saw us coming. He must have smelt a Somalian rat, for he bolted for the *duka*, to the Somalian shouts of: " 'Tis he, yes, that is the man. Kill him!"

I was out of the car pretty fast, not really to protect my driver, although I did need him to drive the big truck, but to try to quieten the situation. With excitable Somalis, anything can happen.

Well, on this occasion, I quickly borrowed two hundred shillings from the gasoline *duka wallah* and handed it, more quickly, to the unfortunate Somali. He thus made one hundred shillings on his investment. And he paid nothing for his five-mile car ride. While making this deal, I was kicking an ample Kamba bottom, continuously, below the shop counter. Later the "bottom" was able to escape safely back to camp.

H CLAASSENS.

Chapter 18
Catalina Finds Her Cheetah

For the next safari, we were host to some perfectly charming people from Mexico. They were the Roberto Sarda family: father, beautiful daughter Catalina, and two sons. David and Anton were helping on the safari. As soon as we met the Sardas we knew we were going to have a really happy time. They had come to me through some of my Texas friends. They wanted to hunt just the usual animals, but certainly elephant. As I recall, we started them off in the Narok area and had some exciting buffalo hunting. I distinctly remember one of the sons clobbering a very handsome bull.

On the first or second day out, Catalina saw a couple of cheetah stalking up on and running a Grant. She was entirely fascinated. She had to have a cheetah! A pet cheetah to take home! We told Papa that we would do our best. Our chances would be better from our next camp in the Mukogodo country. From then on Catalina was just waiting for the move. She took an interest in everything: She hunted, she took pictures, she enjoyed her food and her wine, but she was longing to get into what she now called "cheetah country."

Inside a week, we moved north. We had a night at the Mount Kenya Safari Club as camp was moved, and they all spent one day hunting in the forest. While the party did that, I chased around getting some horses together for the cheetah hunt, checked on the camp, and had a peaceful time.

It is so wonderful to get away from it all now and again! It's better for your strength than a two-pound rump steak. By the time the guests arrived in camp, which was a very pretty spot by the wayside, under the shade of monster yellow thorn trees, below a rolling hill called Doldol, our good steeds were tethered, munching lucerne hay in readiness for the chase. To my Gypsy mind, I felt that the success of this safari hinged on the catching of a cheetah. From all reports there were quite a few of them about. It sounded like a foregone conclusion that the cheetah was in the bag.

The next morning, David and Anton took the Sarda family out. They were looking for an elephant or two, possibly a greater kudu, and would put up a lion bait. That left me to go out and catch a cheetah. To catch a "falling star" would have been easier!

I saw several cheetah, but each time they jinked round the wrong bush, swept me off my mount by a low branch, or played some other nasty trick. The net result was that, after a hard morning's work, I collected nothing but some bruises and a few thorns. Not only were those sensitive parts hurt, but also my pride. I decided I'd have another go the next day. The result was the same, except that the bruises were more and bigger and the parts were more sensitive! As I somewhat painfully took my seat before the campfire that evening, my two sons let me have it.

Said David: "You'd better let Anton and me catch the cheetah. Maybe you can't bend round the trees anymore."

"That's right," agreed Anton. "Leave it to us, Bunny, we'll nail him."

198

I did not demur. I wanted to get a cheetah; that was the main thing.

Off they went, bright and early the following morning. They saw cheetah at once but were completely beaten at a sand river crossing and lost them. Then they hunted all the morning without seeing any more. The next day they tried again. No luck. It just appeared that we were not fated to catch a cheetah. They saw a sufficiency of them, but for one reason or another, they could not catch up with one. They had their troubles, too.

Catalina was very sweet and tried to hide her disappointment, but she was nevertheless a little down in spirit. I then made inquiries to see if I could find any of Raymond Hook's old retainers. I knew that some of them had retired to these parts. With luck, we found a couple. They were ready and willing. Believe it or not, they failed as we had. It was just not written in the book that we should catch a cheetah. Catalina was marvelous. "Don't worry, Bunny, you have tried so hard—I'd love one, but—it appears as if I can't have one." The other hunting had been doing well enough, however, and it was still going on.

Then one evening Roberto asked me if the car could take him up to the little village on the hill. Catalina wanted to buy a *kanga* or two that she had seen in a *duka* there. I sent Tabei with them, as we were all a bit busy marking and numbering their trophies.

In about half an hour they were back. All three in the car had broad smiles on their faces. I thought that they must have done a very satisfactory deal. They had! As the car came to a halt, Catalina uncovered what she had in her lap. It was a quarter-grown cheetah. What a perfectly wonderful end to the safari that made! Catalina, quite rightly, was delighted at her success. Where everyone else had failed, she had succeeded. While shopping in the main street of Doldol, which proudly boasted three tumbledown *dukas*, along had come a young Ndorobo *ndito* leading the cheetah. Tabei arranged the deal. The cheetah passed hands for five-hundred shillings. Catalina named her Sheba, and she at once settled down to camp life. She already had the rudiments of being tame when she arrived, and under the loving hands of sweet Catalina she became quiet as the proverbial kitten.

By the time we got back to the Norfolk Hotel, Sheba was worshipping the ground that Catalina walked on. It really was very touching. An interested spectator of this animal-human partnership was Charlie Chaplin. He happened to be staying with his family in a nearby cottage.

Chapter 19

An Interesting
Experience

Part of a well-known family from Austin, Texas, arrived for a general hunt. They consisted of Al Robinson; his wife, Charlotte; a brother, George; and one son, Spike. Al and Spike, I gathered, wanted to hunt all and sundry, brother George would take anything going, and Charlotte wanted to shoot a few animals but definitely wanted a buffalo. So, for me, the success of this safari hinged on Charlotte's getting her buffalo. She was a good, sound shot, she could do her share of walking, and she would do what she was told.

Against that, she was not amazingly agile. You would not want her to run after buff, twist and bend round bushes or under trees. And most of all, she must not have to run away. In fact, we needed to find her a nice passive buffalo to hunt, if there was such a beast! Well, there was, but dear Coley Coles didn't recognize it. I so well remember the morning when Coley took out Charlotte. She was excited and full of hope.

There was a buff under every tree and shrub. True, most of them took to their heels without the chance of a shot. One or two charged. And then there was the one in a million that you find lying down, waiting for the hunter. Coley saw that one later in the morning—but he failed to recognize it!

As they returned to camp, I noticed Charlotte getting out of the car rather despondently. And I could see that she and Coley were not on the best of speaking terms. Very certainly something was wrong. I made the usual commonplace remark: "Well, how did it go? Didn't you see anything?" To which she replied, pointing to Coley: "Oh, I dunno, ask him." Now, Coley, nice man and able hunter as he is, can be very flat at times. That day he was horizontal.

I cornered him as soon as possible. "Now, what is it, Coley? What happened?"

"Look, Bunny, I'll tell you. We saw a poor old buffalo just about to die. It was missing one horn, blind—completely, I think—and it couldn't get to its feet."

I immediately retorted, "My God, Coley, that was a tailor-made buff for Charlotte. You must be mad."

"What, shoot that?" replied Coley.

I could see that he was already uncertain. I went at once to Charlotte to sound her out. I could tell she was keen to have a go, so I said, "Coley is doubtful about the quality of the horn, but I suggest . . ." That was as far as I got. Charlotte broke in: "Oh, sure, Bunny, let's go get him. I'd like to have a buff." And that was that. She'd heard about the great strength of the African buffalo. She wanted one. She was not after a record head.

In a very few minutes we headed for the "dead" buffalo. By the time we got there it was alive again. It was old, certainly, and blind to some extent, but it did get up on its four feet for Charlotte to shoot it. That she did with a good 'un, straight between the eyes. The buff had a complete head. It was a very peculiar shape, certainly, yet full of character. This was a very good old bull to put down. It might well have done an injury to some unlucky wight had it gone on. What is more, Charlotte was very pleased, and Al, her husband, gurgled contentedly. Even grumpy old Coley was happy. "D'you know, Bunny, I think that buff might have hammered somebody if we hadn't finished it off." He looked quite kindly, and a smile creased his face.

Once more it was time for the Dorns to arrive. They consisted of Dale and Jean and their one son, Tucker. A close friend, Tebo Bowman, was with them, and his son Maclean. We went quite a long way south into Tanzania. They were after sable and roan antelope primarily, but would also take good elephant if we found them. As it happened, we were so beset by tsetse fly that it became, for some of them, about the shortest safari on record.

We were about a hundred miles south of Itigi, in perfect sable and roan country—and perfect tsetse country. What is more, that year must have been a magnificent breeding season for them. The tsetse were bigger and better, more ferocious, and more numerous than ever before. After three days, going different ways to try to avoid the flies, Jean gave it up. We had to send for an aircraft to take Dale and Jean away. "Never mind, Bunny dear," Jean said. "We'll try some other place some other time."

That was typical of Jean, who was a wonderfully good, brave girl. And that's exactly what we did about a year hence. In the meantime, the balance of the party—Tebo, Maclean, and Tucker—bashed on to get their trophies. Mind you, Tebo was as tough as old boots. I reckon that when a tsetse bit him, it immediately rolled off and died. Anyway, the three hunters went bravely on, bitten to bits at times.

Late one evening I had a most unusual experience while out with Tebo. He had really completed all the hunting he wanted to do, but Tebo was a chap who loved firing off his gun at the slightest provocation. I stopped the hunting car up on the slope of a little hill, looking out onto a *miombo* forest glade that stretched in all directions for several hundred yards. I had seen some vultures flying overhead and wanted to check on them. I climbed onto the roof of the car for a better look. Tebo had meanwhile wandered off a few yards with Tabei in attendance, carrying his rifle. I had just started sweeping the glade with my binoculars when a shot rang out. Then I saw a huge warthog legging it for all it was worth. I turned to look at Tebo. He was laughing like a schoolboy, smacking his thigh with glee. "See him go, see him go," he kept repeating between his chuckles. He had fired behind the hog, just to see it run!

While he laughed, I returned to my glassing. And what a surprise I got! There, not two hundred yards away, were a couple of lionesses. They had raised their heads in alarm at the sound of the shot. But that was not all. A few yards farther to the right a slight movement under a bush turned out to be a very large leopard. In between the lions and the leopard was a large warthog, still kicking. It had been laid low by one or the other of them. As I watched, the leopard came from its hide and moved *ventre à terre* (going to earth) toward the kicking hog. All the while, the lions continued to watch us.

I let Tebo know what was going on and cautioned him to silence. This whole thing could build up into a very interesting experience. I glanced again at the leopard. It appeared to have given the hog its quietus and was dragging it to the hideaway bush. I had a quick look around and decided to get a little closer to the astonishing performance.

We left the car and found a slight fold in the ground that got us just above the performers without their knowledge. We were now looking down on them from about fifty yards. A perfect royal box view! It was magnificent, and Tebo was as excited as I.

From this new angle we saw more. A little behind the leopard's bush was another one, with its overhanging branches almost reaching the ground. In among this boscage were two well-grown leopard cubs. Mother was trying to pull the warthog to them. It was a hard drag for her, the hog being quite a monster. Also she continually stopped to look up to check on the lions.

She had made about ten yards of the twenty-five she had to cover when the one lioness came at her with a roar. The second lioness was still looking over to where we had left the car. When the charging lioness got to within ten feet or so of the hog, she pulled up, having driven the leopard away to her hide. The lioness sat down. She certainly was not hungry; she looked very well fed. Very shortly she lay full length and appeared to go away into dreamland. The other lioness still kept watch across the glade. In

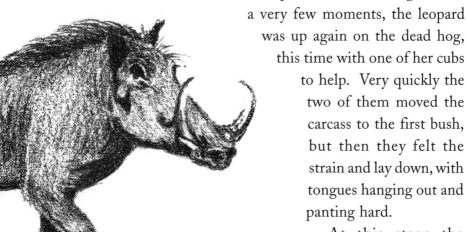

a very few moments, the leopard was up again on the dead hog, this time with one of her cubs to help. Very quickly the two of them moved the carcass to the first bush, but then they felt the strain and lay down, with tongues hanging out and panting hard.

At this stage the lioness watching the glade turned her attention to the hog once more, and seeing what was going on came in a rush past her sleeping companion, straight for the leopards. These made appropriate rude noises as they slunk away to the farther bush. It really was a tremendous performance. Tebo looked at me with a splendid smile on his face, and shook his head to and fro in disbelief. Yet the show was not over.

The two obviously very well-fed lionesses rolled over together and lay in the cooling breeze. The leopard immediately came to the attack once more, this time with both cubs to help. They yanked the hog over to the second bush. Here, after a very few moments' pause, they started to tear meat off the carcass. The lionesses left them in peace for a few minutes; then one of them lifted its head, shook it, got up, and this time stalked slowly toward the leopard family. It had gotten to within about five yards of them when a growling sort of rumble came from the leopard. This brought the lioness to a halt. The lioness just stared into space, or so it appeared. However, that did not satisfy the leopard. After a slight mumbling conversation among themselves, all three of them came with a roar at the lioness. They were joined by a large male leopard that appeared from another bush and which, up to that point, we had not observed. This was altogether too much for the two lionesses. The one nuzzled the other and they both rather slunk off the scene with their tails slightly between their knees. I really felt rather sorry for them. Their pride was hurt. In fact, when they had wandered off about two hundred yards they paused, their tails once more arched with superiority. I was glad.

Meantime the leopard family was making short work of the monster warthog in their shady dining room. They were hungry. The degree of their hunger may have had quite a lot to do with the performance that we had just witnessed. The lions were very well fed. Had they been hungry, would they have given up the kill so easily? It was a nice point, which I discussed with Tebo as we left the scene.

"But my, Bunny, what a show that was. Have you seen the like before?"

"Never, but there is something new to learn every day. Some people think they know it all, lose interest in life, and just wait to go. I know there is so much more to learn that I intend to live forever."

Early the following year, we were able to take Dale and Jean Dorn to a better area to get their trophies. We went before the heavy rains, before the main breeding season of the tsetses, and it was quite bearable. We were lucky; the hunt took place between heavy storms. Dale and Jean were able to complete their African hunting.

After they had flown off home, we spent a month or two at Chestnut Cottage. We had to go over all the tentage and safari equipment and see to repairs and replacements, to make ready for the bumper to bumper season ahead. I was greatly looking forward to the next safari. It was for Betty Coates again, of San Antonio. She had asked me the previous year, when I was visiting the States. She herself had never been on an African safari, although her husband, George, had been out several times. Yet Betty was an accomplished hunter and a good shot. She was a very charming, good-looking woman and always dressed perfectly: a pleasure and a privilege to have at one's side.

I will always remember that when Betty broached the possibility of her safari, she gave a rather sidelong look at me, sort of sizing me up. Then she came out with her thoughts: "D'you think I ought to get somebody to come along with me?"

I laughed a little in replying: "Why, are you nervous? Do you think I might do you wrong?"

"Well, you know, people are funny. They might think I—they might think I'm not being quite proper."

"In that case—best bring someone, someone to guard you against my advances!"

We went off to a nice little club for a dance or two. Betty was such a good dancer that she made even me perform quite well.

Before Betty left me that night she said: "I'll tell you what, I'll probably bring Betty Roberts—you know, my daughter."

We camped first near Doldol, a good chance for a leopard. We at once got a bait or two up, one right in the forest of Mount Kenya, forty miles away. In the meantime, David, Anton, and Jens Hessel had their camp right up in the forest, about ten miles from our leopard bait. Their customers were also Texans, and they knew the two Bettys.

On the second day, the forest leopard bait showed signs of a cat. I asked my Betty, the senior Betty, which of them would go to sit over the bait that evening. Much to my surprise she said that her daughter should go. I naturally had to accompany her, because it was my bait. I knew the complete setup. My associate on that hunt, white hunter Peter Mann-Jones, did not. Consequently, I advised daughter Betty: "You'd better pack a little overnight bag, because if there is nothing on the bait this evening, we might decide to stay over and take another look in the morning."

"And we stay over where?"

"Oh, up at David's camp on the mountain, right nearby."

"I'll just go talk to my mother about that."

Peter and I heard them chattering away for a few moments, and then they both appeared. Mother Betty started the ball rolling: "Betty says you two might be away for the night. Is that so? Is that necessary?"

I answered at once: "No. It is just a possibility. It might be the best chance of getting a leopard. I just can't say until we are on the spot."

Lady Betty shrugged her pretty shoulders and slipped on her safari jacket: "Let's go and get the gerenuk," she said to Peter, as she walked over toward his car. From now on I'll call her "Lady Betty," because she is very classy. Always beautifully dressed— even her safari outfit was the smartest I'd ever seen. Her daughter, Betty, was also a fine-looking girl but a size larger. Anyway, for the nonce, things seemed settled. Betty packed a little bag and we went off to spend the night if necessary.

We drove the forty-odd miles without exchanging many words. There were just the three of us: Betty and I were in the front, with the faithful Tabei behind. As we approached the end of the car journey and started the walk, I explained the geography of the land around the leopard bait and the blind. She grasped the idea and plan quickly enough. We now had to wait for the leopard to come along. These waits are always tense and sometimes interesting, even though the leopard does not appear. This particular wait was not so. It was dead flat. No noises from the forest, no birds twittering, nothing. No smile from the pretty customer. It was bleak and deadly. No leopard could possibly come on an evening like this! And of course, no leopard came.

On this occasion I did not wait until it was too dark to see the gun sights, which is the usual form. We crept away from the blind still in a fair light. Back in the car, I told Betty that we would drive back by way of David's camp to see how things were going. She quickly queried: "But we won't stay the night there?"

"As you like," I answered. "Tomorrow morning will probably produce a leopard."

She took her time to answer, as I negotiated a nasty piece of the track, then: "Why don't we leave the leopard for Mother?"

"Right, I was only following instructions. We'll have one drink at this camp and then head for ours."

From that moment on, she was a different girl. She chattered the whole way home. The fact of the matter was that in the few days' hunting we had already done she had taken a shine to Peter. She was missing him. These little close ties happen on safari. They certainly do!

Back at our camp, Lady Betty and Peter appeared quite normal. She saw we were back empty-handed and she immediately said: "Sorry, Betty; I'll have to go back tomorrow. Yes, that's too bad."

For the morrow, I decided to give the early try a miss and go just for the evening. Consequently Lady Betty and I set out, much as her daughter and I had done the previous evening. Although Lady Betty said: "Bunny, let's get back for the night here in our camp," I rejoined: "Right ho, with a leopard." She crossed her fingers. I think we knew we were going to get one.

This time everything was more promising. She chattered happily all the way till we left the car. From then on we left all the noisemaking to the birds. Of this there was plenty. Lady Betty was sitting very contentedly, with her rifle lying comfortably within the hole in the blind carved out for it. We had been sitting for just about an hour. The light was beginning to fade in the dark forest, but there was still enough light to shoot. We had not heard anything except the birds. I had glanced at the bait the previous moment. There was nothing there. Now there was!

The leopard was feeding, leaving the whole of its shoulder exposed. I had a sideways glance to Lady Betty, but she was already there and teed up to fire. I mouthed a "yes" to her. The next moment a bright flash and a loud report exactly coincided with the leopard's disappearance. I was aware of a slight movement of the spots into the deep bush.

As we ran out toward the bait, all I could hope was that the shot had been a good one. This was no place, and no time of day, to have a wounded leopard out of one's hands. The light was rapidly going, and even now in the thick bush it was as bad as dark. I was a little worried, to say the least, when we did not find a dead leopard at the foot of the tree. All we did know was that it had gone off to the right. We could see no tracks whatsoever. I asked Lady Betty to stay at the foot of the tree with her rifle, while Tabei, armed with a club and a knife, and I, with a shotgun, had a look around. Tabei went rather more right than I. I was looking in some lower-lying ground. It was dark now and extremely eerie.

Just when I thought that all was lost, there was a jubilant cry from Tabei: "*Iko hapa! Bwana, iko hapa!*" He had found the leopard. What a relief. "He's got it, Betty," I cried, as I went to join Tabei. She had hit it good and true. A heart shot, a leap, a forty-yard run, and down and out. Tabei was pleased; Betty was very happy. I was relieved. We drove back to our camp to celebrate. We drank a lot, ate a lot, laughed a lot, and played a little. When I was allowed to go to bed, I slept better and deeper than the "just"!

Having completed our hunting in the Doldol area, we moved to our next camp on the Ngare Mara River, a few miles north of Isiolo. Here our chief excitement was with lion. Each girl wanted a lion. Our camp was a pretty one, under sweet-smelling thorn trees, with desert roses sprouting up in all directions. Buffalo Springs was not far away, and the distant view of Mount Kenya was really beautiful. So if hunting were a bit of a flop, you could always take the client swimming (with or without!) and point out the pretty trees or the lovely shrubs or the grandeur of Mount Kenya. Also there was always the chance of tripping over an elephant, a buffalo, or a lion.

In fact, that was almost exactly what Lady Betty and I did one day.

We had taken quite a walk along the sandy, dusty, rock-strewn countryside and were heading for home. Tabei was keeping his eyes wide open and would point out this and that as we proceeded. However, even his wonderful eyes could not see in every direction at one time, and on this particular occasion it was my eyes that saw one of the many rocks move. I called a halt. Tabei, seeing where I looked, himself saw the lion at once. For, indeed, it was a lion. But it was definitely pretending to be a rock. The beast was crouching right down without even the flicker of an ear, in amongst rocks about the same size as itself. Even the colors matched.

Betty had about the sharpest eyes of any woman I had known, but she could not spot this lion couchant. It was about 250 yards from us. I whispered to her: "It's a good enough lion. We'll walk up on it until you can see it." She nodded. We walked. We made about twenty yards before the lion moved. Then it was up like a flash and behind a large rock before Betty had the slightest chance of a shot. We walked up the incline as fast as we could go, in and among the rocks. I sent Tabei up ahead to spy out the lion if possible. He was there almost the next moment, peeped around a large rock, and then signaled us to hurry. When we arrived, Betty was puffing a little, yet a fair shot awaited her and she took it. It was a good solid hit. The lion took off at express speed. I gave it two shots as it went, but I merely killed two rocks! Meantime, the lion disappeared from sight over a rise in the ground. We got to the top of the incline as fast as possible and peeped over, but we saw no sign of the lion. Tabei and I moved over a few yards to peer round a great round boulder. As we looked, there was suddenly a shot from Betty—and a dead lion, 150 yards away!

The clever girl had spotted it going slowly as it came out from behind another big rock. We hurried over. It was quite a good lion. Betty looked at me. I looked at her. Without a word I took her in my arms and gave her a great kiss of relief. She responded with feeling. And that is what happens on safari. One is inclined to get carried away on a wave of emotion, which may be caused by joy, fear, or stress of some sort or another. This wave will run its course, whether it be for the hour, the day, the safari, or forever.

All that remained now was getting the poor lion back to camp. Then the other Betty had to get her lion, which she did, and off we went to the next stop, Voi. There we hunted elephant and buffalo and had some good bird shooting, and here Peter's wife visited him. She is a sweet and lovely girl, but, as I've always said, a safari camp is no place for a wife or girlfriend. It definitely throws a wrench into the works. I could definitely see that both Bettys were annoyed, so I immediately suggested a run into Mombasa to get some seafood. Lady Betty at once jumped at the idea, saying: "Oh, yes, Bunny, I can get my hair done. Let's have a night there."

We packed, and off we went. Just before I got into the car, Peter came up to tell me that his wife was leaving the following day.

"Sorry about this, Bunny. She had to talk to me about a coming safari."

"Yes, I know how it is. Give her a kiss from me and ask her not to do it again."

Lady Betty and I had a nice drive downhill to Mombasa. She was just in time to get a pretty girl to do her hair, while I ran down to the club to get us rooms. Betty was really lovely company. She liked her room, she liked her food, and she liked her drinks. When I kissed her good night, she was ready to go to sleep.

We drove happily back to camp next day, loaded with some good seafood, fresh vegetables, and fruit. On arrival in camp, a radiantly smiling other Betty greeted us: "How was it, Mother?" To which Mother replied, "It was the best hairdo I ever have had."

"Oh, that's what you call it!"

We all laughed our way into lunch.

David Allen with hippo on Lake Birigi, Tanzania. 1973.

David Allen and his trophies from the Selous, Tanzania. 1971.

Ben H. Carpenter and Bunny Allen with the large record-book lion killed by Ben in the Moyowasi Swamp of northern Tanzania while on safari with Bunny Allen. 1972.

Anton Allen. 1960.

Four generations of male Allens. (left to right) Back row: Jesse Allen (Bunny's nephew) and Petal Allen. Middle row: David, Jerri, and Bunny Allen. Front row: John Allen (David's son) and Benjamin Allen (John's son). 1998.

Hunting sitatunga in the Moyowasi Swamp.

Franzi Kummel, his wife Hanni, and David with big forest elephant near Lamu.

Hippo with Anton, Martita and Frates Seeligson, and Jens Hessel at Lake Burigi.

Ben Carpenter, Jens Henssel, and Bunny at Los Colinas, Texas, Ben's development.

Bunny making a toast at Thady and Lavinia's wedding. Mt. Kenya Safari Club.
1968.

Jack Soames and Kikunyu (Bunny's right hand man for many years). (Photo
courtesy of Carla and Anton Allen)

Anton, Bunny, and David at a Game Coin Conference, San Antonio, Texas. 1977.

David Allen and wife Petal on Franzi Krummel's safari in the Northen Frontier District. 1973.

Ahmed, whose tusks weighed nearly 150 lbs. each, below Marsabit in December 1973. This is probably one of the last photographs taken of him alive. He died of old age in January 1974. (Photo courtesy of Carla and Anton Allen)

Kenya Honeymoon Safari. March 1994.

Returning from a successful sitatunga hunt with a sitatunga in the back of the canoe. Moyowasi Swamp.

Gunbearer, Anton, Frates, and Kiroi are happy with Frates's sable.

Merisie, Tabei, Bunny, Dave, and Anton on Bunny's last safari. Tana River. 1977.

Ahmed near Marsabit. 1970.

Lion with his umbrella in Loliondo. (Photo courtesy of Carla and Anton Allen)

Dave and large Mount Kenya leopard. (Photo courtesy of Carla and Anton Allen)

Left to right: Ben H. Carpenter, John W. Carpenter III, and Bunny Allen. Lion killed by John Carpenter in the Selous region of Tanzania. 1972.

Good use of the nose—reaching for food in the top branches.

Sidney Lindsay and Martita Seeligson have a successful elephant hunt.

John W. Carpenter III, age 12, and his father, Ben H. Carpenter, with the elephant killed by John with a single brain shot in Hunting Block One of northern Kenya. Professional hunters on the 1964 safari were Bunny Allen, Henry Poolman, and Sten Cedergren.

Good buffalo in Loliondo. (Photo courtesy of Carla and Anton Allen)

Crossing the Athi River. 1961. (Photo courtesy of Carla and Anton Allen)

John W. Carpenter III, Sandy Thompson, Dr. L. S. (Buddy) Thompson Jr., Bunny Allen, and Ben H. Carpenter. Taken on an airstrip in the Moyowasi Swamp of northern Tanzania during a safari. 1972.

Bunny and Dave resting during a hunters' gathering at Cottar's Camp in Masai Mara. 1970.

Masai giraffe in Masai Mara.

Old Turkawa woman at Doldol. (Photo courtesy of Carla and Anton Allen)

Vulture at sunset in the Masai Mara.

Illicit gains: These rhino skulls and the buffalo skull were found at a poacher's camp.

Bunny and Jeri Allen with Mick Jagger and Jeri Hall. Lamu. 1980.

Bunny and Jeri's Arab-style mansion, "Smugglers," in Lamu.

Bunny Allen at the East African Professional Hunters' Association reunion at Glen Cottar's Camp in Masai Mara. 1990.

Bunny holding his. 450 Westley Richards double rifle beside the Uaso Nyiro River in northern Kenya.

Bunny Allen (left) with David. 1980s.

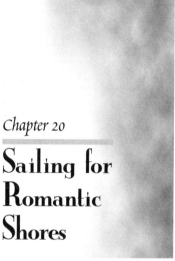

Chapter 20

Sailing for Romantic Shores

I n no time at all, the Robinsons from Austin came again:
the whole Al Robinson family—father, mother, son and
his wife and two daughters, plus the husbands of the
two daughters. David and Anton and Jens Hessel were
hunting for them, with me in reserve.

I always will remember my first impression of this safari.
The whole lot were sitting out under the thorn tree in front of
the New Stanley Hotel. They were chatting away, laughing,
crying. I didn't know who was who. I saw a very pretty young
girl and, seizing a chair, I sat myself right next to her. She was
talkative and lovely, and I soon got her life story. She said she
had four children "back home." She was just a child herself—
a beautiful blonde child. I guessed, of course, that she was one
of Al's daughters. Yes, that was correct; she was Carla. I asked
her why her husband had not come on the safari as well: "Oh,
but he has, he's right over there." She pointed across several
tables to a nice enough looking young man who was chatting
with another chap.

I looked in wonder at Carla: "It's hard to believe that you are married and have four children. You are a child yourself." Then I noticed, over the next couple of days, before they went on safari, what was going on between Carla and her husband. I saw quite a lot of them, but in all the time I saw them together they were just not together. He appeared to take no notice of her. Never a tender word, never a tender act toward her, such as helping her into a chair. And yet he knew the form—he was a gentleman—but they were apart. When they were sort of together, there was no fusion between them; rather there was confusion! There was no spark of warmth. No hand-holding. In other words, Carla was ripe for a safari love affair. It stood out a mile, in a very few days, that she and Anton were sailing for romantic shores. It was just so lucky that they met each other at that time. They are now living happily ever after.

Al Robinson was heard to remark: "Why do my daughters always choose to fall in love with the hired hands?" Apparently the other married daughter had fallen in love with a cowboy on the ranch and subsequently divorced her husband to marry him. I understand that she, too, is living happily ever after. Love should be a fairy story!

During this time, Coley Coles was taking care of Patti and Rollins Wofford over at Ikoma, where I hastened to join them. There was dear old Coley, doing a splendid job of looking after the Woffords in a heavenly camp on a little river, just a few miles from Fort Ikoma. Coley was engaged in his favorite pastime: He was pulling succulent butterfly fish out of the river for our delight. How I wished I had had these to offer Lady Betty. It might have made her fall in love with me.

While we were in this Ikoma camp, we were joined by Tebo Bowman for a period. He had come over from another safari camp some few miles away. "Bunny," he said, "I've got friends over in that camp. I'd like to bring them over to you to get a good meal." So it was arranged.

It turned out to be Bing Crosby and his party. Some of these people happened also to be acquaintances of mine. Lawrence Wood was there with his beautiful wife, Lorraine. John Connally, governor of Texas, was there. These I knew. As luck would have it, my good girl Jeri came flying into camp with a couple of friends, just before the rival camp came to dine with us. Therefore we had a brand-new lot of goodies to offer them to eat and drink. That was sheer good luck, but fortune favors the lucky!

Anyway, for those that came we had a wonderful meal, and the campfire did overtime that night. We all slept well, and the next day it was our intention to set about the Grumeti lions, although it did not happen that way at all. We did not set about the Grumeti lions. Nor, in fact, did the Grumeti lions set about us—but they certainly had the laugh on us.

We put a nice big fat old buffalo out as a kill for the lions. All according to plan, a large pride or maybe two prides of lion had fed on it. There were at least two huge pads to tell us that. So a good trophy had probably been there. Furthermore, these lions had water in a riverbed, right close at hand. They wouldn't move away until the buff was completely stripped. The vultures were out of luck this time. We had a nice covered approach to the kill, with a bunch of bushes that we had hollowed out a bit to view from.

When we came near our natural blind, we could hear the lions on the kill. There was every kind of grunt and growl and roar, with an occasional whimper from a chastised cub. It was a splendid chorus. I was already beginning to feel a bit sorry for the poor old lion we were threatening to take. We peeked our noses through the bushes—and what a sight for sore eyes. There must have been twenty-five lions of various sizes: from cubs of three weeks old to huge lionesses and two monster lions. When our noses first protruded from the shrubbery, Rollins could have shot one of the monsters as easy as pie. Thankfully, he wasn't ready! For the rest of that evening, there was never another chance to take a shot. Always, the big lions were shadowed by a lioness or a half-size lion or three or four large cubs. Always there was something in front of the lions to prevent a shot. It was fantastic and wonderful. I must say I was not being fair to Rollins, the client; I was cheering for the lions.

It became time to go. As we walked back from the hide, we discussed what we had seen and the chances for the morning. In the end, Rollins said: "D'you know, Bunny, I just don't know that I want to shoot one of those dandy lions now. That was such a show."

"Yes, it certainly was." I looked at Rollins. "Anyway, isn't the lion you've already got enough?"

"I reckon you're right. It's good enough. Let's go back in the morning and take pictures."

That is exactly what we did, and my word, it was rewarding. We did not hurry the next morning. We wanted a good light, so we had a brave breakfast and arrived at the scene with the sun. It was all bright and beautiful—but there was an addition. There was another kill! One more buffalo had been laid low, a gigantic cow. The spread of the horns must have been at least fifty inches. They were long, and narrow, and looked pretty mean. The boss was thin but large enough to carry a passenger. The lions had eaten quite a bit of the meat already, yet the original kill still had meat left on it. It appeared to me that the pride of lion was so large that they needed two dining tables!

At the moment of our arrival, the lions were sitting around in groups, with some of the cubs playing like kittens. There was a massive munching of chops as they licked their lips and pawed their faces. They were all replete, and they were not tearing a piece of meat from the kill. In fact, a small group of about twenty buffalo was only twenty-five yards away, gradually grazing in the direction of our hide. The fully fed lions were taking not the slightest notice of them, and the buffalo for their part hadn't a worry in the world. It was as though a truce had been arranged.

Rollins reached over to my ear and whispered: "Bunny, this is great." And it certainly was. I had never seen anything like it, and I'm prepared to bet I'll never see the like again.

However, one of the splendid beauties of this hunting racket is that there is always something new going on. I am always in happy anticipation of what is going to happen tomorrow. There is never a completely dull day. The nearest thing to that is when one is shut up in a tent on a pouring rainy day with a girl who is not interested in parlor games. I believe that seldom happens. Always one will find that if she is not interested in Ludo, or Snakes and Ladders, she will be interested in Patience. In fact, often Impatience will save the day!

On this occasion with Rollins, we had a real tip-top show. The buffalo were grazing closer and closer to us, with some of the lions no more than eight paces away, taking not the remotest

awareness of them. Now the buff were right upon us, stretched out like a small arc, and I noticed that almost all of them, if not all, were bulls. We could hear them tearing the grass out as they grazed, the snorting, the grunts, all the noises of living close. Until this moment I must say I had not felt nervous. Maybe there had not been time even to think of such a thing. But now, with these three or four enormous bulls right on our doormat and casting their eyes over their backs to view the golden lions just behind, I, for one, felt a little spare. And there was a new, hollow noise. Was it my knees knocking together?

At that very moment, the leading two bulls threw their heads in the air and the next moment came at our hide. Rollins had a rifle in his hands in a flash, the cameras fell to the ground, there were three quick shots, and two buffalo lay dead, just about as quick as that. Thankfully, the rest of the buffalo turned and, with tails high in the air, took off. The lions barely reacted at all. The youngsters yelped and scuttled around a bit, but the big chaps hardly lifted their heads. They were in command and they knew it. We retreated a little, however, and continued to watch from another clump of bushes.

All in all, it was a thrilling experience. Several of the younger lions came up to nose the two new offerings. They did not eat at all; they were well enough fed. Rollins and I looked at one another and shook our heads in disbelief. That was the end of the story. We did not return to the scene. I was against it. Something deep inside me told me to let well enough alone. We had chanced our arms sufficiently. The lion and the buffalo had put up a wonderful performance.

The previous year, I had arranged to do a month's safari for Alice Clayberg and her three children. I had met her at the San Antonio Game Conference. She was a charming, marvelous girl, and I was certainly looking forward to taking her on safari. As I understood it, Alice wanted to hunt quite a lot, as did her son, Mike. Her eldest daughter, Chuyla, was a keen naturalist. She wanted to study everything and take a lot of photographs. The young daughter, young Alice, wanted to tag along and shoot a few birds and a little camp meat. They were a sweet lot, not always seeing eye to eye with one another, but individually, each one very, very nice. I enjoyed them all immensely.

I had "old" Coley Coles along to help. He was just cut out for this sort of safari; he was so good with the young people. His patience was inexhaustible. So for the most part I took charge of Alice, usually accompanied by one or another of her daughters; in fact, it was almost always young Alice.

Alice and her daughter Chuyla were a trifle inflammable when together. I found it best to keep them apart. As a matter of fact, from the very start Alice had advised me to do this. It was more than sound advice. It was the only thing to do. Basically they had a great love for each other, but they could "fall out" over the smallest triviality. It was a matter I had to guard against throughout the safari.

Like most Texas girls, Alice was a very good shot. She seldom required a second for any of her trophies. Yet we did have one sad note in her hunting: the buffalo that got away. That really was my fault and not the fault of Alice. Up to this point, her hunt had gone absolutely according to plan. Mike too was doing pretty well with Coley, and young Alice was having a lot of fun getting a bird or two and a very smart impala. She was a sweet girl with a delicious turn of humor. Also the slightly tricky Chuyla was, at least, a dear, lovely girl. You just had to iron the grumps out of her. Personally, I loved her company, and it was a constant source of joy to me. To kiss her good night was to see her natural shyness turn to a warm expectancy. I often wondered what the future had in store for that lovely girl. I bet she made a first-class beautiful wife for some lucky chap, then became a wonderful mother. Yes, they were an odd assorted family, yet they were close-knit and proud of each other. Also they were all proud of being of the clan of the great King Ranch.

Late one evening, as we returned to camp, we spotted a lone buffalo bull in tall grass. We made a sally toward it, and it ran up onto a slight rise in the ground. There it stood, about seventy yards off, in rather poor light. Maybe I should not have said: "Take it in the heart, Alice." But I did, and she took it. I also gave it one, and one of our shots went careering off in a loud whistle to land up in some palms about half a mile away. The buff was in thick cover in a moment. It was really ugly-looking bush. I asked Alice to go to the car, a hundred yards back on the track. She didn't want to go. I squeezed her hand, smiled at her, and she knew she had to go. The bush ahead was a horrible tangle and no place to take her. In fact, I should have gone without Tabei, but I was not brave enough and in any case he would not have let me go alone.

We watched Alice, with the other gunbearer, until they were almost back at the car; then we crept into the bush. There was a clear-enough blood spoor immediately, but it was ghastly bush to go into: a mess of short, thorn-covered palms in among elephant grass, all growing out of black cotton soil, with small hillocks every few feet. It was clammy and dark in there. I must say I expected the buff to come at any moment. There was a great deal of blood, and at that stage I imagined the beast to be well hit.

Suddenly Tabei paused, and held up one finger, and I heard a slight rustle ahead. The buff had slipped away. In a few moments we came to where it had been standing. There was quite a lot of blood, which we examined closely. There was no lung blood in it. We continued on the trail. It was slow work, and all the time we were in a crouching position. It took us at least twenty minutes to do, I suppose, about forty or fifty twisting yards. In one or two more places the buff had dwelt awhile. At the time, we thought it had stopped because of its wounds, but in retrospect it was, I believe, just to listen for us.

In the end we had to give up our search. It would have been madness to go on. It was black in there. Every place looked like a waiting buffalo. We would have to take up the search again in the morning and hope to find a dead buffalo, but by now I had my doubts.

It was with a feeling of great relief that we got out of that eerie swampland bush and made our way back to the car. Alice came forward in the darkness to meet us. She was very sweet and immediately tried to take the blame.

"I'm sorry, Bunny. I made a real bosh shot. I thought it was a good one. I failed us, and you and Tabei might have got hurt."

I replied: "My dear Alice, don't worry. We'll get it in the morning. I think your shot was a good 'un. Now, it's too dark." I gave her a soft kiss and helped her into the car. I was just gentling her along, really, because in my own mind I did not think that we'd find that buff. I felt that it had gotten clean away. Tomorrow would tell.

Having returned to camp, I learned that two people had set up their camp about a mile downstream from us. As was the custom, I got in touch with them at once. I found that they were studying butterflies. They were a woman of about young to middle age and a somewhat younger man. They seemed quite pleasant, so I asked them round for dinner with a drink or two before. Well, they certainly knew how to drink!

We, in our party, were not great beer drinkers, but we had some. That disappeared first, and at a great rate of knots. Then quite a bit of whiskey was disappearing—too fast. I called Coley aside. He was a brandy drinker. I said: "Coley, come to the rescue. I don't want these bloodsuckers to drink all of Alice's scotch; she likes it. Please bring a bottle of the brandy along, the South African stuff. We'll poison them with that." Coley nodded knowingly, and we switched our guests to brandy. At dinner they sank a couple of bottles between them. As they got up to go home, they were feeling no pain.

She was a very bossy girl; you know, she took the driving seat and all that sort of thing, and I, with my horrible mind, could imagine her steering the young man, in a short while, into her bed. I don't think she was just after butterflies! As they were about to leave, thankfully, I remembered the wretched buffalo. "Half a mo. I've had to leave a wounded buffalo down there near the main track." Neither one nor the other, however, seemed interested. They had their sights on other things, maybe. "Anyway," I went on, "I'm going out first thing in the morning to complete my search. I'll let you know. For a start, don't go in that direction." They waved acknowledgment and happily went their way.

The children, large and small, ambled off very tired to bed, leaving Alice, Coley, and me to have a last drink before retiring. As we drank, I asked Coley to pass by the game department post at Garsen the following morning to report my wounded buffalo. "But tell them I am still looking for it. I'll report again when I have something to report."

After a while we all went off to bed. As I escorted Alice, she said: "Bunny, I wish you would let me come along with you to look for my buffalo." I took her hand, held it, and warmly patted it. "Look, Alice, there is just no room in that bush for you, but you can do something, let me tell you. You can take a stand on the other side of the thick bush. If the buff is still inside there, we will spook it out, and you can have a fair chance of nailing it." She was pleased with that. She was a fine sporting girl. I had great admiration for her.

Next morning, we had a good early breaking of the fast and set off with several extra helping hands, just in case. First I took Alice to her position beyond the horrible bush. I sat her in a safari chair until such time as the car came back; then she would sit in it, or on the roof for better spotting. I left two men with her. Tabei and I then returned in the car to the spot where the buffalo had taken cover the previous evening. A driver then returned the car to Alice.

From that point on the hunt was completely anticlimactic. The buffalo had certainly gotten away. It had moved off and had never stopped. In half an hour we were back with Alice, having followed the buff's tracks, which passed within fifty yards of where we had placed her. The blood spoor had ended completely well inside the bush, and during the night the buff had crossed the open country to the riverine forest beyond.

As we drove back toward camp, Alice spoke to me: "So you think it got away—is that all right?"

"Yes, I believe your shot hit high in the neck, just a flesh wound. It bled quite a bit at first, dried up, and I reckon it to be as good as new."

"And your shot?" she quizzed. "You didn't miss?"

"Yes, I missed. I know my shot hit a nearby tree and then went whistling off into Africa."

"D'you know, I just don't believe that—you missed?"

"Yes, Alice, I can tell you, I often miss, but I seldom admit it."

Before going back to our camp, I diverted into Garsen to make my report to the game department. In camp, much to my surprise, we found the butterfly dame waiting. She did not have her male companion with her. She advanced on me, grim-faced and tight-lipped. "Well, and what about the wounded buffalo? Do you realize what you are doing? I think it a disgrace that such people as you are allowed to go hunting—when you leave wounded, dangerous animals all over the place."

She paused for breath. I took the opportunity to guide Alice toward her tent with a caressing pat on her very shapely bottom. With an understanding smile, she went her way. And now the butterfly woman fairly bared her fangs and came at me: "Now tell me, what do you propose to do? We might get killed."

At this point I tried to get a word in. "It is all—" That's as far as I got in telling her it was all safe now, because she took over once more: "That is the exact place we wished to work today. I'm going on now to complain to the game department. I'll get you chucked out—you'll see. I'll get you chucked out."

By now she was frothing at the mouth as she bounced from one foot to the other. The woman was demented. I fancied I knew what was wrong with her. I reckon she was a nymphomaniac whose lover had not come to scratch that night. There was only one quick remedy—but I was not prepared to administer that. Perhaps Coley would volunteer? All I wanted for the moment was to get rid of her. "Yes, that's right," I replied in answer to her last outburst, "that'll save me going in."

That did the trick. She looked like thunder, stomped off to her car, but I had the satisfaction of opening the door for her and handling her in. As she crashed the gears her mouth opened to produce a throaty gurgling noise, somewhat akin to what might come from a sex-starved puff adder, but louder, much louder. My God, that woman was a real bitch. I decided to guard dear old Coley from her. The best way to do that was to encourage him to search out a whopping big elephant for Mike, the son.

Coley was nonstop on the job. I couldn't keep him in camp; morning till dusk he combed the brush for a hundred-pounder. He had little hope of finding it, but they found lots of jumbos of various sizes well below that mark. What was just as important, Chuyla, the photographer, was able to get plenty of pictures, and they were a happy trio together. Coley had a sweet way of dealing with young people. All the young girls fell in love with him. He had his own type of fairy story to tell them, and he completely held them while he was telling it. The girls would swoon and the boys would hang on every word.

Mike didn't get his elephant, yet he had a lot of fun. Chuyla got a splendid lot of photographs. Meantime, young Alice spent most of her time with Mama and me. And baby made three!

Chapter 21

Lady Fortune
Is with Us

Time came to move camp. While this was being done, we all slipped onto Lamu Island for a couple of days. Jeri and Alice got along very well together. Alice picked up her mail and was pleased to find a letter or two from her brand-new husband-to-be. He was apparently upset because he had not had a letter from Alice. He probably didn't realize that on safari it is sometimes quite difficult to post and collect mail. Also, very often there is little time left over to write a letter in camp. Anyway, this particularly keen lover boy was obviously beginning to feel that when one's fiancée is on another continent, thousands of miles away, love is not a bowl of roses. He was missing her, and that was sad. She undoubtedly was missing him, but she was not sad. She was too busy. No time for sadness. Thoughts, yes; sadness, no.

I mention this matter to illustrate that there are times during a safari when something happens that might well mar its success, its happiness. Thankfully, on this occasion Alice was in wonderland. She was completely understanding, and saved the potentially unpleasant situation in the form of a sweet letter. We then settled down and had a happy safari ever after.

Our final camp was on the Northern Frontier. I remember one classic shot Alice made on a lesser kudu. It was quite a way off, going in great leaping strides, and she got it in midair. It was a very fine shot by my standards. Then we settled down to planning a leopard's downfall. In this, unwittingly, we were considerably helped by some poachers.

One evening Alice decided to stay in camp to write a letter. I took a turn up the river to see what I could find of leopard signs. I found signs. Without a doubt I found signs. Furthermore, I found a bait already hanging in a tree and a hide made ready for use in a hollow baobab. The poachers had been there before me!

Tabei called me out of the baobab tree and pointed to pug marks in the sand behind the bait—a large leopard. He suddenly looked up and across the swampland. My eyes followed. There was a small group of people across there, with a few dogs. I put my glasses up. They carried bows and arrows. Poachers! I at once drew my rifle to my shoulder, aimed a bit off to the right, and squeezed the trigger. With the bang and the crack of the whip the group went in all directions. I gave them one more joy as they all disappeared over a rise. I turned to find a grinning Tabei, approving of my actions. "*Wata-kwenda tu,*" he said, as his hand intimated that they had gone for good. I certainly hoped so, in order to give Alice a fair chance on the leopard. It was a perfect setup, and we would try the next morning.

As Tabei and I returned to camp, we discussed the situation. I did not want Alice to get involved in any way with the poachers; we had to keep them away. Tabei reckoned that they would keep away, at least for a while, as a result of our brush with them. I did not mention the poachers to Alice. But I did take very special precautions. While we sat down for our drinks by the campfire in the evening light, Tabei and a trusted follower slipped off, back to the leopard bait. I instructed them to find a lay-up for themselves close enough, yet safe enough, to watch what went on. They would meet us as we arrived to inspect the bait in the morning. I must say I hoped for a negative report.

Alice was excited about the leopard. She went to bed happy and keen for the morning. With the first dawn light in the sky, Alice drank a morning cup of tea with me. We talked in misty whispers so as not to disturb the rest of the camp. They were getting up later, and Coley was going to take them fishing on the Uaso Nyiro River.

Tabei and his companion met Alice and me at the agreed rendezvous. Thankfully, there was nothing to report—no poachers had come anywhere near. I now just hoped that we could conclude the hunt without interference. Tabei said that he had heard the leopard grunting up toward the river but had not actually seen it. It could be that it was now on the bait! We had an excellent covered approach to our baobab tree hide. The wind was perfect. Everything pointed fair. There was only one snag. The poachers were in the hide! They had slipped in just ahead of us while Tabei was away to make contact with us. By sheer luck and Tabei's wonderful eyesight, we had spotted the poachers before they spotted us. Now—what to do? Was the leopard at the bait or, for that matter, anywhere around? So far we had neither seen nor heard it, but just now the baobab tree hide was blocking our view.

It is at these moments of uncertainty that one needs a stroke of genius or a stroke of luck. While Tabei and the other gunbearer were peering ahead for both the poachers and the leopard, I suddenly recalled the wise words of Piramus Berners, my Gypsy mentor: "Look around behind you—it might be there." I slowly turned my head—and—there it was! Stalking along slowly in a slight draw, just below us, came a very fine leopard.

I alerted Alice, then whispered close into her delicious ear: "Take it as soon as it stops, or when I touch." Now was the time for quick thinking. There were three important factors—the leopard, the poachers, and Alice. Alice wanted to get the leopard. I wanted to chase off the poachers. I didn't want Alice to know about the poachers. Thankfully, the leopard's slow progress down the draw gave me a few seconds for thought.

I intimated to Tabei to keep on watching the poachers. I got my trusted Rigby double ready for action, just in case, and then waited for the leopard to stop in its approach. Lady Fortune was with us. The leopard pulled up in a completely open spot a mere fifty yards off. The light was perfect. Alice made a first-class shot, and it was a dead leopard. Meantime, Tabei, watching the reaction of the poachers, informed me by a hand signal that they had come out of the hide and run for it. So far, so very, very good. While I took Alice down to see her trophy, Tabei went off to check on the movements of the poachers. I then took a look at the bait hanging in the tree, still untouched by the leopard. As I had surmised, it had been well dosed with poison. These poachers had two ways of getting a leopard: If they failed with their bows and arrows, the poison would do the trick in double-quick time. They used the same poison that they put on their arrow barbs. It was from the roots of a wild bushlike tree called *murishu*. This grew in abundance in many parts of Kenya.

By the time Tabei came back to report on the poachers the car had arrived, and we loaded the leopard for the return to camp. Tabei told me that the poachers were across the river on a rise, watching what was going on from a safe distance. I deemed that they would return later to inspect what we had been doing.

Once again I left poor Tabei on guard, this time with a shotgun loaded with no. 6 shot. I called him aside to instruct him to pepper an arse or two if he was able to do so. He was thrilled with the idea. His eyes lit up considerably. I left him with a pot of nice sweet tea, and with the balance of the party I drove back to camp. I instructed the skinner to prepare the leopard as quickly as possible and gave instructions to pull the camp down at once. I did not intend to stay in those parts longer than was absolutely necessary. These poachers could become a real nuisance. I could smell that!

This episode was the first time, ever, that I had felt menaced by poachers. Of course, over the years I had had frequent contact with them. Time and time again there had been evidence of their being about, but they kept away. We had a type of ungentlemanly disagreement: They went their way, and we went ours. This time they were being more than a little saucy! They could easily attack our camp, and I was further led to believe in that possibility when Tabei returned.

He had peppered an arse successfully, but some of the other poachers had screamed abuse and threats. Also, as he left the field of battle, he had seen one man on the far slope carrying a gun of some sort. It was time to go. I would make my report to the game department as I passed their post. I had valuable clients with me. I could take no risk.

Before I draw the curtain down on this particular safari, I would like to hand a little bouquet to Alice. Alice was a sweet, charming woman—always understanding of every situation, good or bad. I suppose I have escorted, or semiescorted, around 350 women of all ages on safari in my time. To my mind, they were all wonderful in one way or another. Sometimes, it was two ways and another! Of those 350 wonderful women, I should say there were ten or twelve who were completely outstanding: either their beauty, loveliness, sexiness, sheer goodness, or whatever. Alice was one of those. She was superlative!

It was at this time that I expected to have a slight spell with my delightful friend Diana Vanderscut. We had kept in touch as we had promised, and on my way to the San Antonio Game Conference we met briefly in New York. And I do mean briefly. She met me at the airport as I arrived, rushed me to the Plaza Hotel, and after a slight spell asked me to put on my smartest suit. We then descended to a massive party given by the New York Safari Club or some such. This consisted of cocktails, a rather fine dinner, and then dancing to all hours. However, Diana, like the wise, beautiful girl she was, whispered in my ear: "Honey Bunny, I'm slipping up to bed. I've got something to do up there. Come when you can."

Immediately I decided to go when I could. This was fairly soon. I had one more dance with one of my tablemates; it was not a howling success. Her two legs kept fouling one of mine, with the result that I fell forward onto her rather ample breastworks. She received my apologies with a comfy smile as she squeezed my hand. In handing her back to her seat, I suggested another dance later, to which she nodded acquiescence. There never was a "later." I wandered over to the elevator and took myself up to the little girl's room. I found the "little girl" lying in bed reading and giggling. She was scanning the unexpurgated notes of my safari experiences!

All beautiful things have to end. The next morning we parted and went our separate ways. Diana had to go to join her mother for a European trip, and I headed for the San Antonio conference. There I met lots of old friends, had a joyous time, relived some of the old times with old customers, and got thoroughly exhausted.

By arrangement, I met up again with Diana in London. I was staying at the Naval and Military Club, Piccadilly, and Diana was just opposite at the Ritz. I met her at the Ritz, but she warned me that her mother was completely puritanical. She'd have to watch her step lest she get cut off with the proverbial shilling. Therefore

Diana left her mother to go off shopping and then popped over to see me at the "In and Out." However, we had only two days of this, because I was headed back for Kenya, which was calling to me.

Since the parting, I have neither seen nor heard from Diana again. She just disappeared into thin air. I had noticed on this meeting that she was not quite her old self. She was still very wonderful, still very lovely, but some of the old fire was missing; there was not quite that spark in her eyes. Also, to my mind, she had gone rather too thin. It was very sad. She was a great girl. Certainly she is numbered in one of my ten or twelve!

The Wheel of Life

Chapter 22

Frates– Professional Client!

T hat splendid fellow, Frates, was back again. Once again I had the joy of having him and his lovely wife, Martita, on safari. They were accompanied by a very charming man friend, Sid Lindsey. The only slight snag was that he was of truly massive dimensions. With Sid it really was "once round him twice round the gas works." We had to have special chairs for him and almost special aircraft! But what a lovely chap. It was worthwhile to turn the world upside down to have him on safari.

Also (although how it came to be I do not quite know), we had two very sweet "Tex lasses" with us. They just happened to be in Nairobi at the time we set off and they just happened to come along. I rather fancy that my sons pressured them somewhat.

We traveled a long way on this trip. We camped near the great Malagarasi Swamp in southwestern Tanganyika. There was a good selection of game there, including the rather rare sitatunga. There were thousands of buffalo—certainly more than I have seen in any other place—and the biggest lions in the world. The lions there live entirely on buffalo. One sees dozens of buffalo around the swamp that have suffered lion attacks and gotten away, but they bear the scars. During this particular safari, I witnessed a most tremendous fight between lion and buffalo.

I had gone out to scout for sitatunga and was skirting the edge of the swamp. In doing this, Tabei and I continually had to avoid buffalo. There were hundreds of them, and we saw several herds that numbered in the thousands. From time to time we would come on the remains of a buffalo that a lion had killed and devoured. It was wild country, and there was continuous movement everywhere: always some animals slipping out of or into the reeds, the pounding of buff, the mooing of calves, the grunt of a lion and then, from time to time, the splash of a sitatunga as it skied across the weeds and water. It kept us on our toes. Then we turned a corner in the swamp—and saw the sight of a lifetime! It was a fight to the finish between two buffalo and one huge lion. This was certainly the biggest lion I've ever seen. In thinking it over afterward, I judged that it must have weighed seven hundred pounds.

These three animals were in a sort of natural arena of fairly level ground. The fight must have just that moment started, for we could see no blood. The three fighters were circling one another, rather like boxers in a ring. In fact, that description really fits, because while one buffalo and the lion were sparring, the second buff was standing slightly aside like a referee. While this was going on, we had the chance to study the lion. It was truly magnificent. Huge, as I have said, and of the most unusual, wonderful shade. It was rufous in color, with its long mane and tail of a deeper hue than the body, indeed almost blood-red to black. The whole time the lion kept its eye firmly fixed on the buffalo, which now stood stock-still as though mesmerized. The second buffalo had altered its position somewhat, putting itself a little farther away on the lion's left flank, about twenty yards off. We were watching from behind an anthill fifty yards away. All three animals were completely oblivious to us. The balance of the herd were milling around a couple of hundred yards away, mooing and lowing, while white egrets flew above them.

The lion was gradually creeping up, foot by foot, closer to the transfixed buff. Meantime, the second buff was also doing its share of creeping. It was now almost directly behind the lion and closer; something was bound to happen soon. The advancing lion was a bare ten yards from its target, which was still holding fast. The lion now stopped completely and sank down on its haunches, but not relaxed or slack. It was absolutely taut and ready to spring. The second buffalo had edged up still closer, within about ten yards of the lion. As we watched, the lion's tail coiled like a whip and lashed out a couple of times. With that, it sprang. The old buff roared out a tremendous grunt and threw its heavily bossed horns high in the air, turning them to the right a little as it did so. They gave the lion a heavy body blow in midair, but nevertheless the lion landed fair and square on the buff's body, stretching from neck to rear. That brought both animals to the ground with a resounding thud. During all this, number two buffalo had not been wasting its time. It had come from behind and now laid into the lion before it could get properly to its feet.

At this stage, there were certainly some grunts of painful disbelief from the lion, together with amazing bellows from the downed buffalo. As suddenly as if a bell had proclaimed the end of the round, the antagonists parted from one another. Once again the two that were grounded were on their feet, went off a few paces to their own corners, recovered their breath, and sort of licked their wounds. And wounds there certainly were. The downed buffalo had a great lion-fanged gash high up on one rear leg and a lot of blood spilling from a stomach wound. Even the second buffalo had not got off free. It had a heavily bleeding claw wound on one front leg.

As for the lion, it was hard to assess the damage. It was very certainly hurt and going short on one hind leg, but it didn't appear to have any bleeding wound. It had certainly been buffeted really hard. It would be very bruised and might even have some internal damage.

For the first time since the battle had been joined, Tabei and I were able to exchange glances. I feel that we rather nervously smiled at one another during this initial letup in the combat. Tabei had just started to shake his head to and fro—a habit of his when he was pleased because of some unbelievable happening, which this certainly was—when the second round started.

The badly mauled buffalo was beginning to walk slowly offstage and the referee had backed away a little when the lion thought it time to strike again. With a great roar it sprang, as though completely unhurt, and landed smack on the mauled buff, tumbling it over. All four of the buff's feet were in the air, and now the lion thoroughly set on. There was a tearing of flesh amidst loud bellows. But here the second buffalo came back into the fray. It came charging at the rear end of the lion, but as it struck, its opponent deftly swung round and caught merely a glancing blow on the buttock. Even so it was a goodly strike, and it drove the lion a few yards from the downed buff, which was up quite fast and trotted into nearby bushes.

Now it was time for the lion and the referee to have a go. This they proceeded to do as soon as they had drawn breath. The lion still appeared to be in fair condition; I was no longer aware of a limp in the hind leg, but it must have been badly bruised. As for the buffalo, it had the deep gash on the front leg but nothing else to show. That was soon to change. The buffalo turned slightly, as if it were moving off. At that moment the giant lion sprang, emitting the most tremendous roar as it did so. It tore a large piece of flank off the buffalo as it paused momentarily, then went on past. The buffalo turned around as fast as a polo pony and came as quick as lightning at the turning lion. They met head-on with a colossal crunch, the buffalo's huge boss meeting the lion's forehead sweet and true. The impact sent both animals back a foot or two, and there they stood, weak-kneed, eyes rolling, and heads ashake. The pair of them were all but "out"! For several minutes they stood shaking thus—then each turned its back on the other and tiptoed away as if nothing had happened.

Tabei and I exchanged not a word. We simply looked at one another, turned, and side by side tiptoed away. After that episode, everything else that happened on safari had to be anticlimactic.

Frates was his usual wonderful self, full of good humor and a splendid host. The lovely Martita bubbled over with joy every day, and her cup was full when she collared herself a very fine lion trophy. And it was a splendid specimen—a real copybook animal, hair parted in the middle with a black mane. But, for me, there was only one lion—the battered one wandering the swamp. I was waiting to see it again. I felt I would.

Before we finished the hunt, Frates got himself a good sitatunga. Mind you, he had to work hard for it—day after day, up to his neck in water, ploughing through the swamp. In the end I reckon he sprouted web feet and then wings. He came out smiling. And the two young Tex-lasses kept the young white hunters—Jens, David, and Anton—guessing until the last day, or shall we say, night?

We had a lot of fun. That huge, splendid fellow, Sid Lindsey, naturally wanted to shoot an elephant. We really wondered if we could get him up to an elephant, he was such a huge target himself. We pulled his leg unmercifully in camp on the subject. He took it all in good heart, and I will always remember his last retort: "I'll show you fellas. And don't you forget it, I'll show you all." And he certainly did. When the time came for him to creep up on his bull on the edge of the swamp, he was as silent and quiet as a mouse. He brushed softly past bushes and marsh grasses with never a stir. Then he put in a perfect shot. A great fellow was Sid, in more ways than one!

Over the next few weeks, the monster fighting lion was very much on my mind. I wondered what had been the finish of it all. Had the first buffalo gored gone into the bush to die? Or had it recovered? And the second bull—what happened to it? Finally the lion: It was certainly sorely smitten, but I did not fancy that it was about to die. The next safari was going to give me the answers to some of these questions.

H CLAASSENS.

Chapter 23

Ben Carpenter's Lion

We did a quick refit and were on the road again—or rather, in the air. The same party of white hunters this time had our old friends, Ben Carpenter, Doc Thompson, and their respective sons, John and Sandy.

We flew into the ready-made camp in the delightful Selous hunting country of Tanganyika. The rather rough airstrip was only a very few miles from camp, situated on a small range of hills looking out on the hunting area in all directions. To the south was the flatter country with the little memorial stone marking the spot where the great hunter Frederick Selous met his end during the Kaiser's War. A German sniper got him while he was leading a patrol.

To the west the land dropped away to the tremendous Rufiji River, with its thousands of crocodiles and thousands of hippos. It was fascinating, very wild country, and it looked as if it should have been full of game. But it wasn't. There was precious little game on the plains or in the glades.

As we got down close to the Rufiji there was a little more evidence of game, but even there not much was on view except, of course, for hippo and crocs. It was quite astonishing. There were pockets of tsetse fly here and there, which kept the cattle away. There was very, very little evidence of man.

After a while we found a poacher's snare or two, a poacher's hide, a poacher's pit in an animal track, and so on. There was certainly evidence of poachers, and we found more and more as the safari proceeded. The roaring of lions kept us awake at night, and one wondered what they had to roar about. Were they roaring in anger—or in hunger?

There were quite a few lions about. Both John and Sandy collected a good one each. They were in very good condition, well fed, with beautiful, silky coats. We really puzzled over what they were feeding on. If it had not been for the birds that we shot, we would have been hard put to feed the camp. There were also some small lakes nearby that gave us some ducks; they were stocked with hippos as well.

During our stay in the Selous, which was about ten days, we shot only two lion, one roan, one waterbuck, one warthog, and two impala. It was truly lovely country, though, and it was a thrill to walk the footsteps of that great adventurer and gentleman, Frederick Selous.

Before we moved on, we did find out the secret of the good condition of the lions. They were feeding almost entirely on young hippos! The fat from these feeds accounted for their silky coats. One day we had the luck to see lions hunting hippos. We witnessed one successful hunt and one failure.

In this remote country, hippo appeared to wander around and away from the river at all times of the day. There was a constant flow of a few at a time to and from the river, and to a lesser degree to and from the lakes. What we saw was a couple of lions go for a quite large, but not full grown, hippo as it headed back to the river. The hippo was a little behind the main group, and it tumbled over quite easily and speedily with hardly any noise at all. An assault on the top of the neck appeared to kill it, and then, as it tumbled to earth, the lions went for the throat. A little later in the day we saw a pride of about six lions set on a small band of hippo, trying to cut one out to kill. In that they rather failed.

To start with, everything appeared to be going well for the lions. As was their habit, the hippos had formed into a single file on one of their regular tracks down to the great river. They cropped and grazed and browsed as they went. There was constant movement. At the same time, the lions were creeping up on them. In fact, the lions were steadily coming along, walking, hardly lowering their heads at all. There was no need.

When a hippo is on its way, it does not look behind, especially when partaking of succulent morsels en route. Rather, it gets a benign smile on its smug face, somewhat akin to the expression one will see on an elderly gentleman's face in a London club as he sets about a fine dish of springtime English asparagus.

Well, it was at this stage, when all the hippos had a good mouthful of their special asparagus, that several lions ran across the front of the file and caused a slight hippo panic. Amidst loud snorts, the hippos broke file and went in circles. The lions very deftly singled out their prey and immediately tore a slice or two off it before the hippo could slip away toward the river. Several lions darted after it, but a phalanx of hippo confronted them, more by accident than design, which caused a halt. The wounded hippo made it to a pool in the river, but the other hippos immediately broke from their position and headed for the water, with the lions pell-mell after the blood spoor.

Almost as if by accident, three lions were in quite a deep pool in the river. Two scrambled out quickly, leaving the third one still there, and it appeared to be having a tussle with a hippo or two. I noticed the two lions trotting off to higher country with their tails very much between their legs.

The third one managed to break away from the hippo and made for the shallow end of the pool. There a couple of waiting crocodiles that had undoubtedly smelled the blood from its wounds set upon it. Eventually it managed to dodge the crocs, but it was a very sorry-looking lion that finally crawled up the bank of the river. It was lame in one foreleg and was bleeding quite a bit. It went and sat under a tree away from the rest of the pride. After a while a large lioness came over, and I noticed that she licked its wounds. Lions do not always win, and sometimes they have quite a hard time.

In a few days we were in among the buffalo and the lion of the Malagarasi. I once more thought a lot about the huge lion.

I was sure I'd see it again. We had all missed the beautiful Selous country very much indeed. With its rolling hills and placid lakes at the eastern end, and the plains and gladelike openings going down to the great river at the western end, it was truly beautiful.

As we flew in to the camp airstrip, we viewed the thousands upon thousands of buffalo in and around the swamp. We also spotted some lions here and there. When we flew a little low, the lions always looked up but never ran away. The buffalo did not look up but always ran for cover. We must have seen at least a dozen sitatunga, grazing, skiing in the swamp, or basking in the sun on its edge. Yet when we hunted them there was never a one basking there.

As we drove into camp, we saw sable, roan, elephant, and signs of a leopard. It was encouraging. But the camp itself was dreary: a little opening in the *miombo* forest, letting down to the swamp. It improved after nightfall, with a good campfire burning and a loud chorus of animal grunts, squeals, roars, snorts, and trumpetings coming from the swamp and land around. With a good large whiskey in one's hand one felt one could face the night.

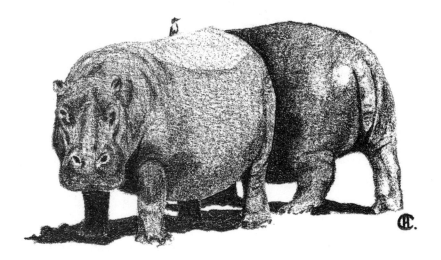

For the customers, we were keen for both Ben and Doc each to get a lion. For the rest, we needed a sitatunga or two, a sable, a roan maybe, and whatever came on offer. For myself, I wanted to find that lion. I wanted to know that it had not been a daydream, a hallucination; I wanted to be quite sure that it really existed. During time spent near the swamp, I slipped away whenever possible to look for my lion. It eluded me for quite a while.

Ben was very keen indeed to get a sitatunga. It was not going to be the easiest hunt for him. He was in for a real tough time: hour after hour, pulling his legs through water and thick water weeds, and always up to his knees, often up to his waist, and sometimes up to his neck. He worked hard for several hours, yet failed. He would stalk for half an hour, an hour, get close up on his quarry, only to hear it splash away.

"Bunny," he said, "I think I'm done. Those sitatungas want nothing of me."

But he gave it one more go, and we found a place where a little signaling helped a bit. We located some sitatungas in a spot where the swamp narrowed. This allowed Anton and me to sit on a bit of higher ground and watch the hunt going on across the swamp. We had arranged several specific signals by means of a small white flag. From our little high spot we had a very good view of the land down below and across. It took some time for Jens to get over there and in position. Meantime, we had covered the whole area very well and had seen two families of sitatunga. At last this seemed a real possibility for Ben to get his trophy. We all hoped so. He had worked hard enough.

We signaled across to Jens the position of the one big buck we had observed going into the tallish reeds. He caught on all right, being the bright Dane he is. He got Ben in a good position and then sent a couple of men in from behind. They were to try to beat the buck out of the reeds and toward or across Ben. It worked just that way.

Poor Ben had a very unsteady shot. Standing on floating weeds and reeds is hardly conducive to good shooting. Nevertheless, he hit the target good and solid, yet it went on and into the reeds before Ben could deliver the "coup." It took them another full hour to catch up with and collect the very wonderful trophy. While all this was going on, Anton and I could merely watch. It was the most enjoyable morning's hunting that had come my way for at least a couple of moons!

After that it was the lion—nothing but the lion—except that by now he was not just a lion. In my mind, he was Rufus, on account of his unusual coloring. Doc got himself a very good lion with a huge black mane. He was very proud of it, as well he should have been. It was a first-class trophy; he stalked it well and shot it expertly. But it was not Rufus. I was after Rufus. I couldn't find him; yet I knew he was there. At least once a day I spent about two hours scouting. I saw plenty of lions, but no Rufus. However, I did not give up hope. Everywhere Tabei and I found buffalo carcasses. The lions of these parts lived entirely on buff, and there was no shortage of them.

One evening in camp, Ben asked me, "What are you on, Bunny? We don't see you about much." And Doc followed up quippishly: "Yes, what goes on? Found some dancing girls?"

"How did you know, Doc? You're exactly right. And I hope to produce the dancing master, in the form of a great big monster lion, for Ben any time now."

It was magnificent to see Ben's eyes light up with expectancy. We all knew that he so much wanted to get a good, a really good, lion. I said, "Ben, give me a couple more days; be patient. Tomorrow I want to take Anton, with his keen eyes, to help me. I know where to go. I want his eyes to ferret him out."

And that is exactly how it happened. The next day, we found Rufus.

Anton and I used a combination of safari car and walking, and we climbed every bit of slightly higher ground. We took the whole morning, glassing every bit of open country we came across. Finally we came to what appeared to be the end of the swamp. The *miombo* forest came right down to the water's edge on a slight knoll. From this knoll we sighted Rufus! Anton got him. By sheer luck he was sitting on top of a large anthill, way off in the distance. After watching him for a few moments, Anton said: "He's got his family below him. I can see at least six."

In a short while my eyes were on Rufus, too. I was delighted to see at least a couple of youngish lions ready to step into Rufus's shoes, should we take him. As we trudged back to the car, tired but satisfied with our efforts, Anton remarked: "I say, what a lion. There can't be many like him. He's colossal."

On our way back to camp we must have come across the remains of about a dozen buffalo, all very recently killed by lions. Over and above these were old and new buffalo bones in all directions. Even so, there were thousands of buffalo, wherever one looked. The larder was not going to be bare for quite a while.

The next morning, after a good breakfast, we set off for Rufus. It was quite a long way and extremely slow going. Having reached the *miombo* forest promontory, we all got out—I say "all" because we were quite a party: Ben, Anton, myself, Tabei, and three other assistants. And how grateful I was for those three other assistants. We could have done with three more!

At the promontory, we glassed the swamplands in all directions. Some of us were up trees, the better to get a view. But alas! No Rufus in sight. After a slight discussion, we decided to make the promontory our headquarters, leaving two men there to continue to watch. They were to keep in constant visual contact with us, in case we wanted them to come along behind, or even to join us.

We then proceeded over the completely uneven ground—sometimes through water, sometimes through mud; into ditchlike holes, and over mounds and anthills. There was never one piece of level going. It was hard work, and very slow. From time to time there would be the snort of a lone bull buffalo as it shot off from us into the swamp, the grunt of pigs, and once the whistle of a sitatunga announcing its departure. But up to this time, not a sign, not a sound, of Rufus. We were standing on a completely dry piece of ground with a view of at least half a mile all around us when, from way down the swamp verge, came the most colossal roar of a lion. It was tremendous. The ground, in fact the very hummock on which we rested, fairly reverberated beneath us. We were on our feet in that same moment, while the ground still shook. I said: "That has to be Rufus!"

Meantime, that ever-seeking Tabei had climbed another hummock a few yards away and was looking intently into the distance. I watched him as he gently lowered his glasses, came down toward me, and with a smiling face, said: "Bwana, he is there." He pointed: "He is there."

Anton was up on Tabei's hummock at once. He looked quickly, nodded to me, and motioned with his hands to let me know that Rufus was coming in our direction. We all advanced slowly, with great caution, and before very long we could see the great Rufus and his family. There were six or eight others with him, but he stood out head and shoulders above them all. It was

249

apparent that there was a family argument going on: grunts and howls, screeches and rows. Twice I saw Rufus make a rapid advance on one member of his family—he appeared to be an up-and-coming young son—to dole out a handful of claws. This was accompanied by a great yowl of pain.

Rufus did not appear to be in the best of tempers. A very few minutes later, Ben was able to draw a good bead on him, at about two hundred yards. Ben made no mistake. He got him good and square in the heart. Rufus rushed off for fifty yards, stopped and stood, to make one great roar of defiance in defeat. Then he toppled into a majestic silence. We kept completely quiet, including our Africans. We had just witnessed the fall of a king.

We went up to him. He was no optical illusion. He must have been the biggest lion that ever existed. We measured him to stand 6 feet, 6 inches at the top of the shoulders—that is, the height of the withers on a horse. His body coloring was a golden red and his mane rufous red, as were the great tufts of hair from his elbows.

Then we moved round to study his huge sun of a head, also surmounted with long rufous red hair. This had tumbled over his forehead and eyes. I was intrigued. I wanted to know that this was the lion of the buffalo battle of several weeks ago. I was certain he was, but I swept the hair back from his forehead and then I was sure. He had a swelling on the middle of his forehead the size of an ostrich egg. This was full to the bursting point with pus. God! That must have caused a great headache for poor old Rufus. No wonder he was so bad-tempered!

Back in camp, when the skinner got to work, we found that there was also a large crack in the skull bone. The bull buffalo had left its mark, and the gallant Rufus had not been much longer for this world. Ben felt better. We all felt that this had turned out a "mercy killing."

Ben started to smile again. He talked about the lion: "My, what a size. Ain't he a dandy, though. What d'you reckon he'll weigh, Bunny?"

I'd already thought about that. His legs were as thick as a buffalo's. He had almost a four-foot chest depth, a huge head, and feet the size of pudding plates. "My guess is 800 pounds," I answered. Of course, we never did ascertain his actual weight. All we knew was that he must have been one of the heaviest lions that ever roamed Africa. And one of the handsomest.

The sad part of Ben's lion was that he never did get it! Somewhere along the line between East Africa and Dallas, Texas, someone had made a change of trophies. The lion I saw in Ben's trophy room a year or so later certainly was not Rufus. There are some very mean people in this world. The more I know of people, the better I love lions.

Note to the reader: Just after the time of this writing, on 22 July 1983, my wonderful gunbearer and friend, Tabei Arap Tilmet, died. He had appeared as buoyant and full of life as usual. We had taken a walk together along the beach to see how some work was progressing. He then repaired the lawn mower in order to be able to mow the lawn—the lawn of which he was so rightly proud. A little later, I saw him erecting some shades over recently planted citrus trees. Late in the afternoon he complained of stomach pains. He was in great pain. I massaged him, which seemed to give some relief. We put him to bed

with a hot-water bottle on his stomach. I gave him milk to drink. That appeared to soothe him, and he appeared to be better as night fell.

In the morning, Mwenji told me that Tabei was just about the same but wanted some tea. By the time that was taken to him, Tabei was on his way to the happier hunting grounds. I closed his wonderful eyes and we buried him under a tamarind tree.

Tabei had always been my right-hand man. He so often was my eyes; continually he was my sixth sense. His judgment saved me time and time again, and his humor salvaged many an awkward situation. After so many years—over fifty—to say I miss him is an understatement.

I can fairly say that if my hunting life has been any measure of success, it has been so to a large extent because of Tabei's help and guidance. He had the heart of a lion, the strength of a buffalo, and the demeanor of a gentleman.

After Tabei died, one of his sons took over the job as my gunbearer. His name is Kipchoge Orkip.

ne particular hunt was rather a sentimental journey for me. In 1947, I had had the pleasure of escorting several American millionaires on a safari. One of the men employed on that trip was a splendid young white hunter named Owen McCallum. I rather took him under my wing, and we got along fine. We teamed up and were a success. Several times after that Owen worked with me. It was always a pleasure for me and always a good safari. Sadly, after a few years, he became ill, suffering from some wretched malignant disease. Nothing could be done for him. Those who knew him missed him very much. Thankfully, he had some children to carry on his good work. One of his sons, Danny, helped me on this elephant hunt. Like his father, Danny was a charmer as well as a good hunter.

On this hunt we had two clients from the Midwest, but I can't remember their names. I just remember Danny and one particular elephant—Danny because he was such a splendid man, and the elephant because it led me to some delicious wild fruit. The customers were not the nicest in the world, and not the easiest.

Danny was so good, so patient with them, that he took a great load off my shoulders. All I could think of was to get the safari done with so we could all go home.

We were camped on the Tana River within thirty or forty miles of its estuary into the Indian Ocean. It was a nice shady camp, and with pleasant customers we would have had an enjoyable time. Anyway, Danny knew my feelings, so he realized that I wanted to get the safari over and done with. It was just a matter of getting two "good enough" elephants. We both agreed that the one man (call him Bill) was a better chap than the other (I won't mention what we called him!); consequently, we hoped Bill would get the better jumbo.

Danny took turns with me in taking the men out, yet for three days we saw nothing but herds of cows and calves with an occasional "toothpick" of a bull accompanying them. However, the clients got in some good bird shooting, including some splendid wild duck, so we did not starve. We also had the luck to come across a Galla lady tilling her acre. She sweetly produced some beans very like peas, some mint to go with them, and herbs strangely like sage. Thus we did not lack for stuffing. Bread and onions, of course, we had in camp. Good food was the only saving grace of the safari, so far as I was concerned.

After that third empty day, I got hold of Danny and said, "Look, Danny, something's got to be done; I can't stand much more of this . . . of them."

Danny nodded his head. "You're right; but what can we do to hustle the hunt?"

"Well, I tell you what; I'm going to burst into some new country. I'll go along the Lamu road and strike into the bush toward the coast."

The next morning I set off with Bill's friend on what I intended to be just a prospecting journey to see how the country lay. But, as so often happens, surprise smashed all our plans. Each of the men got an elephant that day, and of course it had to be the dreadful one who got the bigger jumbo!

We had gone down the road toward Lamu only a few miles, then turned off onto a little track into the bushland created by the charcoal burners. Less than a mile down the track we saw a large gray leg disappearing into the bush about two hundred yards from us. We advanced swiftly yet quietly and soon heard the tearing of leaf and limb from the trees. Our elephant was feeding and obviously enjoying its eats. Almost at once we saw its massive grayness reaching into a tallish tree and pulling down what appeared to be a vine covered in luscious fruit. The elephant appeared, in fact was, quite unaware of us. In looking at its tusks, I was able to catch the look in its eye. It was one of absolute ecstasy.

It was bad luck for the poor old jumbo that it had a very fine pair of tusks. But I'll say that it had a very glorious five or six final minutes. The fruit was simply wonderful. It was on a vine and looked like a smooth-skinned litchi, and tasted much the same. We harvested and took back to camp all that the elephant had left behind. It was the brightest thing about the whole safari.

✕ ✕ ✕ ✕ ✕

Shortly afterward, I was in the company of the highly amusing Stach Sapeiha, that splendid and dashing prince of Poland, or Lithuania, or some such fairy-tale place. Stach had a house on Lamu Island that he visited from time to time in order to get away from the clamor of Nairobi. He was a good hunter and had done several safaris with my customers—always, I might add, with success, and leaving a pleasant taste in everyone's mouth. And that, I can tell you, is no mean achievement. I believe that the secret of his success was his tremendous sense of humor. Not only could he laugh with the best of them, but also he could laugh with the worst of them. And that, if you follow the implication, is a passport to success.

Our safari was supposedly for elephant; we both had licenses to expend. As an elephant hunt it was a complete flop, but as a full-of-fun little trip it was an unqualified success. It rained and it poured every sort of wetness out of the sky. None of the tracks off the main Lamu-Garsen highways could we use, and oftentimes the highway was out. Yet, one way and the other, we thoroughly enjoyed ourselves, and laughter in camp was nonstop.

We parked just off the main track, under some friendly but wet, bushy trees. We walked day after day in different directions, looking for the elusive elephant. We never once went together. We each of us had our hunches and followed them. They never worked. The clever old jumbos were always a move ahead of us. But, no matter, we enjoyed ourselves, and we did not come back empty-handed. We brought home several lovely desert rose plants and several sacks of fine runner grass, and we had full bellies. The desert roses went into, and further beautified, our respective gardens. The runner grass was the start of our lawns, and I can tell you now that those lawns have to be seen to be believed. They could be some of those running down to the verge of the Thames from beautiful houses at Maidenhead. So, how's that? No ivory but lovely lawns?

And we ate well. Stach was mighty fine with his shotgun and kept us always in birds—snipe, quail, duck, and guinea. I brought home wild asparagus, wild spinach, wild sage, mint, and thyme, together with a little type of crab apple (called *kunasi*) and a portion or two of the fabulous wild litchi. Then was the famous day, in fact the only day, I saw elephant, when I also saw a field of mushrooms. I left the elephant and took the mushrooms. I brought back to camp three kilos of mushrooms, all about the size of the old English half-crown. They were magnificent. As luck would have it, they coincided with Stach's bringing in half a dozen splendid quail. I will always remember the look of ecstasy on Stach's face as he smelled, from the kitchen, the aroma of the mushrooms cooking. The meal that followed was worth a dozen jumbo tusks! It was a meal fit for princes.

In after days, Stach and I always referred to that elephant jaunt of ours as the si-pare safari. The African appears to have a marked dislike for words of a single syllable. Thus they don't like the word "spare"; they prefer to say si-pare. I had always noticed that fact, but Stach had not until I continually used the word on this safari. In fact, seeing how the probability of our getting elephant was so remote, I began referring to them as completely si-pare to our safari. To tell the truth, for myself, I really gave up looking for them after only two days.

But I had some lovely walks, saw hundreds of buffalo and a few very silky-coated lion, and (this was the biggest treasure of all) found the wonderful previously mentioned grass. It was in thick riverine forest, where little glades opened up here and there. There was grass growing in great profusion and cropped so close by the buffalo as to resemble a well-kept lawn. And I can tell you this: There are not many grasses that will grow out of plain sand. This one did, and does. It also grows in the deepest shade. The value and the pleasure of my lawn have well repaid me for my going to bed with two elephant licenses.

Also, as a further benefit from the si-pare safari, I was able to discover several camping sites for future short safaris and get an idea for a semipermanent camp. Both these possibilities had been building up in my gray matter for some time. In fact, I had already been approached by a Lamu hotelier to take out some of his visitors on bird-shooting and other short safaris. And I thought that, in conjunction with these, I could also use a permanent type of camp as my base. I wanted it to be on the seashore, with a good beach, in pleasant country, and with wild game about. Any other "game"

I'd take there myself! In my own mind, I rather thought of it as "Bunny Allen's last stand."

With these ideas in mind, I started to get the whole thing organized. I found two or three nice campsites. Also I found an exquisite camping area on the beach. This was adjacent to some old ruins from bygone days. One of these was the perfectly lovely remains of a little coral-pink mosque. It was a real gem of a place, called by the local fishermen *Moskiti Wanali Sabaa*. Apparently, in the bad old days of about 100 or 150 years ago, the raiding Wagalla from southern Abyssinia constantly caused havoc amongst the Swahili people living on the coast. On one famous raid, the locals hid seven very valued little virgins in this mosque; they escaped unharmed. From that day the place was known as the Mosque of the Seven Virgins. Thus when the time came to make my camp nearby, what other name could I give it but Virgin's Camp? Even though I stipulated that all girls of that category could come to the camp free of charge, I cannot recall one application!

I gathered that the majority of people coming on these hotel hunts would be Italian. It seemed that I'd need an Italian-speaking helper in the camp. By sheer good fortune, I found that the Comtessa Sieuwke Biseliti was staying from time to time in her house on Lamu Island. Somewhat against her will, I managed to persuade her to help me on these hunts when she was able to do so. She was a real godsend. Quite apart from the language, she was so good and sweet with the clients in every way. Sieuwke made my work much easier, and she was such a lovely companion.

I remember one occasion when we had slipped down a little pathway to have a dip in the sea. While we were besporting ourselves in the water, Sieuwke suddenly looked up the path, and there was a giant maned lion, sitting on its haunches looking at us. It was a fine sight and made our swim so much the better.

Mind you, Sieuwke had a close affinity with lions. After all, she did so much handling of them for the Elsa pictures, and had bred lions for years.

I had several very amusing safaris with our Italian friends shooting birds, and Sieuwke made the whole thing understandable. But I'll say one thing: You had to keep your weather eye on those sporting Italians. They shot at anything that got up, from a canary to a marabou stork. I will always remember one of those Italian safaris for its three elements of humor, danger, and satisfaction.

This particular safari started off for a party of five, including a man and his wife. They were just bird shooting. The dear Sieuwke and her charming nephew

H.CLAASSENS.

were helping to make the show a great success. Then the married couple, Adolfo and Clementina Delecto, one day saw a herd of buffalo. That was it! He immediately wanted to get one, and in this desire he was very definitely egged on by Clementina: "Si, si, 'Dolfo, get one for me."

"It is possible?" asked 'Dolfo.

Through Sieuwke, I told him that it would be possible; they'd have to stay on a few days longer and we might have to move camp. So it was all arranged. Unfortunately, Sieuwke could not stay on for the buffalo hunt—she had a job to do in Lamu. I would have to manage alone with regard to the Italian language.

This tale of 'Dolfo, Clementina, and the buffalo is really about the safari ants that joined us. The wretched *siafu* almost always have a certain part to play in any safari. In this one, they produced a little humor, considerable annoyance, and a splash of danger. There was everything: from the initial tickling nip, through the infuriating pain of mass bites, and, finally, to the surprising climax with a modicum of fear. However, all that came at the tail end of the safari.

When Sieuwke left, I got a young English army officer, Nick, who was on leave in Lamu, to join us. I felt I had to have someone I could talk to! Both 'Dolfo's and Clementina's knowledge of the English tongue was minimal, and my knowledge of Italian was about the same. The episode of the safari ants, I must say, caused at least Clementina and me to have a much better understanding of each other.

We set off from the original bird-shooting camp for a spot where I had often found buffalo. Sure enough, there they were, fifty or sixty of them, with a nice bull in the middle. Leaving Clementina and Nick under a shady bush, I advanced with 'Dolfo to within seventy yards of the little herd. We hid behind some tall grass as I pointed out the bull. The splendid 'Dolfo took aim and shot . . . and wounded a cow! I of course made him follow it. After quite a chase we finished it off. He still had no trophy, and I should have left it at that. But no, we went on, collected Clementina and Nick, and followed the buffalo into a piece of riverine forest.

As we went up a slight incline, I signaled 'Dolfo to stay put while I went a yard or two up the slope. Then things happened— fast! A buffalo suddenly appeared and I crouched down, apparently giving the good 'Dolfo a fine view of him between my widened legs. That was too much for 'Dolfo. He let fly at the buff, using my bowed legs as a foresight. Thankfully, he missed everything—the buff by a wide margin, and my precious parts by a narrower margin. I was aware of the heat of the bullet as it went past.

I turned to study the little group behind me, as Tabei gave me a sort of gentle shake to check on me. My smile assured him that his bwana was in one piece. 'Dolfo stood there looking a little puzzled—nothing more. Nick, standing with Clementina slightly behind, was shaking his head from side to side in disbelief. Finally, there was Clementina. She had her legs tightly wound together, almost twisting one on the other, with her hands clasped in front as if in protection. Her eyes were working overtime, trying to open wider than possible.

We followed the buffalo spoor for a while. There was not a spot of blood. The buff had gotten clear away. Both it and I were lucky. Dear 'Dolfo never did make any form of apology to me. I'm sure that he did not realize what he had done. That is what Nick thought, too. As we left the forest to go back to the car, Nick said: "By Jove, that was close, Bunny. I thought he was trying to de-man you!" He laughed as he added: "But do you know, I'm sure, with his one eye closed, he didn't even see you. You know, in the heat of the moment."

We had a bird shoot that same evening, after we had all had a restful afternoon. The following morning Nick had to go back to Lamu. Somewhat like a fool, I suggested to 'Dolfo and Clementina that we go to a camp on the Tana River and have a final crack at buffalo. After a great struggle in broken English and fractured Italian, I put this across to my clients. Why I was so keen to do this I really can't say—or can I? It was, maybe, partly the fact that I did not want to be a failure in getting a buffalo for 'Dolfo (although he certainly had thrown away his chances and did not deserve one); it could also have been that thoughts of Clementina urged me on. The end was all very sudden and very unexpected and, for some of us, very successful. The safari ants—bless them—arrived.

Whilst we were setting up this camp, some of the camp staff got set on by safari ants, and with great hoots of pain two of them set off speedily and jumped in the nearby water. They were soon out again, having washed off the *siafu*, and great laughter ensued from one and all. I then carried out a thorough inspection of the spot where I intended putting up the clients' tent. Not a sign of *siafu*. So up it went. Meantime, the watchful Tabei had seen a nice big bull buffalo go into the bush right near our camp, alongside a pool of inland flood water. We quickly got organized, and I took 'Dolfo around to the far side of the bushes. However, before I left, I placed Clementina on a little hillock, with a bush cover, put a .300 with a solid bullet in her hand, pointed to the bush, and pointed to the middle of my forehead. She caught on all right; she was a quick-witted girl. I left a reliable gunbearer with her, and I knew that if she had the good fortune to get a shot, I would be with her the next moment. Also, her position on the hillock was quite safe. At this stage, my thinking was that 'Dolfo's unsteadiness might yet again wreck the chances of obtaining a buffalo trophy. Little Clementina, in her secure position, was another string to the bow, however. How right I was!

Tabei, 'Dolfo, and I crept into the thickish shrubbery, having noted that the lazy bull had not come out. It was in there, and in fact the very next moment we heard it tossing its head and swishing its tail as it browsed. I halted Tabei, and turning to 'Dolfo I pointed to the front of my head and then the side, indicating that he'd have to take the brain shot. He nodded his understanding, and I led him on, foot by foot, through the bushes. I then pushed 'Dolfo ahead of me on the very narrow path. There was just not room for the two of us. At that precise moment the buffalo threw its head in the air, and, I must say, 'Dolfo wasted no time. There was a bang from his rifle, a bellow of rage from the bull, and then a crashing of brush. This was followed by a shot from Clementina. The buffalo crashed into the bush, and the next moment we saw the old buff, down and out. Clementina came running hand in hand with her escort, making Italian whoops of joy.

They had got their buffalo.

By the time the congratulatory kisses were done with, the light was fading from the sky. I called over the skinners from the camp, which was just across the bend in the river. Tabei and the other help had, in fact, already put their knives to work. They were going to take just the head and the front feet that evening. The rest we would see about in the morning.

For the time being all was happiness in the camp. After several failures, they had their buffalo. It did not matter that it had been a shot from Clementina that did the job. Poor 'Dolfo had merely taken a slice off the buffalo's boss and caused it a nasty headache. However, I did not point that out to 'Dolfo. I saw no need. Everyone was satisfied. That's all that mattered. We had a drink or two. We all toasted one another. We had a nice meal, and very soon we went to bed, tired out and ready for sleep.

I cannot say at what time the disturbance took place, but it was certainly after the camp staff had dropped off into their slumbers. And I must point out that they were sleeping about fifty yards away from our tents. I was first aware of a call for help and then an agonizing scream from the clients' tent. It could be nothing else. It had to be safari ants! I had heard that cry before. I was out of my bed in a sleepy flash, girded a *kikoi* around my loins, seized a flashlight, and ran to find 'Dolfo and Clementina already at the entrance to their tent. They were quite a sight: he without a stitch on and simply covered in *siafu*, and she with the flimsiest raiment about her waist, also with a covering of ants.

'Dolfo, with an agonized thrashing of hands about his body, and a distressing cry of *Prego, PREGO,* burst past me and headed for the water, just as he had seen the Africans do earlier in the day. Meantime, I had a simpering Clementina on my hands. I immediately reached for a kerosene lantern from the verandah table, tipped kerosene into my hands, and quickly rubbed it as gently as possible onto the affected parts. I asked Clementina to hold the flashlight so I could do the job better. By now she had discarded the *kanga* from her waist and was hopping from one foot to the other as the wretched *siafu* nipped her in her most private places. The kerosene served good purpose and Clementina was pretty well cleaned of the damned insects, but I noticed that the floor of the tent was rapidly filling up with them once again. I seized her hand, pointed to my tent, and away we ran.

My tent was completely free. Once in the tent I carried out another search on Clementina and picked off what I thought was the lot. She meantime flicked a few off her pretty breasts. Then she uttered one more excruciating yell of pain as she brushed away at her pubic hairs. Now it was her turn to plead, "*Prego, prego—prego*, Bunny," as she pointed to the affected quarter. She sat on, then lay back onto, the bed, the better to allow me to search out the offending *siafu*. I then had to hold the torch with one hand while with the other I searched. Eventually I found what had to be the absolutely biggest ant, feasting itself at the very entrance of her "delicacy." It must have been painful. I got hold of the ant and yanked it out rather too quickly, with the result that the head got left in! I had to fumble and feel to complete the job. But by now the pain had disappeared from Clementina's face. In its place was a look of expectancy. And the expected is exactly what happened.

A plaintive cry coming from the river, "Bonny— Clementina—*prego-pre-ego*," broke into our idyll. I must say that little Clementina quickly came back to reality. She was out of bed in a flash, found the torch, found a *kikoi* to drape round her—all before I did a thing! Then, I was ready with a *kikoi* girded round my own loins and a flashlight in my hand. My other hand seized a hand of Clementina's, and we ran toward 'Dolfo. We soon had him in the beam of the light, splashing around in the water.

Apparently, in his wanderings to get rid of the *siafu*, which took him some time, he had gotten stuck in some thick, deep mud, and he was anchored there. As we walked down to get closer to him, I heard a splash in the water up toward the buffalo carcass. I turned the flashlight in that direction. Three tremendous crocodiles were in view: two feeding on the buffalo and the third swimming toward us. A terrified sort of groan came from 'Dolfo, "*Oh-h-h—uggh—oh-h.*"

I turned my hurried attention back to him, whilst poor Clementina wrung her hands and took another undecided step toward her husband. I grabbed her and pulled her back. I couldn't afford to have the pair of them stuck in there! I could not reach 'Dolfo with my hand. I tore my kikoi from around me and flung one end to him. He caught hold, and from my firm foothold I managed to pull him out, foot by foot.

It was quite sweet and fetching to see the reunion of Clementina and 'Dolfo. They had been hurriedly separated, each on a rather different sort of little safari. Now they were together again, and nothing else mattered.

I have often had the occasion to wonder, though, exactly what would have happened if the buffalo remains had not been there.

Chapter 25

A Virgin's Camp

or the next few months, I kept myself fairly busy doing shortish safaris—of never more than two weeks' duration—either on the coast or adjacent to the river. I was never more than eighty miles from Lamu Island. During this time I had some successful hunts with some charming people and a lot of laughter and fun. Also over this period I gave thought to Virgin's Camp, and in fact gradually built upon it.

Funnily enough, two of the first girls to use the camp probably qualified genuinely for a "free seat"! It happened thus: I was going on a gentle jumbo jolly with Peter Mann Jones. We each had elephant licenses and we could afford a few days to expend them, if possible. Also we could fish, play around on the Tana, and maybe get a crocodile or two. Two rather sweet young maids who were staying with friends and relations heard that I was going and asked if they could come, too. Of course I said: "Yes"— rather too quickly, methinks. The two young maids conferred together slightly aside from me, then they stepped forward and the one said, a little shyly, yet firmly: "Oh, Bunny, we do want you to understand that we are coming to see elephants—we don't want you to think—"

I cut in here. "Yes, yes, don't you worry. In any case, you are coming as free guests. You have to pay to get extra treatment!" We all three of us laughed, and the bargain was sealed. Each night I gave them a kiss as they toddled off to bed. No harm was done, and I know they enjoyed themselves. For several days we walked them in and out of elephant in good open country. We did not shoot any. We were looking for seventy- or eighty-pounders; all those we saw were around fifty. They also saw Peter make a very good shot on a crocodile, right from our campsite. Caroline and Lovelace were returned to "store" as good as new. They still talk of the nice adventure, and so do I.

Shortly after I got home I was delighted to have a letter from my son David, asking me to join his safari the following week. He and Anton were bringing a hunting party from Vienna to camp only a few miles inland from Lamu. So I jumped into the work Jeri had awaiting me at home, and then she packed me up in her efficient way to send me off with her blessing. My faithful Tabei, of course, accompanied me, and within fifty miles we found the camp.

It was sign-posted in the usual safari way, with a cut limb of a bush here and a blazed tree there. It proved a very pretty spot, right on the edge of a large water hole, full of clear water and clumps of woodland all around. However, it was not far removed from the country where I had come across the poachers a year or so earlier. I pointed this out to David. He was quite assured in his reply: "Oh, I think it is all right. We are just keeping to the south of the main track."

"Well, in that case you should be safe enough. Just tell everyone to keep his eyes open."

They had a very jolly party out: Franzie and Hanii Krummel, a couple of their friends, and a chap from Munich who, because he was a very good photographer, quite often got a free ride on these trips. His name was Emil, and we all had known him for some years. All told, they were a nice lot. I got particularly fond of Hanii and Franzie. They were a happy couple. There was a laugh a minute.

Elephant were in great numbers, but it was hard to find a good tusker. A big moon got up and gave us great entertainment as the elephants came down to the water. We tucked ourselves in the trees and bushes, while the elephants were in a light almost as bright as morning. Certainly, we spotted for a big elephant, but we glowed at the antics. It was a marvelous performance. They were positively playing games, and each night for five nights we watched them. The waxing moon was just right for us. The finale was at the full of the moon. We had to walk only five minutes from our campfire to take our positions in and around the trees and bushes. Luckily the wind was very steadily in our favor.

We went in little groups here and there, more or less aimlessly, yet sometimes by design. Usually Hanii was there to hold my hand. She was a very sweet little companion, and we had a good understanding. In the full moon, Tabei's watchful eyes had seen a rather larger than usual movement of elephant at the far end of the pool. I got hold of Anton, who happened to be quite close, and whispered: "I'm off over there a bit; Tabei has spotted something." I pointed away to the left. Anton nodded his understanding.

As I left with Tabei, a hand took mine. It was Hanii's. I was expecting it. We took ourselves into the shadows, by a convenient fold in the ground, and got quite close to the new lot of elephants. Most of these were actually in the water, having a real frolic, but a few were still up on land. Suddenly, the clever little Hanii pressed my hand and pointed still farther to the left. And there had to be the elephant Franzi was looking for. It stood out, head and shoulders above the rest. It was an absolutely tremendous fellow, and, true to form, some of its pals were zealously guarding it, in fact, completely surrounding it. So much so, in fact, that up to this point I had not seen its ivory.

I think I'll go further—I know that this was the tallest elephant that I have ever seen. Surrounded by others, it started slowly moving down to the water. Every now and then I'd seen a flash of ivory in the moonlight. The three of us were kneeling down, enjoying every moment of this thrilling spectacle.

A delicious little mouth awakened my ear. It whispered: "It is *wunderbar.*" I nodded a "*Ja*" as we looked again. Now they were at the water. Our big fellow, still covered up, was drinking thirstily. Then suddenly, I saw a great gleam of white ivory. It was long; it was thick. This was the one for Franzi. I exchanged a smile with Hanii as I stuck both my thumbs in the air.

At that very moment, I heard Tabei clucking his tongue. Looking quickly at him, I saw him shaking his head to and fro as a moonlit smile creased his face. Something was wrong! I looked again at our elephant. There it was, standing quite alone in the bright full moon, its head held high for all to see. It was proudly defiant, as well it might be. It stood head and shoulders above those about it. All its strength had gone into its enormous body. It will go on living forever. It hadn't got a tusk in its head!

Of course, I had seen a few tuskless bulls in the past, and positively dozens of tuskless cows, but never before had I seen such a huge animal. The tusks I saw in the moonlight must have been those of another animal—probably a cow: that, and moon, and probably a bit of blissful thinking! But now the fairy story was over. Reality had returned, and we retired to the dinner table.

✕ ✕ ✕ ✕ ✕

Hunting bongo is always very difficult, hard going, and physically exhausting: up hill and down dale, through ice-cold mountain streams and thick bamboo, never knowing when you are going to be confronted by either an irate elephant or a snorting rhino. And even though the "experts" say we are running out of rhino, in bongo country there is always a rhino around one corner or the next—or lying in wait.

On one particular safari, as I recall, however, we had no trouble in getting a bongo. In fact, three clients each got a bongo in one morning!

It was not at all like hunting bongo in Kenya. It was like hunting bongo in the Sudan, where, certainly, they can be a lot easier. There they are of a somewhat different type, rather smaller and lighter in color.

My two sons, David and Anton, Jens Hessel, and I were in the same camp in which I had entertained Abie and Babie some years previously. We had left camp after a hunter's breakfast and advanced up into the Aberdare Mountains. After a mile or so, the valley we were following split in two. Consequently, the hunting party split also. Two clients followed the bigger valley and one the smaller. Where possible, and for the most part, each party kept to one ridge of the valley. Yet owing to the heavy bosky cover, from time to time they were forced down to proceed along the valley bottom. It was heavy going, but the hunters were young men, and there were no elephant, no rhino, and no buffalo. All they encountered was one giant forest hog. It came, snorting, rushing out of the herbage beside a stream. The charge scattered a hunter or two in its path without harm to man or beast, and then the hog continued, at a trot, up the incline of the valley. Unbeknownst to us, and to the hog, it was heading straight for a herd of bongo, grazing in a small forest glade. We heard the joyful noise of them as they whistled in alarm upon the arrival of the hog. We heard the distinct, yet light, pounding of their hooves as they broke and ran—then a forest silence. When we told the clients what was going on, their faces lit up and the hunt was on.

271

Kip, one of the gunbearers, got the bit between his teeth and hurried along up the slippery forest path. He and another sharp-eyed gunbearer went ahead to get a clue or two if possible. They awaited us in the pretty glade, with forest on one side, bamboo on the other, the icy stream in the middle, and verdant grazing all around. There were steaming telltale bongo droppings, a sight heartwarming to the hunter.

Kip had made a rapid assessment: He held up the fingers of one hand plus two from the second—seven bongo. A nice little group. We pressed on quietly yet urgently. At the top of the ridge the forest thinned considerably. We could see patches of open grassland both on our ridge and on the ridge that David and his client were hunting.

As we searched these little grass patches, we suddenly became aware of the clash of horns, not far from us but out of sight. Then a fine sight met our eyes. A fight was on between two bucks, one a fine big master and the other an up-and-coming male who had obviously poked his nose a little too far into forbidden territory and was now being disciplined—or that was the idea! In actual fact, he was having the best of the duel. He had already gored the big fellow quite badly and was now definitely on the offensive. As he who had been king backed away and turned to run, he was laid low by one of our clients. It was a splendid trophy and one presented on a hot plate, so to speak. Almost at the same moment, we heard a single shot from David's ridge. Could it be another bongo? It was.

As yet it was only about 11 A.M., so we bashed on. "Follow luck," said Anton, and on we went. One, two; and in the third grass glade awaited a bongo. We collected it, and one can safely say that never again will three bongo fall so quickly and with so little effort.

Chapter 26

Two Beauties

I really looked forward to my next safari. It was for Ervine Nutter of Xenia, Ohio. I had met him at one of the San Antonio conferences. He had not hunted in Kenya before, but he had hunted in various other parts of Africa as well as many parts of the world. He had a great desire to get a big elephant. His previous elephant hunts had proved unsatisfactory, I gathered. I think he had always hunted them in thickish bush country where one often has to shoot the animal before even having a good look at it.

Anyway, I told Erv that I could take him into kinder country where he would be able to see all right. I certainly did not guarantee that he would get a big elephant, but he would, at least, be in a big elephant locality. He also wanted to hunt a few other animals that he had not had a chance at before, such as lesser kudu, Grevy zebra, gerenuk, and Hunter antelope. To start with, we camped midway between Lamu and the Tana River. We had a very pleasant camp under giant mango trees, planted many years ago by the Arab slave traders, I have not a doubt.

Erv was a very pleasant companion, enjoying camp life to the fullest. He did not have just a sole object in mind—collecting a trophy. He also loved sitting in camp, watching the birds and listening to their song. He wanted to talk about my experiences in the bush, both with the wild beasties and the humans. We spent hours in this manner. We had a lot of laughs as we swapped hunting experiences. Of course, he touched on the safari romance side of things, but when he realized I was not to be drawn out on the subject, he did not pursue it.

I agreed with him, however, that such things did go on. As indeed they did. And how lovely they were. Those loving days, and loving nights. Saying "Good night," knowing you would meet again in the morning. And I believe that those romances seldom caused any hurt to anyone. Certainly some of them developed into something more permanent. Well, if that happened, and it broke up some other linkage, it probably meant that the previous arrangement was already rusty at the joints! I always found that the golden rule in this kind of thing is to keep quiet and don't talk. Talking about it "does more harm than doing it." And never be drawn into talking of personalities. Whenever a name is mentioned, I shut up like a clam.

Well, Erv and I did a lot of chattering and a lot of laughing without being unkind to anyone. We also did a lot of hunting— we had to. That particular year there appeared to be herds and herds of cow elephants, all up and down the Tana River. For many days we were in and out of these herds, looking for a shootable bull. It was exciting, but we failed. Then one evening, in perfect country, we saw a bull on the edge of a small herd. It looked to me a seventy- or eighty-pounder, with very pretty tusks. Erv wanted to take it, but the bull was about 120 yards away and I didn't like him to risk the shot.

Anyway, soon the bull was on the move into the bush, over the hill, and away. He had got our wind. Erv a little ruefully remarked: "I could have taken him." "Maybe," I replied, "but that was a tricky shot."

In retrospect, I feel that Erv very well might have gotten the bull, but at that stage I did not know what a good shot he was. He proved his shooting ability on the Hunter, the Grevy, and the lesser kudu—all long shots, and, on the Hunter and kudu, running shots. But the milk was spilt; it was no use crying about it. Anyway, at that stage of the hunt, with still quite a few days to go, I think my sights were set on a rather heavier tusker for Erv. It was later, when we were running out of time, that we settled for a 60-pounder. However, it was a really exciting hunt and, I believe, an eye-opener to Erv. He did not realize how close one can get to an elephant.

The one in question came strolling toward us in fairly open bush country. It was cropping odd succulent bushes. I moved Erv up quietly to a nice thin cover of thorn trees and *swaki* (toothbrush bush). Tabei was meantime keeping a close watch on the wind, which luckily kept completely constant. The old bull was now no more than fifteen feet from us. I glanced at Erv. He was as steady as a rock, his eyes wide in anticipation and wonder. I knew that the "old man" would very soon have to go down, or else it would tread us into the ground! It paused for a moment to snip off a juicy piece of wild asparagus, and then took its last step toward us. Erv's shot was straight and true. Up to that point Erv had displayed no sign of excitement, but now, with the job done, he became quite warm with nervous reaction. "But Bunny, it was so close. . . . I had no idea you can get so near." He shook his head as he clicked his tongue.

Some little time after Erv's hunt, I met him in New York, together with his very attractive wife, Zoe Dell. We had a fine time together, followed up with a further meeting at the San Antonio Game Conference, and finally he sent me a ticket to fly out to his lovely home in Ohio. It is worth doing safari work if only for the wonderful people you meet and the fine friends you make.

During all this time, I was slowly building up Virgin's Camp and using it as a base for any safaris in that locale. I had one or two highly amusing ones—sometimes a little trying, but the laugh they created made them well worthwhile. These Virgin safaris were in the main for my friends. They paid their fee, but I did them so well from the point of view of both food and drink that I did not hope to make a million from the venture.

Quite a few of the people whom I had helped to build Arab-style houses at Lamu came out to see and stay a few days at Virgin. Everyone loved it, and we used to see quite a number of animals. One day, in the middle of the morning, a grand old man of a lion came to take a drink out of the birdbath! Then it sauntered down to the beach and went up it very slowly northward, grunting gently the while. It is an odd fact that the lions on the coastline never roar: nothing more than a rather subdued grunt. It is as though they do not wish to compete with the roar of the sea. The episode of the lion was one of the most unusual things that happened at Virgin. Actually, there was always something going on. Elephants were continually in and around the camp and on the beach—a waterbuck, a bushbuck, a warthog, and always a troop of baboons. Then again, at the right season, it was a great place for the turtles to nest: forty or fifty eggs in one nest, and here and there their great tracks, like a caterpillar tractor, as mother turtle herded her young to the sea.

While at Virgin I always expected and eagerly awaited a beautiful mermaid to offer herself, but, alas, I had to settle for the human. Shame on me, should I complain! I had no cause.

Some delightful people visited me at Virgin. I remember one most interesting girl from Chili. She turned up completely unexpectedly at Lamu, sent along by a mutual friend. As luck would have it, I was able to take her to the camp. She saw the lovely and lonely sandy beach stretching for miles in each direction, and she offered to dispense with her clothes and walk au naturel. With the glorious backing of golden sand, every shade of coral rock, and the patches of green and blue sea, my stripped nymph looked pretty good. She said: "Why not join me?"

"Right I will—half a mo."

I ran up to my *banda*, collected a pair of canvas gloves, and rejoined my Beauty on the beach. I pointed out to her the coral rock pools left by the tide, and then, in the "first stage of love," hand in hand, we proceeded on.

On the way, Beauty suddenly saw a pretty shell and bent down to examine it, and in doing so she presented her exquisite shape to me. It really was beautifully revealing. Back up to the erect posture, she must have seen the look in my eye. She said sweetly but firmly: "Say, Bunny, I do want you to realize that I'm not here on a—a little—you know?"

I finished her sentence for her: "You are not here on a little sexual jaunt. Is this right?"

277

"That's about it. Mind you, I'm loving it, but—I don't want to go—"

"Whole hog. All right, my Beauty. We'll just keep to the first stage of love, only 'hand in hand.' With that, I took her by the hand and we walked on to the coral pools. Once there I passed her the gloves and pointed to the lobsters swimming about, and in a trice she was in the pool catching our lunch. Beauty was quick on the uptake! In all she was a most pleasurable companion.

Taken all in all, I much enjoyed the stay at Virgin's Camp with Beauty. She was a clever girl. She talked well on many subjects, wrote well, and read very prettily. Also, she was a clever artist. She made some very nice sketches of the camp and the shoreline. Then, while I was writing and dreaming she made a sketch of me. It was too good. I said to her: "Beauty, it's wonderful—but it's not true. There's not a line on my face—I look twenty years old." She looked at me with a slightly crooked smile, then: "Hey, mister, I ain't finished!" She then completed her task. In a minute or so she passed the sketch me. The lines were there. I looked like a dried-up old prune! She was fun.

✕ ✕ ✕ ✕ ✕

Oh yes, I had all sorts at Virgin's. Well, perhaps not quite all sorts! But I had a great amount of interest, a lot of beauty, and plenty of laughs. I remember on one occasion I returned to our Lamu Island home, and Jeri greeted me on the doorstep with: "Bunny, you'll be tickled to death; I've got two lovely girls for you to take to Virgin's." There was not a wicked twinkle in her eye. It sounded genuine. "Tell me more, darling. When do they want to go? Are they paying customers? Do they get free seats? Or are they on the 'old friend' basis?"

Jeri picked up her little Yorkshire terriers, and each one nuzzled me a little as Jeri answered: "Well, as a fact you just might have to pay them! Work it out when you get there. They want to go the day after tomorrow for a few days."

When I met the girls I certainly was delighted. They were in their early twenties, and both were very pretty and girlish. When all arrangements had been made, Jeri admonished the girls: "Now, I warn you, don't let Bunny take advantage of you. Watch him!"

If only she had known, it was I who needed the warning!

I set off with my two pretty girls for Virgin's. It was an enjoyable car ride down the coast road under any conditions, but on this occasion it was special.

We saw a whole mass of game in the glades alongside the road from beginning to end. There were a few elephant under the big shade trees, hundreds of topi, dozens of waterbuck, and the odd family of "shorty warty hogs." This is to mention just a few. The girls were completely thrilled. The one sitting next to me in the car would from time to time take my hand with a gentle and, I thought, encouraging pressure, while the other reached across to pat my shoulder, as she mouthed: "Wonderful."

I must say at that moment I felt, in the words of that wise poet of days gone by: "How happy I would be with either!"

Then we passed through the dusty, sleepy village of Kipini and on to the track, which I myself had forged out of the forest. A short distance from Virgin's mosque stands a great baobab tree, well known to the elephant. It is possible for a hundred of them to shelter under its great shadows, against the midday sun. On this occasion we looked in on the monster tree to find thirty or forty elephant relaxing in various ways, as only elephant can. More hand pressures, pats, and little movements and gasps of excitement as we "bush-bashed" through the coastal forest belt until our camp, one mile on.

I must say the two girls went into ecstasies of delight when we turned round the last corner in the forest, entered the campsite, and had revealed to them the beauties of the sea, the sky, the beach, and the coral strand. There was every color under the sun—all the blues, all the greens, blue-white, milky white, and cream. Brown, black, pink, and red of the coral; yellow and golden shadows from the midmorning sun. It was a great hash of everything beautiful. There was even a mass of wildflowers of many hues among the carpet of grass, brought along by the recent rain.

But that was not quite all. As we alighted from the car, my fine captain of the camp staff Mwenji signed to us to follow him. He led us to the little thatched bar standing on a small cliff overlooking the sea. From here he pointed to the beach and . . . there to cap it all were two elephant besporting themselves amongst the incoming waves. "It can't be true," said one of the girls. "I don't believe it," said the other. They wrung their hands together and kissed one another, and then each one kissed me. We watched for a while until the two jumbos went "trunk in trunk" along the beach. It was a once-in-a-lifetime sight.

I showed the girls their *bandas* (small rooms made of poles and thatch roofs). They each had a *banda* but preferred to share one, which was natural enough.

I gave them a good lunch and told them to get their heads down for a while.

"And what are you going to do, Bunny?" asked one girl.

"Yes, while we rest, what do you do?" asked the other.

"Oh, I've got one or two things to do. Then, after an early cup o' tea and a digestive biscuit, I'll take you out to see some game . . . maybe a lion."

"Lovely," they answered in unison and headed bedward. Then I took myself off to my *banda* to do my "one or two things." One, put my head on a pillow, and two, have forty winks!

At the right hour, Tabei took the wheel of the hunting car to drive us out to the fifteen-mile stretch of *vlei* between the sand dunes and the tsetse fly belt of forest. I got myself up in the hatch with these two beauties. Our good fortune continued. In this little heavenly haven for game, in amongst the cold springs, hot springs, and nice sweet grass, we found elephant, buffalo, and a small pride of lion and lesser game of all sorts. The girls' chatter was continuous and delicious. In their excitement and contentment they pressed up against me with their firm and softer parts. I soared up into the realms of expectancy as we turned for camp and home.

Later, as we sat round the campfire, at a little distance from it certainly, with a drink in our hands, we discussed the outing, and the sweet girls were in clouds of happiness. One remarked: "D'you know, we two have had lots of trips together, but never one so wonderfully fantastic as this." And the other: "And, Bunny, we both love you for it." Things sounded all right. At this stage I wondered which would it be!

The second speaker went off for her bath. The other came and took my hand. I fondled and kissed it. I felt a slight pressure of her leg against mine. She said, "I'm off to take my bath. See you very soon."

She ran off to join the first girl. I continued with my drink. In no time at all the first girl was back with me. She took my hand as I rose to greet her. She then somewhat folded into one of my legs. I thought, *Ah, this is the one.* Before I could get beyond that thought, the second girl was back among us. She joined me on the other leg, and then they sort of played a game of "shuffle cock" with me! It wasn't bad, but I was uncertain of my next move. I need not have worried; they made all the moves!

We wined and dined and they played me all the while. Came the romantic time of sitting round the campfire. Each girl took one of my hands; I could barely find the opportunity to partake of the after-dinner drink. Then the first girl excused herself and tripped off to their tent. The second girl murmured something like "Lovely" and took me by both hands. I thought, Ah, here it comes, and passed one arm around her, slightly pulling her to me. Her lips met mine for the briefest of a flutter, then left me in midair as the first girl arrived back on the scene. She took over guard duty and the game went on. It continued, and finally, to my great relief, they both decided to go to bed. I found myself exasperated, frustrated, and somewhat exhausted by the girls' performance (or, should I say, lack of performance?).

Next morning, as I passed the girls' tent, the secret was revealed. With the slight murmur of the bed came the sweet whispers of love. I had been deadly dull not to have tumbled on the truth before. Later in the day they completely enlightened me.

Ever since school days they had enjoyed this love of theirs. Such has been their lives, that they were able to be together constantly; now they were a little ashamed for having me "on string." They had intended to do exactly what they did, and I rather suspected that little Jeri had been in the plot! But, the truth being out, we went on to have another several most enjoyable days. They were a couple of really nice happy girls.

Before they finally left me, I admonished them thus: "Look here, you sweet girls, I'd just love to take each one of you on safari . . . separately. I'll do my best to convert you!"

Chapter 27

Romantic Lamu Island

I suppose that, like everyone else in my profession, I've had every type of safari with every sort of person: good, bad, and indifferent. But I must say, for my part, that they have nearly all been good—some indifferent, and precious few bad. And what is more, very often the humor of a situation becomes its saving grace. I well remember two such safaris that took place along the coastline.

The first was for a very attractive girl I had met in the States. She was, unfortunately, accompanied by her latest boyfriend. It would have been nicer to be with her alone! That wasn't to be, however, and I made the best of it.

As I understood it, the safari was to be for her alone to hunt. The boyfriend was merely coming along as "exsex" baggage. It was not until we were well out into hunting country that I gleaned that Master Robert wanted a trophy or two. I remonstrated, albeit rather mildly, saying: "But you have no license to hunt."

"Suzie has. Surely I can hunt a bit on hers?"

Well, the upshot of it all was that Sexy Sue turned on her sweetest charm, and I fell like a load of bricks. I am very weak with women when it suits me! Robert did a bit of shooting.

Suzie proved a very steady shot and collected some nice trophies. I especially recall her buffalo epic. We had located a small herd in a thick bundle of bush, close to some inland floodwater from the Tana. The tracks showed that there was at least one large bull.

Just the three of us—Suzie, Tabei, and I—went on the narrow path after them. In but a few minutes, we could hear the buff grazing just ahead of us. Suzie had her rifle in her hands. We slowly advanced, with the trusty Tabei in the lead. He slowly raised his hand. We halted as he turned to us and pointed with his thumb, over his lowered shoulder. That meant that the buffalo was just in front—near indeed!

At this moment, with a great bellow of rage, a bull buffalo came charging out of the bush to

Suzie's left. I could not shoot, for she was directly in my line of fire, but that brave little girl raised her rifle, remaining as cool as a cucumber, and fired, to bring the old bull down a mere few feet from us. She had brained it good and proper. Suzie then reacted as all nice girls do on such occasions: She crumbled in my arms and made sobbing noises. Had David Niven been on hand she would, of course, have turned to him for strength, but he was otherwise occupied. So, without any hesitation, I restored her shattered nerves in the approved way. What is more, I told her in no unmeasured terms how splendidly she had done: "Suzie, that was wonderful. You did beautifully. You were very courageous and certainly saved several of us from a bad goring." Tabei also joined in the praise. He knew how well she had done. She had saved the situation. And what is more, she had got herself a trophy. It was a good, strong head of forty-seven inches. Eventually, we called the boyfriend into the arena. He carried on with comforting Suzie where I had left off, little knowing that I had completed the job.

After the hunt, they expressed a wish to take a look at Lamu, at the previous invitation of Jeri. Consequently we motored to the little jetty at Mkowe and took a boat for Lamu Island. They stayed several days at our house and wandered here, there, and everywhere. Finally Jeri suggested they should take a little sailing boat across to the island of Manda. Suzie had expressed a wish to Jeri that she wanted to get her boyfriend in a really romantic place for a final love frolic. The ever able and helpful Jeri suggested the lovely Manda beach as a "frolicful spot." Over they went, Suzie full of hope and desire. Suzie later told Jeri:

"Yes, do you know, he was doing just fine. I had closed my eyes and heaven was just around the corner, when I was aware of a shadow over my eyes and a strong smell of fish. I looked over Robert's shoulder as I cried out, 'Oh, Bob.' He faded as we both turned and gazed at an old fisherman, standing looking at us. In his hand he carried half a dozen fish. Robert immediately shouted at the man and signed for him to go, which eventually he did. But, alas, Robert, too, had gone; certainly not to return that day! It was a shame, he was doing so well. Jeri!—what a time to try to sell us fish!"

My very next safari followed a somewhat similar pattern, bar the fact that the clients, a boy and a girl, wanted to see game and not shoot it, except for the pot. We did very well. They were very loving and sweet with each other and me. Eventually we went across to Lamu for our great elephant experience. This time it was an elephant, not a fisherman.

One night the lovers took an after-dinner walk on the moonlit beach. Romance was in the air, and the beach had little human traffic at that hour to interfere with their idyll of love. They walked closely as they talked sweet nothings. After a while they settled down on a firm, dry piece of sandy beach. The lovemaking was well under way when a girl and boy elephant came onto the scene. They were also taking a romantic walk.

Our boy and girl were fully employed when the girl spied, over the shoulder of her swain, the gyrations of loving elephants. In her own words: "I tried to scream, but I couldn't. Only a sort of gurgle came from my mouth. I was terrified."

And from the boy: "I knew something was wrong. Following her wide-open eyes, I turned my head. There, not more than twenty feet away, were two elephants playing the love scene in full."

By this time, all thought of sex had departed from our hero. He was as petrified as his girlfriend. Thankfully they kept quiet and moved little as they watched the antics of the jumbos. Eventually the elephant lovers trundled along the beach as the young bull caressed the young cow's rear end with its trunk. When the lovers returned to the house to tell their tale, I accompanied them back to the scene. All the evidence was there. Even did we hear the playful squeal of the young cow, a few hundred yards off.

✕ ✕ ✕ ✕ ✕

I fondly remember a Texan family: the handsome, tall Dan Harrison, his lovely diminutive wife, Ann, and two very good-looking sons. They were an absolutely charming family: close-knit and a pleasure to be with. I cannot even recollect anything outstanding that occurred on their safari—they themselves were so outstanding that nothing else could be in the same category. But we had a lot of fun and got trophies sufficient for their needs. Like all Texans they were good shots. We did not have to follow up one wounded animal; that alone is a proud record.

I do remember one idiosyncrasy of the Harrison family. They simply had to eat sweets. This especially applied to Dan. He chewed them all day long—even directly after a meal, and forever and ever. We had to keep a plentiful supply in the camp. Good old strong mints were the favorites, as I recall.

It was a gentle, easy safari: no strain by anyone, for anyone. The Harrisons accepted it all as it came along. At the end all were content and happy—clients, camp staff, and I, although I would have loved to have "chanced my arm" just a little bit more with that lovely Ann!

Dan and the boys went off home first—they never all flew together—and then my son Anton appeared from nowhere to help Jeri and me see Ann off. We took her to dine, had a little dance, she packed, and we took her to the airport for the midnight flight. We all fell in love with her, and she liked us. She said so, but she also said: "And now I go home to those lovely sons and that magnificent Dan." She was so right. Dan was a splendid chap, and what a fine family!

Before I close this chapter, I want to tell of one incident of which I am not proud, but perhaps it had to be. It was another girl-and-boy affair—both nice enough in their own way, but not the finest in the world. I blame him entirely—of course I would! But if it had not been for him, the unpleasantness would not have occurred. It was a case of Sadie, the girl, having the money for the safari, and Albert, the boy, coming along for the ride.

All went peacefully, more or less, for a couple of weeks. Sadie explained to me that "her Bert" wanted to shoot an animal or two. Would it be all right for him to shoot on her license? Knowing full well that she did not intend to shoot her full quota of game, I at once agreed. However, I did add: "But mind you, Sadie, he must not shoot overmuch, and certainly not any big, dangerous game, except perhaps a buffalo." All parties understood and agreed. I had several times in the past made this sort of arrangement. No harm was done. Usually I did so with the agreement of the game department, knowing of the desire when purchasing the licenses.

Once again I arranged the hunt entirely in the coastal area, between Garsen on the Tana to Ijara on the Garissa road. There was a nice lot of game about, but I made them walk quite a lot. Sadie was grateful, but Master Albert did not like the walking. He was keen to sit in the car, drive as close to the animal as possible, then get out and shoot it. This I did not allow him to do, and he got peevish as a result. In fact, the start of the unpleasantness hinged on this slight beginning. I made him walk as far and as often as possible. It was a little mean of me, but I can be rather a nasty fellow. Anyway, he was on the soft side; he needed hardening up.

So the safari ran its course with no real harm done. I did nothing more with dear Sadie than kiss her good night, and that only after she had cleaned her teeth to get Bert's foul-tasting cigarette smoke smell from her pretty mouth. We returned to Nairobi, and then came the crunch.

I made the mistake of taking them to Muthaiga Country Club for the night as my guests. While we sat there having a drink, a friend of mine came up for a few words. I, of course, introduced him to my client and "lover boy." In the course of the conversation, my friend turned to Bert and said: "Well, I bet Bunny gave you a good time. Did you get all you wanted?"

Dear Bert puffed himself up like a small frog, blew through his stupid mustache, and replied, loud and clear: "Nope . . . I didn't get a lion. . . . I didn't get an elephant. . . . I didn't get . . ." At this point I cut in. It was just too much: "And you didn't get a license." My remark deflated Bert immediately. He retired into the depths of his chair, rather like a slug to his slimy lair. I could take no more. As my acquaintance took himself off, so indeed did I. I excused myself to Sadie and went.

I immediately took myself to the men's bar and ordered a drink at a writing desk. I composed a brief yet adequate letter to Sadie. Under the heated circumstances in which I wrote, I do believe it was, nevertheless, a nice letter. It read:

Dear Saidie,

I am afraid I can do no more for you and your boyfriend. I find him impossible. I will arrange to sign all your club chits until you leave tomorrow morning. All your expenses here, of course, I will meet. I have arranged for a taxi to take you to the airport at 6 A.M. tomorrow. You will be called at 5 A.M. I am indeed sorry for not being able to bid you good-bye, and I'm sorry for the unpleasant ending to your safari. It is no fault of yours. I feel it is no great fault of mine.

Bon voyage,
Bunny

I subsequently received a kind letter from Sadie, exonerating me from all blame. At the same time she was loyal to her lover. I reckon Sadie was a pretty splendid girl.

H CLAASSENS.

Chapter 28

Simone and Lorenzo

When I returned to Lamu, I was pleased to get a letter from my sons asking me to join them on a safari. Franzie Krummel and his wife were coming with friends from Vienna. I was delighted at the prospect. The safari was to start on the Tana River, in the Garissa area. It just gave me time to organize things at home, explain to Jeri that I was off wandering once again, and take two very nice Italian friends to Virgin's Camp for a few days. Jeri was always understanding—in fact, so understanding that I almost felt that she was pleased to see me go! She flatly denied that. Let us say that she never made a fuss about my comings and goings, and she was continuously sweet and helpful.

Simone and Lorenzo were bringing along a girlfriend. It sounded as if it would be a pleasant few days. I looked forward to it: a few days of complete rest and relaxation before a hard working month's safari with David, Anton, and party.

However, it never rains but it pours. Just as I was setting out for Virgin, more friends got in touch with me regarding a visit to my camp. Derek Mangnall, his sweet wife, Gillie, and two girlfriends wanted to come. They were all such good company that I did not intend to miss that treat! Consequently, I arranged for them to come to the camp immediately after Simone and Company had left. I got in touch with David and Anton to say I'd be a few days late on the Tana and laid in more stores for Virgin.

The weather proved lovely, including a hunter's moon. Game was plentiful, and, what is more, the turtles were nesting. A stroll on the beach always produced turtles, turtle eggs, or at least bags of turtle tracks. One evening, as Simone and I returned from a little turtle-ing, we decided to drop into the ocean for a dip. We left our things on the sandy beach, including my gold neck chains with my various attached medals—earned either for good conduct or misconduct! We toyed with the sparkling water for a while and then went to retrieve our belongings. The chains were missing.

At first I thought that Simone had taken them as a joke. I asked her: "Simone, did you hide them?" but the shake of her head and the honesty in her lovely eyes assured me that indeed my "bank balance" was missing. We got down on our hands and knees. We searched—and got a clue. There was a slight chain drag over the damp sand. It led for eight or ten feet and descended into a crab hole. I was about to put my index finger down the hole but was arrested just in time by Simone: "No, Bunny, let me use my finger; maybe it is more sensitive." How right Simone was. I reckon that her fingers are the most sensitive in the world. In fact, the whole of Simone vibrates with sensitivity.

Well, she found my wealth and gradually opened up the hole. There in the smallest corner was the minutest pink crab, sitting on my gold trinkets. I whispered to Simone: "Treat her gently." (I thought it surely had to be a female!) Simone very gently lifted up the crab and we watched it scamper off to the next hole. I think it waved good-bye as it disappeared!

On our final morning I had a good laugh. I had noticed during our days together that the two girls pulled Lorenzo's leg quite a bit. He was so precise that his leg cried out to be pulled. For example, he asked to be called in the morning at 6:15—not 6:10, not 6:20. Everyone laughed except Lorenzo; he was in deadly earnest.

On this morning, Lorenzo expressed a wish to breakfast at 8 A.M. and leave camp at nine. So it was all laid on to do just that. I noticed Lorenzo consulting his watch continually during breakfast. After one of these consultations, which lingered somewhat, he asked for another cup of coffee. The two girls smiled and had a snigger together. Another look at the watch and Lorenzo strolled over to his tent to check the baggage. He supervised its loading into the car to the last detail. I tried to help but to no avail. He, and only he, knew where every box or bag had to go. The girlfriend quietly pulled me aside to say, "He has to do it. Only he knows. Leave him to it."

Finally, he placed himself behind the wheel, then signaled the girls to get in. He consulted the timepiece again, then fiddled with the choke, the lights, and various other panel instruments. The girlfriend smiled at me and pulled my ear to her quite delicious mouth. She whispered: "He's waiting for 9 A.M. Then he'll go."

I shook my head to and fro and took advantage of the proximity of her lips to kiss her good-bye once again. At that moment there was a sort of Ahh of satisfaction from Lorenzo as he let out the clutch and they were on their way. Nine o'clock had arrived! Lorenzo the perfectionist!

Some months later, Simone showed me some excellent pictures taken on this little safari. In one I had Simone and (goodness, what was her name?) on either side of me with my arm round each of their waists. And what waists they were. As I looked at this picture I said to Simone: "But what a superb figure Bridget . . .

Bridgette . . . Bridgend has got. Why the hell didn't I make a pass at her?" Simone replied: "Bunny, it would have been no good. She's very much in love with her husband." But you never know on safari. The wind of romance often blows people off their normal course!

Chapter 29

The Last Safari
1977

And so, we moved on to what proved to be the final hunting safari for me.

I knew the area where I would find David's safari party and, without overmuch difficulty, I located the camp, cunningly tucked away in a wide bend of the river with riverine forest all around. It was a bright, moonlit night, and as I arrived I heard the whole party besporting themselves in the river. They called for me to join them, and I, covered in the dust of the journey and nothing loath, was with them in a flash. I cast off my clothes on the bank of the sleepy river in passing.

Franzi and Hanii seemed very, and genuinely, pleased to see me. There was a kissing on the lips and a clasping of hands. I was wetly introduced to several boys and girls, and got the same treatment. While this was going on, a chorus of hippo snorts, puffings, and whistles went on from a school of hippos upstream. Then, from one of the party still on dry land, the beam of a flashlight lit up a sandbank across the river. There a dozen or more reddish, yellowish, in fact sunset eyes reflected back at us.

A few crocodiles were passing the time just in case a free meal happened to come their way. But with the noise and splashing of the night bathers, there was little chance of that.

When I more formally met the safari party at dinner a little later, they proved to be a jolly lot. Of course I knew Franzi and Hanii—they were always fun to be with—but also their friends were very nice. They were well stocked with wine, and corks popped merrily. There were two more couples apart from Franzi and Hanii.

Besides David, Anton, and myself, we also had Jens Hessel to help with the hunting. In this first camp, the main idea was to get a certain number of good crocodile skins and, of course, a huge elephant for Franzi if one happened to come along. Some of the party were hardly hunting at all. They were there just to enjoy safari life, get some birds, and have a good look around the countryside.

While in this Tana River camp, I had one memorable experience. It happened on a day when a car full of the visitors had gone off sightseeing. I was rather luckily left with a charming girl by the name of Trudi.

Franzi said to me, with a twinkle in his eye: "Bunny, we are leaving Trudi in your care. Can you manage her?"

And from that little minx Hanii: "You'll do all right, Bunny. We'll be back before night. I know how nervous you are in the dark."

I nodded in reply as I looked at the smiling Trudi: "I'll do my best. I'll try to keep her happy and contented."

Trudi added: "I have faith in you." I thought that was kind of her.

I suggested that we take a walk up the river through the bush, riverine forest, and past the various floodwater pools. "Oh that'll be great," responded the green-eyed Viennese. She had been in America for a few years and consequently used quite a number of Americanisms.

In a matter of minutes we were on our way, with the trusty Tabei leading. I knew we would see hundreds of baboons, also some warthogs, and maybe a bushbuck and waterbuck or two. We would watch fish eagles at play and indeed hear them, which is always a joy. Guinea fowl too would gladden our eyes, together with the beautiful and rarer forest variety. I knew we would see enough to keep Trudi happy and smiling and make her hungry for lunch on her return. I did not allow for the tremendous sight we were in for. For the excitement, fright—and the aftermath!

Within a couple of hundred yards of camp the baboons started jabbering at us. They coughed and barked, as they always do. There were the usual squeals and yelling and bawling from the youngsters as they were chastised by their mama or grabbed at by their papa. The noise was continuous, and it grew louder as we penetrated into the thicker forest. We were still only a bare mile from camp. Trudi's eyes were pushing out of their sockets at the cacophony. I had turned to look at her. Her eyes were full of surprise, delight, and a little fear and expectancy. For myself, I must say I was somewhat surprised. Baboons en famille are always noisy, but this was something special.

At this moment, when I was exchanging looks with Trudi, a brand-new noise came into the scene: the very savage, loud, and long growl of a leopard. Trudi took a short step forward and her hand was in mine in a trice. We felt nice and frightened—together!

After the great growl, a complete silence reigned for some moments—it seemed like minutes. Then all hell let loose, when seemingly every baboon in the locality jabbered and chattered full blast. In the middle of it all there came one scream from a young baboon.

Tabei softly said: "*Chui ameshikwa mtoto tu.*" I passed on to Trudi the news that all the rumpus was because the leopard had caught a young baboon. While the noise of battle went on just ahead, we hurried to try to catch up with it. This we did in another thirty yards. There, in a small clearing, the fight was in full swing. A very large leopard was crouched over a big young baboon that appeared to be disemboweled yet not quite dead. The leopard, meanwhile, was snarling in very mean fashion at eight or more large baboons circled around it. These were jabbering away nonstop, and then as we watched they started to dart in and attack. The leopard, of course, answered back very forcibly, but as fast as one baboon was driven off, two more came to fill the breach. The wounded baboons, some of which were clearly dying, crept away into the bushes. But the leopard was also beginning to appear very sorry. Those cruel baboon teeth were giving it a dreadful mauling.

The end of the battle came suddenly. It was so sudden that it caught Trudi and me completely unawares. Two large baboons swung themselves onto the leopard at the same moment. One of them appeared to carve a large slice of flesh from the thick part of the leopard's neck. With a pained scream, the leopard took the easiest way out—that happened to be where we stood! Even though it was sorely smitten, it came on quite fast. I pushed Trudi out of the way and then rather fell after her. In doing this, I hooked my leg in the fork of a fallen tree and wrenched it very badly. Meantime the wounded leopard snarled its way past us and crept into the thick woods. I at once picked myself up, or at least I tried to—but I failed. I wanted to assist and comfort Trudi. However, it was I that needed the assistance! My leg would not sustain my weight. Trudi was quickly on the job, and my trusty Tabei soon saw my predicament. Between them they got me squarely onto my feet, but I was extremely wobbly on my left leg.

They helped me back to the camp: It was a slow and painful safari, yet we made it. Trudi at once ran over to her tent and was back in no time with two powerful painkillers. She said: "Bunny, these will knock you out in just a few minutes. Have a good sleep. Later I will come to massage you."

"Do you promise?" I asked. She nodded, blew me a kiss, and left.

My pain gradually left me as I slept. It was a deep sleep, and I woke still lying on my right side, as Trudi had left me. My guardian angel was sitting in a chair a few feet from my bed. As my eyes opened she leaned over me to soothe my fevered brow with a cool hand faintly savored with the perfume of sweet herbs. I mouthed a "kiss me" to her and she did, gently yet firmly. As I raised my arms to encircle her, she made her escape to the tent doorway. From that safe distance, she said: "Now, Bunny, you just lie quietly until I come back. I will bring your English four o'clock tea. You need it; you missed lunch."

After a few moments, I tried moving my legs into a different position. The tablets were doing their job; I was easier. I closed my eyes and was once again in the Land of Nod. Next, I was aware of a delicious aroma. I opened my eyes to see a prettily laid tray beside my bed and on it the most wonderful dish of Viennese pastries.

While I slept, the clever and sweet Trudi had created these with the connivance of the camp cook. "Oh, how beautiful!" I exclaimed. "You are amazing, Trudi. I feel better already."

I eased myself into a better position for eating. Then she passed me one of the scrumptious pastries on a plate and watched as I enjoyed it, betwixt swallows of good tea. "What a joy," I remarked as I tucked into another. "God, you are clever."

She was pleased and replied: "Well, you know, years ago my mother thought I was rather wasting my time, so she sent me to do a pastry cooking class at Demel's, the leading pastry, cake, and chocolate establishment in Vienna. I have kept up the practice. I'm glad. They are doing you good." She repeated: "I am glad."

A little later Trudi came back to massage my wretched leg. With the help of Tabei, I had hobbled into a very hot bath and was still steaming from this when Trudi returned. First of all she gave me two sleeping bombs and a brown capsule.

"What's that?" I asked, pointing at the brown job.

"Oh, that's just a little quietener," she replied with a slight smirk of her pretty face as she handed me a good glass of whiskey to wash them down. Then she arranged me in bed, stomach down.

As she was about to anoint me with some rather sweet-smelling unction, I said: "Half a mo, Trudi, I've got some better stuff. Over there near my shaving kit." She moved over, picked up the indicated jar, took off the lid, and smelled the contents. She pulled a wry face: "Pooh, for goodness' sake. What is it?"

"Lion fat," I replied. "Don't worry, a little hot water will clean your hands right up."

With that assurance, she set about me. She certainly knew how to massage. Having done a sound job on the back of my leg—and I could really feel the goodness of her hands—she turned me over on my back. I arranging my *kikoi* to cover me somewhat, thinking: "Oh, dear God, keep me under control." But I need not have feared or worried. While Trudi worked away on me, I was as good as gold! When it was all over, I thanked her and ended by saying, "My word, you make beautiful pastry, and you massage like an expert. Did you also take a course in that?"

"No, Bunny," she said. "That comes naturally. Any woman should know how to massage a man!"

As she was about to leave, I fired one more question at her: "Trudi, when you turned me over onto my back, don't you think I behaved well—under control, and all that?"

"My dear Bunny, that was not you; that was the little brown capsule!"

My leg gradually improved, but for the rest of the stay on the Tana River I did precious little and remained close to camp. The sweet Trudi continued to minister to me, but she also had to take care of her swain, so I did not see as much of her as I would have liked. Soon came the time to move camp. While Anton and I did that, up to the highlands, the rest of the party flew down to Lamu for three days.

Anton and I had quite an enjoyable trip up to and around Mount Kenya, setting up a splendid camp under the yellow thorn trees of Doldol. By now my leg had improved vastly. Trudi did come to Doldol camp. She manipulated my leg a couple of times, and before she left she pronounced it as good as new. Of course, it was not as good as new, but considering my years and my past mishaps, my leg did still have a fairly good secondhand trade-in value. While at Doldol, it took me up rocky hills and down thickish dells pretty well as I searched for elusive greater kudu, a mighty eland, or a monster record elephant.

As the safari packed up and left Doldol, so did Trudi and her three friends. Her final words to me were: "Bunny, you must come to see me sometime in Vienna. We will give you a good time, and I will cook for you as well." When I did ultimately get to Vienna a few years later, I could not find Trudi. The "other lovely girl" told me that she had heard that Trudi had gone back to the States—probably taking a course in blueberry pies for some lucky fellow!

It was only a day's journey back from Doldol to the final camp of this "last" safari. Here things were somewhat complicated by the fact that David had arranged a French-speaking safari in the same vicinity. He had a French white hunter in charge of it, together with a couple of Kenya hunters. We also had two charming French-speaking girls taking it in turns to run the camp and act as interpreters.

The one camp for Franzi and his friends was situated quite high up in the Aberdares, while the parlez-vous camp was in a

H.CLAASSENS.

forest on the lower slopes of Mount Kenya. They were about twenty-five miles apart, with David's house on the Naro Moru River about midway between them. As both camps were looking for leopard, and as we had enough white hunters, I got the job of putting up baits for the two camps and checking on them. In doing this I found it convenient to make David's house my base, working out from there to the two camps. So sometimes I slept there, and at other times in one or other of the camps. In doing so, I saw quite a lot of Petal, David's wife. She is a really charming girl and a great help to David in his work. She was constantly in and out of the camps, bringing in special "goodies."

Also, I got to know the interpreting girls. Each was a perfect delight in her own way. I had met them briefly in the past, and it was nice to get to know them. From one, Jane, I learned how to make perfectly good finnan haddie out of fillets of Nile perch. We prepared them and smoked them, and the empty plates at the breakfast table proved to us how good they were. A year or so later, Jeri and I visited Jane and her delightful husband, Dick, on their safari barge at Épernay, when we were visiting the champagne cellars of Moet et Chandon.

As I said, I was constantly in and out of the camp, giving my news of leopard baits. I knew that some other Austrian friends of Franzi's had come into the Aderdare camp; they took the place of Trudi and Company. I had not as yet met them, but I knew two of them: Harald Prinzhorn, from some years before at Lamu, and his son, Peter. However, as yet I had not seen them in the camp. Each time I was there, they and their party were out. Very often I was in the camp for only an hour or so, and then off to other fields of sport. But one great occasion will always stay in my mind. Even now, years after, I say to myself: "It can't have been true!"

I had returned to the Aberdare camp in the course of the afternoon, and, having had my pot of tea and a couple of biscuits,

I decided to amble down to some woodland to inspect a leopard bait. It was within a mile of camp, and I enjoyed the little walk. After the recent showers, wildflowers were out in abundance, and all the fragrance to go with them. There was birdsong from all directions and one solitary bark of a bushbuck. I was alone with nature and loving it—but, I was not alone!

As I approached the forest edge, a most beautiful creature came out on a narrow animal track. The first thing I was aware of was her hat. This was a very pretty little brown straw with a chain of yellow daisies around it. As she came into the open, she was picking pieces of lichen from her hat and shoulders. She was so engrossed in this task that she did not notice me at first. Then her eyes lifted up to mine, and I saw how beautiful they were. Then she smiled, and they became more beautiful. "Hallo," I said, "and who are you?"

"I'm Gretl," she answered.

"Then I must be Hansel," I replied. It then was the most natural thing in the world for me to advance, take her in my arms, and kiss her. She responded, albeit gently, but she responded. To this day, Gretl denies that she ever did respond. However, my lips told me and my heart still tells me that she did.

After a few golden moments, Gretl managed to extract herself from my embrace and then proceeded to unwind a bit more tickling lichen. Meantime I was admiring her. Finally I asked her: "You are from the camp back there?" I pointed from whence I had come. "You are one of the Prinzhorn party?"

With great assurance she answered: "I am the Prinzhorn party." We laughed together. Then she continued: "You must be Bunny, David's and Anton's father. Harald has told me all about you—and warned me about you!"

"And what are you doing here, wandering around on your own?"

Gretl looked into the sky, then looked at me again, as she answered: "I didn't feel like going out today. I wanted to be left alone to read and write and think. Harald has gone up on the moors with the others."

"Well, they'll be back soon. You had better be in camp when they arrive or they will be worried."

"Oh, no," she retorted, "they won't be back until it is dark. Harald hates wasting a moment when he is hunting."

That being the case, I was delighted to spend some time with this lovely girl. I invited her to join me on a nice dry-fallen tree, which made a sound seat. We talked for quite a while. She had been several times to Africa and loved it. She talked of her life in Vienna, which she also loved. In fact, I gathered that her life was somewhat of a paradox. She was a complex character. She could be sophistication personified, and yet there was a delightful simplicity about her. I admired her sophistication. I loved her simplicity.

After a while she said: "Well, Bunny, I'm glad I've met you, after having heard a bit about you. Why didn't you come into the camp sooner?"

"I have been in and out of the camp several times. Always you were out. I was out of luck!" I looked at her, taking her in completely. She must have seen my active eyes and sensed my thoughts. She smiled with the knowledge that she had made a deep impression on me.

"It's a pity," she said, rather to herself than to me.

"What's a pity?"

"That you left it so late. Probably David will get the bongo for Franzi tomorrow. Then the safari is over. We go."

"Ah, but I must see you again."

"Yes, maybe in my next life. When I return to Vienna I will consult my Romany girl about my karma. Yes, maybe in the next life."

"But we are in this life. I have met you, and I want to go on meeting you. You are beautiful." She was silent as she thought for a while. Then she looked deeply and truly into my eyes before she replied.

"Bunny—yes, Bunny, Bunny, we come to Malindi every year. Maybe we will meet, but it is rather late for this life. I feel it will be the next life."

I kissed her gently, her lips fluttering like butterfly wings. She turned to go up the incline to the camp while I angled off to the leopard bait.

I watched her reach the top of the crest. She turned, we waved, and she was gone. The last thing I saw was the sweet little brown straw hat with the surround of yellow daisies. Perhaps, perhaps, we would meet next year, or in the next life. "*LABDA!*"